Lecture Notes in Artificial Intelligence 4461

Edited by J.G. Carbonell and J. Siekmann

Subseries of Lecture Notes in Computer Science

T0238826

Sam Joseph   Zoran Despotovic
Gianluca Moro   Sonia Bergamaschi (Eds.)

Agents and Peer-to-Peer Computing

5th International Workshop, AP2PC 2006
Hakodate, Japan, May 9, 2006
Revised and Invited Papers

 Springer

Series Editors

Jaime G. Carbonell, Carnegie Mellon University, Pittsburgh, PA, USA
Jörg Siekmann, University of Saarland, Saarbrücken, Germany

Volume Editors

Sam Joseph
University of Hawaii, Dept. of Information and Computer Science
1680 East-West Road, POST 309, Honolulu, HI 96822, USA
E-mail: srjoseph@hawaii.edu

Zoran Despotovic
EPFL Lausanne, School of Computer and Communication Sciences
1015 Lausanne, Switzerland
E-mail: zoran.despotovic@epfl.ch

Gianluca Moro
University of Bologna, Dept. of Electronics, Computer Science and Systems
Via Venezia, 52, 47023 Cesena (FC), Italy
E-mail: gmoro@deis.unibo.it

Sonia Bergamaschi
University of Modena and Reggio-Emilia, Dept. of Science Engineering
via Vignolese, 905, 41100 Modena, Italy
E-mail: bergamaschi.sonia@unimo.it

Library of Congress Control Number: Applied for

CR Subject Classification (1998): I.2.11, I.2, C.2.4, C.2, H.4, H.3, K.4.4

LNCS Sublibrary: SL 7 – Artificial Intelligence

ISSN 0302-9743
ISBN 978-3-540-79704-3 Springer Berlin Heidelberg New York

Springer is a part of Springer Science+Business Media

springer.com

© Springer-Verlag Berlin Heidelberg 2008

Typesetting: Camera-ready by author, data conversion by Scientific Publishing Services, Chennai, India
Printed on acid-free paper   SPIN: 12265541   06/3180   5 4 3 2 1 0

Preface

Peer-to-peer (P2P) computing has attracted significant media attention, initially spurred by the popularity of file-sharing systems such as Napster, Gnutella, and Morpheus. More recently systems like BitTorrent and eDonkey have continued to sustain that attention. New techniques such as distributed hash-tables (DHTs), semantic routing, and Plaxton Meshes are being combined with traditional concepts such as Hypercubes, Trust Metrics, and caching techniques to pool together the untapped computing power at the "edges" of the Internet. These new techniques and possibilities have generated a lot of interest in many industrial organizations, and have resulted in the creation of a P2P working group on standardization in this area (http://www.irtf.org/charter?gtype=rg&group=p2prg).

In P2P computing, peers and services forego central coordination and dynamically organize themselves to support knowledge sharing and collaboration, in both cooperative and non-cooperative environments. The success of P2P systems strongly depends on a number of factors. First, the ability to ensure equitable distribution of content and services. Economic and business models which rely on incentive mechanisms to supply contributions to the system are being developed, along with methods for controlling the "free riding" issue. Second, the ability to enforce provision of trusted services. Reputation-based P2P trust management models are becoming a focus of the research community as a viable solution. The trust models must balance both constraints imposed by the environment (e.g., scalability) and the unique properties of trust as a social and psychological phenomenon. Recently, we are also witnessing a move of the P2P paradigm to embrace mobile computing in an attempt to achieve even higher ubiquitousness. The possibility of services related to physical location and the relation with agents in physical proximity could introduce new opportunities and also new technical challenges.

Although researchers working on distributed computing, multi-agent systems, databases, and networks have been using similar concepts for a long time, it is only fairly recently that papers motivated by the current P2P paradigm have started appearing in high-quality conferences and workshops. Research in agent systems in particular appears to be most relevant because, since their inception, multiagent systems have always been thought of as collections of peers.

The multiagent paradigm can thus be superimposed on the P2P architecture, where agents embody the description of the task environments, the decision-support capabilities, the collective behavior, and the interaction protocols of each peer. The emphasis in this context on decentralization, user autonomy, dynamic growth, and other advantages of P2P also leads to significant potential problems. Most prominent among these problems are coordination: the ability of an agent to make decisions on its own actions in the context of activities of other agents; and scalability: the value of the P2P systems lies in how well they scale along several dimensions, including complexity, heterogeneity of peers, robustness, traffic redistribution, and so forth. It is important to scale up coordination strategies along multiple dimensions to enhance their tractability and viability, and thereby to widen potential application domains. These two problems are common to many large-scale applications. Without coordination, agents may be wasting their efforts, squandering resources, and failing to achieve their objectives in situations requiring collective effort.

This workshop series brings together researchers working on agent systems and P2P computing with the intention of strengthening this connection. Researchers from other related areas such as distributed systems, networks, and database systems are also welcome (and, in our opinion, have a lot to contribute). We seek high-quality and original contributions on the general theme of "Agents and P2P Computing." The following is a non-exhaustive list of topics of special interest:

- Intelligent agent techniques for P2P computing
- P2P computing techniques for multiagent systems
- The Semantic Web and semantic coordination mechanisms for P2P systems
- Scalability, coordination, robustness, and adaptability in P2P systems
- Self-organization and emergent behavior in P2P systems
- E-commerce and P2P computing
- Participation and contract incentive mechanisms in P2P systems
- Computational models of trust and reputation
- Community of interest building and regulation, and behavioral norms
- Intellectual property rights and legal issues in P2P systems
- P2P architectures
- Scalable data structures for P2P systems
- Services in P2P systems (service definition languages, service discovery, filtering and composition etc.)
- Knowledge discovery and P2P data-mining agents
- P2P-oriented information systems
- Information ecosystems and P2P systems
- Security considerations in P2P networks
- Ad-hoc networks and pervasive computing based on P2P architectures and wireless communication devices
- Grid computing solutions based on agents and P2P paradigms
- Legal issues in P2P networks

The workshop series emphasizes discussions about methodologies, models, algorithms and technologies, strengthening the connection between agents and P2P computing. These objectives are accomplished by bringing together researchers and contributions from these two disciplines but also from more traditional areas such as distributed systems, networks, and databases.

This volume is the post-proceedings of AP2PC 2006, the 5th International Workshop on Agents and P2P Computing,[1] held in Hakodate, Japan on May 9,

---

[1] http://p2p.ingce.unibo.it/

2006 in the context of the Fifth International Joint Conference on Autonomous Agents and Multi-Agent Systems (AAMAS 2005).

This volume brings together papers presented at AP2PC 2006, fully revised to incorporate reviewers' comments and discussions at the workshop. The volume is organized according to the following sessions held at the workshop:

- Invited Paper
- P2P Infrastructure
- Agents in P2P
- P2P Search
- Applications

We would like to thank the invited speaker Raman Paranjape, Director of Special Initiatives from TRLabs in Saskatchewan Canada, for his talk entitled "Macroscopic Modeling of Information Flow in an Agent-Based Electronic Health Record System."

After the call for papers, we received 23 papers. All submissions were reviewed for scope and quality, ten were accepted as full papers, and six as short papers. We would like to thank the authors for their submissions and the members of the Program Committee for reviewing the papers under time pressure and for their support of the workshop. Finally, we would like to acknowledge the Steering Committee for its guidance and encouragement.

This workshop followed the successful fourth edition, which was held in conjunction with AAMAS in Utrecht in 2005. In recognition of the interdisciplinary nature of P2P computing, a sister event called the International Workshop on Databases, Information Systems, and P2P Computing[2] was held in Trondheim, Noray in August 2005 in conjunction with the International Conference on Very Large Data Bases (VLDB).

September 2006   Sam Joseph
                                                            Zoran Despotovic
                                                              Gianluca Moro
                                                          Sonia Bergamaschi

---

[2] http://dbisp2p.ingce.unibo.it/

Organization

Executive Committee

Organizers

Program Co-chairs   Sam Joseph
Dept. of Information and Computer Science,
University of Hawaii
1680 East-West Road, POST 309, Honolulu, HI 96822
E-mail: srjoseph@hawaii.edu

Zoran Despotovic
School of Computer and Communications Sciences,
Ecole Polytechnique Fédérale de Lausanne (EPFL)
CH-1015 Lausanne, Switzerland
E-mail: zoran.despotovic@epfl.ch

Gianluca Moro
Dept. of Electronics, Computer Science and Systems,
University of Bologna, Italy
E-mail: gmoro@deis.unibo.it

Sonia Bergamaschi
Dept. of Science Engineering,
University of Modena and Reggio-Emilia, Italy
E-mail: bergamaschi.sonia@unimo.it

Steering Committee

Karl Aberer	EPFL, Lausanne, Switzerland
Sonia Bergamaschi	Dept. of Science Engineering, University of Modena and Reggio-Emilia, Italy
Manolis Koubarakis	Dept. of Electronic and Computer Engineering, Technical University of Crete, Greece
Paul Marrow	Intelligent Systems Laboratory, BTexact Technologies, UK
Gianluca Moro	Dept. of Electronics, Computer Science and Systems, University of Bologna, Cesena, Italy
Aris M. Ouksel	Dept. of Information and Decision Sciences, University of Illinois at Chicago, USA
Claudio Sartori	IEIIT-BO-CNR, University of Bologna, Italy
Munindar P. Singh	Dept. of Computer Science, North Carolina State University, USA

Program Committee

Karl Aberer	EPFL, Lausanne, Switzerland
Alessandro Agostini	ITC-IRST, Trento, Italy
Djamal Benslimane	Universite Claude Bernard, France
Sonia Bergamaschi	University of Modena and Reggio-Emilia, Italy
M. Brian Blake	Georgetown University, USA
Angela Bonifati	CNR, Italy
Rajkumar Buyya	University of Melbourne, Australia
Paolo Ciancarini	University of Bologna, Italy
Costas Courcoubetis	Athens University of Economics and Business, Greece
Yogesh Deshpande	University of Western Sydney, Australia
Asuman Dogac	Middle East Technical University, Turkey
Boi V. Faltings	EPFL, Lausanne, Switzerland
Maria Gini	University of Minnesota, USA
Dina Q. Goldin	University of Connecticut, USA
Chihab Hanachi	University of Toulouse, France
Mark Klein	Massachusetts Institute of Technology, USA
Matthias Klusch	DFKI, Saarbrücken, Germany
Tan Kian Lee	National University of Singapore, Singapore
Zakaria Maamar	Zayed University, UAE
Wolfgang Mayer	University of South Australia, Australia
Dejan Milojicic	Hewlett Packard Labs, USA
Alberto Montresor	University of Bologna, Italy
Jean-Henry Morin	University of Geneva, Switzerland
Andrea Omicini	University of Bologna, Italy
Maria Orlowska	University of Queensland, Australia
Aris. M. Ouksel	University of Illinois at Chicago, USA
Mike Papazoglou	Tilburg University, Netherlands
Mara S. Pérez-Hernández	Universidad Politécnica de Madrid, Spain
Paolo Petta	Austrian Research Institute for AI, Austria
Jean Marc Pierson	INSA de Lyon, France
Jeremy Pitt	Imperial College, UK
Dimitris Plexousakis	Institute of Computer Science, FORTH, Greece
Martin Purvis	University of Otago, New Zealand
Omer F. Rana	Cardiff University, UK
Douglas S. Reeves	North Carolina State University, USA
Thomas Risse	Fraunhofer IPSI, Darmstadt, Germany
Pierangela Samarati	University of Milan, Italy
Christophe Silbertin-Blanc	University of Toulouse, France
Maarten van Steen	Vrije Universiteit, Netherlands
Katia Sycara	Robotics Institute, Carnegie Mellon University, USA

Peter Triantafillou	Technical University of Crete, Greece
Anand Tripathi	University of Minnesota, USA
Vijay K. Vaishnavi	Georgia State University, USA
Francisco Valverde-Albacete	Universidad Carlos III de Madrid, Spain
Maurizio Vincini	University of Modena and Reggio-Emilia, Italy
Fang Wang	BTexact Technologies, UK
Gerhard Weiss	Technische Universitaet, Germany
Bin Yu	North Carolina State University, USA
Franco Zambonelli	University of Modena and Reggio-Emilia, Italy

Preceding Editions of AP2PC

Here are the references to the preceding editions of AP2PC, including the volumes of revised and invited papers:

- AP2PC 2002 was held in Bologna, Italy, July 15, 2002. The website can be found at http://p2p.ingce.unibo.it/2002/ The proceedings were published by Springer as LNCS volume no. 2530 and are available online here: http://www.springerlink.com/content/978-3-540-40538-2/
- AP2PC 2003 was held in Melbourne, Australia, July 14, 2003. The website can be found at http://p2p.ingce.unibo.it/2003/ The proceedings were published by Springer as LNCS volume no. 2872 and are available online here: http://www.springerlink.com/content/978-3-540-24053-2/
- AP2PC 2004 was held in New York City, USA, July 19, 2004. The website can be found at http://p2p.ingce.unibo.it/2004/ The proceedings were published by Springer as LNCS volume no. 3601 and are available online here: http://www.springerlink.com/content/978-3-540-29755-0/
- AP2PC 2005 was held in Utrecht, Netherlands, May 9, 2005. The website can be found at http://p2p.ingce.unibo.it/2004/ The proceedings were published by Springer as LNAI volume no. 4118 and are available online here: http://www.springerlink.com/content/978-3-540-49025-8/

Table of Contents

Invited Paper

Information Flow Analysis in Autonomous Agent and Peer-to-Peer
Systems for Self-organizing Electronic Health Records 1
  Ben Tse, Raman Paranjape, and Samuel R.H. Joseph

P2P Infrastructure

Hybrid DHT Design for Mobile Environments 19
  *Stefan Zoels, Simon Schubert, Wolfgang Kellerer, and
  Zoran Despotovic*

DANTE: A Self-adapting Peer-to-Peer System 31
  *Luis Rodero Merino, Luis López, Antonio Fernández, and
  Vicent Cholvi*

The Exclusion of Malicious Routing Peers in Structured P2P
Systems 43
  Bong-Soo Roh, O-Hoon Kwon, Sung Je Hong, and Jong Kim

Agents in P2P

Cooperative CBR System for Peer Agent Committee Formation 51
  Hager Karoui, Rushed Kanawati, and Laure Petrucci

Mobile Agent-Based Approach for Resource Discovery in Peer-to-Peer
Networks 63
  Jaafar Gaber and Mohamed Bakhouya

P2P Search

CHORA: Expert-Based P2P Web Search............................ 74
  Halldor Isak Gylfason, Omar Khan, and Grant Schoenebeck

K-link: A Peer-to-Peer Solution for Organizational Knowledge
Management 86
  Giuseppe Pirro', Domenico Talia, and Massimo Ruffolo

An Analysis of Interest-Community Facilitated Peer-to-Peer Search 98
  Elth Ogston

Applications

Mitigating the Impact of Liars by Reflecting Peer's Credibility on P2P
File Reputation Systems 111
  So Young Lee, O-Hoon Kwon, Jong Kim, and Sung Je Hong

A Comparative Study of Reasoning Techniques for Service Selection 123
  Murat Şensoy and Pınar Yolum

PROSA: P2P Resource Organisation by Social Acquaintances 135
  *Vincenza Carchiolo, Michele Malgeri, Giuseppe Mangioni, and
  Vincenzo Nicosia*

Reliable P2P File Sharing Service 143
  Jung-Hwa Shin, Weon Shin, and Kyung-Hyune Rhee

Studying Viable Free Markets in Peer-to-Peer File Exchange
Applications without Altruistic Agents 151
  David Cabanillas and Steven Willmott

Distributed Multi-layered Network Management for NEC Using
Multi-Agent Systems 159
  *Richard Vaughan, James Wise, Paul Huey, Michael Alcock,
  Jonathan Vaughan, Steven Shingler, and Graham Atkins*

Facilitating Collaboration in a Distributed Software Development
Environment Using P2P Architecture 167
  Maryam Purvis, Martin Purvis, and Bastin Tony Roy Savarimuthu

A Peer to Peer Grid Computing System Based on Mobile Agents 175
  Joon-Min Gil and Sung-Jin Choi

Author Index 187

Information Flow Analysis in Autonomous Agent and Peer-to-Peer Systems for Self-organizing Electronic Health Records

Ben Tse[1], Raman Paranjape[1], and Samuel R.H. Joseph[2]

[1] Electronic Systems Engineering,
University of Regina and TRLabs Regina,
3737 Wascana Pkwy
Regina, SK S4V 0R4, Canada
Raman.paranjape@uregina.ca
[2] Laboratory for Interactive Learning Technologies,
Department of Information and Computer Sciences,
University of Hawaii,
1680 East West Road, POST 309
Honolulu, HI 96822 USA
srjoseph@hawaii.edu

Abstract. There are various software applications that are highly suited for development using agent technology. Typically these applications take advantage of some of the intrinsic qualities of agents that include: autonomy, reactivity/proactivity, group-action, and/or mobility. On the other hand, there are many parallels between Agent Systems and Peer-to-Peer Systems allowing the latter to be employed in similar problem domains. This paper presents an agent application in the health care record management domain and then examines how such a system might also be implemented as a Peer-to-Peer System. The management of health care records is in itself a novel use of Mobile Agent technology and in order to understand the Agent System Dynamics, the system is simulated using a limited number of agents and agent platforms; as well as being modeled mathematically. The Peer-to-Peer system is also simulated and modeled mathematically demonstrating a number of behaviors that are similar across both systems.

Keywords: autonomous agents, peer-to-peer, mobility, electronic health records.

1 Introduction

1.1 Electronic Health Records

Health record information access/retrieval is one of the major problems in modern health care systems (Moreno, 2003; Nealon & Moreno, 2003). Ideally relevant information from a patient's complete health record would be available to every practitioner at all times; however prescription information, test results and doctor's

S. Joseph et al. (Eds.): AP2PC 2006, LNAI 4461, pp. 1–18, 2008.

diagnoses are generated and stored in multiple locations such as hospitals, clinics, pharmacies and so on. In reality it is difficult to assemble the relevant information in the correct location at the right time in order to provide the best possible service to the patient. The problem is made more complex by the importance of maintaining patient privacy.

An Electronic Health Record (EHR) is an electronic version of a patient's health information and contains prescriptions, lab results, evaluations by doctors, etc. EHRs can be made easily accessible through an electronic health information network. The advantages of EHRs include: increasing effectiveness and efficiency of clinical staff and health practitioner by simplification of access to health records, rapid movement of health information for better care of patients, simple duplication and multiple/simultaneous access to patient health information, and potential increases in the profitability of the medical practices and/or facilities.

Although EHRs appear to hold great promise, there are many challenges that need to be addressed before they can be fully integrated in a health care system. These challenges include: security and confidentiality, lack of standards (data exchange, data management and data integration) or slow adaptation to existing standards, lack of government and/or private funding, especially in developing countries, complexity of medical data, rejection by health care professionals, and network bandwidth consumption (Dick & Steen, 1991; Johns, 1997).

1.2 Mobile Agent Technology

Mobile agent technology has received a fair degree of attention in academic research in recent years (Kotz et al., 2002). Mobile agents are defined as a software objects that can migrate to different computers over an IP network to perform user-assigned and self-initiated tasks. Mobile Agents are autonomous software programs that may start running on a host computer, stop what they are doing, move to another host computer, and start up from where they left off.

Mobile Agents are best understood through comparison with other related technologies such as mobile code, distributed objects, and viruses/worms. Mobile code technologies such as process migration, remote evaluation, and mobile objects are very similar to Mobile Agents but differ in that Mobile Agents autonomously initiate their own mobility during their execution process. Mobile Agents place an emphasis on location awareness that differentiates them from distributed object technologies like RMI, CORBA, and DCOM (Raj, 1998) which abstract over location. Viruses and worms are related technologies that have negative connotations; however they are essentially mobile agents that use deception or software bugs to facilitate their movement and execution instead of relying upon an agent execution environment.

The mobile agent programs run with the aid of another program called an agent execution environment that must be installed and running on a host computer before the mobile agent program can run. An agent execution environment provides the mobile agents with services for mobility, messaging, resource access, and security. The agent execution environment also provides administration services for running and monitoring the behavior of mobile agents. TEEMA (TRLabs Execution Environment for Mobile Agents) is an agent execution environment that was developed by faculty, staff and graduate students at TRLabs Regina and Electronic Systems Engineering at the University of Regina. TEEMA provides basic services such as logging, agent-to-agent messaging, agent migration, and agent naming. Customized services can be added to TEEMA without any difficulty because of its flexible architecture. More information related to TEEMA can be found in (Gibbs, 2001; Martens, 2001).

A mobile agent system may be viewed as a specific type of multi-agent system that would be classed as a Heterogeneous Communicating Multi-agent System according to Stone's taxonomy (Stone & Veloso, 2000). Stone's survey lists many multi-agent systems and classifies them into: Homogeneous Non-Communicating Multi-agent Systems, Heterogeneous Non-Communicating Multi-agent Systems, and Heterogeneous Communicating Multi-agent Systems. SWARM (Minar et al., 1996; Luna & Stefansson, 2000) and REPAST (Collier, 2003) are examples of multi-agent systems that are particularly popular for economic simulations. Multi-agent systems can be composed of many intelligent mobile agents. These multi-agent systems have been used for various applications including for example: electronic market places (Smith et al., 2001) course scheduling applications (Yang et al., 2004), and network resource management (Wei et al., 2002).

2 Agent System Dynamics and Analysis

In order to ensure that useful and effective mobile agent systems are constructed it is important to study, examine and test their system level behavior. This allows for greater understanding of the system dynamics so that once the system is implemented the dangers of unexpected system behavior are reduced. These unexpected system behaviors result from unforeseen group actions of agent groups, and agent-group behavior that was not directly coded by the agent designers.

The proposed approach is to simulate the agent system with a simplified architecture. This simplified architecture was implemented and the actual behavior of the system examined using executions of the simulation. The simplified architecture can also be modeled mathematically to define asymptotic system behavior.

Several mathematical approaches have been introduced to model and analyze system behavior in multi-agent systems (Lerman & Galstyan, 2001; Tecchia et al., 2001; Xu et al., 2002). Among these approaches Lerman & Galstyan (2001) present a general mathematical approach to analyze the global dynamic behavior of multi-agent swarm systems. Swarm systems (Bonabeau et al., 1999) are typically composed of many simple, task-oriented, objects that travel through potentially hostile environments to search for their task-related items. With no central controller directing how individual objects behave, interesting and intelligent collective behaviors emerge from the local interactions among individual agents and the interaction between individual agents and their surrounding environment.

Lerman & Shehory (2000) applied their mathematical modeling approach to a swarm system in a large scale electronic market, allowing observation of coalition formation behaviors. This behavior, however, was not explicitly programmed into each individual agent but was a spontaneously produced group-action. Similarly, much work has been done in information access/retrieval based on mobile agents; for example Smith et al. (2001) indicated that the full potential of each individual agent is not obtained during unwanted agent-group behaviors. Therefore, the behavior of agents in a multi-agent system must be carefully examined before implementation of an actual system, in order to minimize the chances of system failure and achieve superior system and individual agent performance.

2.1 The Agent-Based Electronic Health Record System

Many current health care systems are distributed among different geographical locations and patients' record are scattered throughout the Health System and could physically be anywhere such as for example in a clinic, a doctor's office, medical laboratory and/or a pharmacy. We propose an Agent-Based Electronic Health Record System using the TEEMA platform. A simplified simulation model of the system is shown in Figure 1 and follows our earlier work (Tse & Paranjape, 2006).

By using mobile agent technology, we add mobility to these records, which allows the record to move independently anywhere within the health care information system. This multi-agent system can be colloquially described as putting a mobile

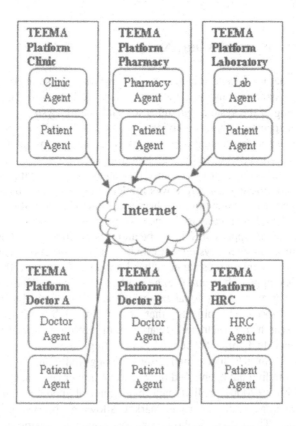

Fig. 1. An overview of the simplified Agent-based Electronic Health Record System architecture; each TEEMA platform represents a site in the system. Patient Agents visit each of these sites in the process of executing the simulation.

agent wrapper around an electronic health record fragment and instructing the agent to move the patient health record fragment to other medical facilities in order to unite and complete the patient electronic health record.

The two critically important aspects of the system are: (1) A complete health record set is defined as every piece of information in a patient's health record regardless of where it was generated united into one consistent and complete set of information. (2) Each agent in the system is self-regulated. This means that an individual mobile agent will accomplish its assigned task without any external supervision or guidance and no concept of what the group goal is. For each agent, its task is to retrieve and/or update the health record for the patient. Each individual agent has no interest in finding out what other agents within the system are doing.

2.2 System Components

Each TEEMA platform represents a certain physical location such as: a clinic, a doctor's office, a pharmacy or a laboratory. In each platform, there are a number of stationary and mobile agents. The location where all patient information is collected and collated is defined as the Health Record Central (HRC). All patient information is eventually sent to the HRC. The system contains five different types of stationary agents and one mobile agent:

Stationary Agents	
Clinic Agent (CA):	Responsible for creating an agent for a patient when the patient arrives at the clinic. The clinic agent also verifies patient identity.
Doctor Agent (DA):	Responsible for managing doctor's comment (health record) for patients.
Pharmacy Agent (PhA):	Responsible for validating the patient's identity and communicating with the patient agent when the patient pickups his/her prescription.
Lab Agent (LA):	Responsible for validating patient identity and communicating with the patient agent when the patient comes into the lab for medical tests.
Health Record Central Agent (HRCA):	Responsible for validating patient agents before they can access/modify/update the health record database.

Mobile Agents	
Patient Agent (PtA):	Is the patient's representative and it (or its clone) can migrate to different platforms to do work on the patient's behalf. It is responsible for updating patient health records, transferring new records to the HRC. If there is a prescription and/or lab test needed, the patient agent will clone itself and migrates to the pharmacy and/or laboratory and ensures that the patient fills the prescription or does the test and that the information is recorded and collected in the system.

Activity At Each Site	
Clinic:	All patients enter the simulation at the clinic. Patients Agents (PtA) are created when the patient enters the clinic. The PtA then checks if the patient health record needs to be updated. If so, it will clone itself and go to the HRC to obtain the necessary data. Then the PtA enters one of the two Doctor's offices. After the visit to one doctor's office the patient health record is updated and this new information is deposited in the HRC. The PtA will again clone itself and transmit the new information to the HRC. In addition, the Doctor may order laboratory tests, and/or medicines from the pharmacy. In this case, the PtA will also clone itself and move to the laboratory and/or pharmacy and wait for the patient to arrive.
Doctor's Office:	When the PtA arrives at the Doctor's office it interacts with a stationary doctor's office interface agent. This stationary agent relays the Doctor's instruction for the patient into the PtA. The Doctor's assessment of the patient's condition, which becomes part of the patient's health record also, is loaded into the PtA. The PtA then takes responsibility of the update of the health record and satisfying any Pharmacy or Laboratory requirements.
Laboratory:	A clone of the PtA is sent to the Laboratory on the instructions of the Doctor. The PtA clone waits for the patient to physically arrive in the Laboratory and then for Lab results to be generated. These results are assumed in this simulation to be available immediately after the patient visit but may in fact require some time to complete. The PtA clone interacts with a stationary Laboratory Agent which provides an interface to the Laboratory technician who is responsible for the operation of the Laboratory.
Pharmacy:	A clone of the PtA is sent to the Pharmacy on the instructions of the Doctor. The PtA clone waits for the patient to physically arrive in the Pharmacy and then for Pharmacy results to be generated. These results are assumed in this simulation to be available immediately after the patient visit but may in fact require some time to complete. The PtA clone interacts with a stationary Pharmacy Agent which provides an interface with the Pharmacist who is responsible for the operation of the Pharmacy.
Health Record Central (HRC):	Is the data center for the Agent-based health record system and is the place where all patient health information is stored. The HRC acts as the repository of all patient information that may be generated in the health care system even when the patient has exited the health

	care system. When the patient re-enters the health care system by coming to the clinic and a doctor's office, the HRC is used to update the patient information. The operation of the HRC is mediated by a stationary agent who task is to maintain the health record information delivered by PtA clones.

3 Experimental Validation

The architecture was implemented and experiments run to assess its behavior. These experimental results can be compared with numerical results from a general mathematical model of the system which will be discussed in section 3.4.

3.1 Simulation Structure and Conditions

Computers in the simulation were interconnected via 100Mbps Ethernet. Two computers were used that each executed a number of TEEMA platforms (the agent execution environment) Each TEEMA platform represents one specific physical medical site; in our experiment these included: 1 Clinic, 2 Doctors in the Clinic, 1 Pharmacy, 1 Laboratory and 1 HRC; leading to a total of 6 TEEMA platforms. The TEEMA platforms for the Clinic and the two Doctor's offices were executed on a single computer, and the other TEEMA platforms were executed on the other computer to represent the Pharmacy, Laboratory and the HRC.

Basic conditions and assumptions used in the experiment are listed below:

1. Doctor evaluations, prescription contents and lab test results are predefined to be the only type of data in the electronic health record. The combination of these components was considered the full health record of a patient.
2. Each TEEMA platform represents a physical medical site, so it will have its own unique IP address and port number. A configuration file is used to gather all TEEMA platforms associated with doctors, clinic, pharmacy and lab IP addresses and port numbers used in the experiment. This file is used as a reference for all the patient agents who need to migrate to different medical sites or TEEMA platforms.
3. Patients' health records are structured based on a file-system structure. So, in the HRC, each file contains an individual patient's health record.
4. A Number scheme was used for the patient name and each file was named using this scheme.
5. There are several random behaviors simulated by different kinds of random sources during the experiments:
   - Patient preference behavior – this behavior describes a patient's wish to choose a specific doctor. For simplicity a uniform distributed random number is used to represent this behavior.
   - Patient necessitated behavior - this behavior describes the need for a specific medical action. This includes the need for prescriptions and lab work. A Bernoulli random number was used to describe this type of behavior. Since the need for a prescription/lab work is

binary the chance that a patient will need this type of medical service when he/she visited the clinic is 50/50.

- Patient arrival behavior – this behavior describes rate of patient arrival at the clinic. For simplification, a constant mean rate of arrival was used and set to one patient arrival at the clinic every minute.
- Professional service behavior – this behavior describes the service time of any medical services provided to the patients. This includes physicians, pharmacists, and lab technician patient processing time. The doctors' service behavior was a uniform distributed random number between 1 and 5 (average service time of 3 minutes) while the lab and pharmacists' service behavior was a uniform distributed random number between 1 and 11 (average service time of 6 minutes).

3.2 Simulation Results

Figure 2 shows a set of graphs of the Agent population versus time for each of the sites with in the simulation. The horizontal axis on each graph shows time while the vertical axis shows number of agents. Patients and therefore Patient Agents were spawned into the system at the rate of 1 patient per minute. The experiment had duration of 30 minutes, and so involved 30 patients and their associated PtAs and clones.

We observe from Figure 2 that the number of Agents in the clinic goes up and down from zero to four agents but in general remains stable within this range. The PtA population does not show system level increases or decreases. Similarly the HRC does not show a marked development in the agent population with either zero or one agent on site throughout the experiment. On the other hand, all the other sites in the system show steady linear increases in agents congregating at the sites. Each of the Doctor's offices as well as the Pharmacy and Laboratory appear to have unsustainably long processing times and the population of patients and patient agents builds up at these sites. After studying these system behaviors the observer may be in a position to suggest mediating action such as decreasing pharmacy and laboratory wait times by adding staff.

3.3 Mathematical Modeling

A macroscopic model that treats agent population at each medical site as the fundamental unit (hence directly describing the characteristic of the system) can also be constructed. The equations used to model the system are presented below. These equations are presented in general form in Tse & Paranjape (2006) but are presented here modified for the specific context of the current experiment. The dynamics of the self-organizing processes can be examined using this model. The model contains a set of coupled rate equations that describe how the agent population at each platform evolves over time. The mathematical model contains one clinics, with two doctors in the clinic, one pharmacy, one testing laboratories and one Health Record Central.

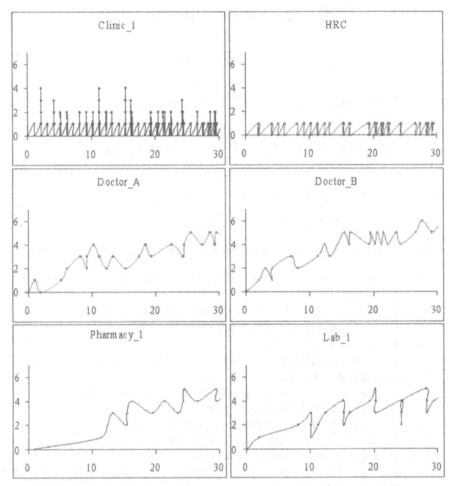

Fig. 2. Evolution of Agent Populations at each of the Sites in the Simulation. These are typical traces showing movements of patient agents in the simulation between six TEEMA platforms for a 30 minutes simulation run. The x-axis is time and the y-axis is number of agents on the site.

The dynamic variables in the model are:

- $N_C(t)$ – is the number of agents in the clinic.
- $N_{CDm}(t)$ – is the number of agents in doctor m's office in the clinic.
- $N_P(t)$ – is the number of agents in pharmacy.
- $N_L(t)$ – is the number of agents in laboratory.
- $N_{HRC}(t)$ – is the number of agents in the Health Record Central.

The equations governing the behavior of the system are given below:

$$\frac{dN_C(t)}{dt} = \lambda + \delta - \alpha_{CD} N_C(t) - \beta_A \alpha_{CR} N_C(t) - \beta_B \alpha_{CP} N_C(t - \tau_{AvgD}) - \beta_C \alpha_{CL} N_C(t - \tau_{AvgD}) \tag{1}$$

$$\frac{dN_{CD1}(t)}{dt} = \alpha_{CD}N_C(t)\beta_{D1} - 1/\tau_{CD1} \tag{2}$$

$$\frac{dN_{CD2}(t)}{dt} = \alpha_{CD}N_C(t)\beta_{D2} - 1/\tau_{CD2} \tag{3}$$

$$\frac{dN_P(t)}{dt} = (\alpha_{CP}N_C(t - \tau_{AvgD})\beta_B - 1/\tau_P)\theta(t - \tau_{AvgD}) \tag{4}$$

$$\frac{dN_L(t)}{dt} = (\alpha_{CL}N_C(t - \tau_{AvgD})\beta_C - 1/\tau_L)\theta(t - \tau_{AvgD}) \tag{5}$$

$$\frac{dN_{HRC}(t)}{dt} = \alpha_{CR}N_C(t)\beta_A + \theta(t - \tau_{AvgD} - \tau_L)1/\tau_L + \\ 1/\tau_{CD1} + 1/\tau_{CD2} - 1/\tau_{HRC} \tag{6}$$

And the definitions of the parameters used in the model are:

- λ – the patient arrival rate at the clinic, which is the rate of agent production.
- δ - the rate of agent cloning that occurs at the clinic platform.
- τ_{CDm} - the examination time of doctor 'm' on a patient.
- τ_{AvgD} – the average of all τ_{CDn}.
- τ_P- the service time of an agent in the pharmacy (prescription fill time + prescription pickup time).
- τ_L - the service time of an agent in the lab (time for a patient to come to the lab + test result production time).
- τ_{HRC} - the service time for an agent in a HRC.
- β_A, β_B, β_C, - the probability of a patient who need an update, or a prescription, or a lab work, respectively.
- β_{Dm} - the probability of a doctor being chosen by a patient. It is set to 1/(# of doctors in the Clinic), since each doctor is to be chosen equally.
- α - the transition rates of agents between different platforms, for example: α_{CP} is the rate at which PtAs leave the Clinic platform to go to the pharmacy platform.
- $\theta(t-\tau)$ - a unit step function to ensure certain variables are zero during t < τ.

For simplicity, we assume the following when solving the equations:

- all α to be uniformly distributed in some space, which set to 1.
- all β to be a constant value 0.5, except for β_{PP1} and β_{PL1} which set to 1.
- τ_{CD1} and τ_{CD2} are set to be a constant value of 3, τ_P and τ_L are set to a constant value of 6, while τ_{HRC} is set to 1. These values are the expected value of the uniform distributed random number in our parameters used in the simulation.
- $\lambda = 1$ and $\delta = 1/3$.

3.4 Modeling Results

A set of graphs indicating the solution of the set of equations above is shown in Figure 3. The graphs show the population of PtAs at each of the sites in the Agent model presented as a function of time over a 30 minute interval. The first and most important observation is that the graphs in Figure 3 correspond closely to the graphs in Figure 2 for the agent population in the simulation.

In the HRC graph, we see that there is a small oscillatory behavior which occurs in the value of $N_C(t)$ at the beginning of the experiment. The reason may be that there are many PtAs being created and they are cloning themselves at the same time, causing an increase in $N_{Cl}(t)$. As the PtAs leave the Clinic platform for either of the Doctor's platform the number of Agents in the clinic platform, $N_{Cl}(t)$, decreases. Thus there are forces increasing and decreasing the agent population in the Clinic platform. As time goes by, the number of agents in each platform becomes stable in the form of a straight line. This suggests that the system adjusts itself to the changes of PtA population in each platform.

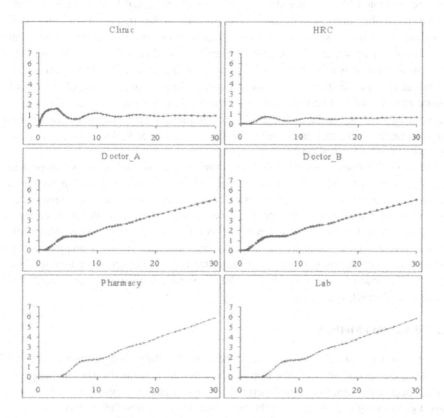

Fig. 3. Asymptotic Behavior of Agent Populations at each of the Sites in the Simulation. These are typical traces showing movements of patient agents in the mathematical model between six TEEMA platforms for a 30 minutes execution. The x-axis is time and y-axis is number of agents on the site.

We can calculate the number of agents in each Doctor platform by noting that 30 PtAs were created in the 30-minute experiment. Since the agents will divide themselves up between the two Doctors platforms each doctor will see 15 patients. Each doctor's examination time is 3 minutes on average, thus at the end of 30 minutes each will have processed only 10 patients leaving 5 patients and their corresponding PtA on each of the Doctor's platform. In fact, this is very close to what we see in Figure 3. Similar calculations for pharmacy and lab platform indicate there should be 6 PtAs in Pharmacy and 6 PtAs in the Laboratory respectively. Again there is good correspondence to what we see in Figure 3.

4 Peer to Peer

4.1 Development of an Equivalent Peer-to-Peer System

Many peer-to-peer techniques are not especially relevant to systems on the scale of the one presented above, since these techniques are designed to deal with situations where particular machines or documents needs to be tracked over very large distributed systems. A scaled up version of the health record system described in this paper could in principle rely on multiple health record centers. To the extent that there were thousands or even tens of thousands of health record centers peer-to-peer techniques such as distributed hash tables (Balakrishnan et al., 2003) could be used to ensure retrieval of a consistent individual health record for each patient. However in a system of the size considered here these techniques are redundant since any request for information can be immediately satisfied by a direct lookup against a list of available locations and dispatch of an agent.

However this does not prevent us from simulating a system that works on peer-to-peer principles, i.e. one that involves the decentralized transmission of messages as opposed to agents. In fact, arguably this kind of system is not a novel peer-to-peer system at all, but simply a decentralized messaging system just like most common network systems today. While much of the web for example relies on a client-server model layered over decentralized messaging systems, many commonly used applications such as email still use a decentralized non-client-server system and have done so for many years; long before the term peer-to-peer was associated with decentralized overlay networks as it is today.

4.2 Simulation Method

A "peer-to-peer" simulation was developed in the Ruby programming language following the specifications of the health record system described earlier in this paper. To be specific the health system described above is a largely centralized system, with most agents being required to pass through a single centralized "clinic" location, with the exception of occasional traffic between the "lab" and "hrc" locations. The possible message pathways are shown in the following diagram:

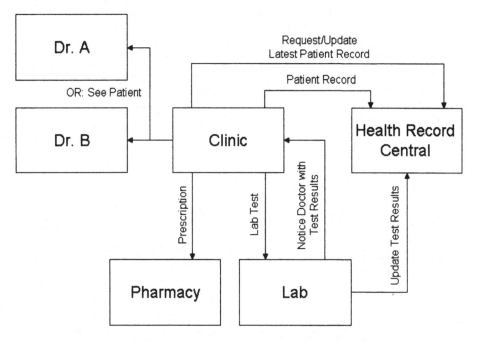

Fig. 4. Locations and information flow in the Health System application

Each location was considered to have a queue for incoming messages, and could be in a "blocked" state if it was unable to process additional messages, e.g. when a doctor was seeing a patient. Message transfer and process time was assumed to take a second, when not associated with professional service behavior, which itself followed a one to five minute Uniform distribution. A new patient arrived at the clinic every minute. The clinic peer would check the locally stored copy of the patient's health record and request an update from the HRC peer as necessary. Assuming a patients health record was up to date patients would be assigned to the doctor of their preference, and a message containing the health record would then be sent to the doctor peer which would start to process that patient and not process any additional messages until the doctor had finished with that patient. Finished sessions with patients would lead to the doctor peer sending notification and follow up requests to the clinic peer, which would pass them on to the pharmacy and lab as appropriate, with the pharmacy and lab peers blocking as they performed their own professional service behavior. The lab and pharmacy peers would then notify the appropriate peers via the clinic peer (in the case of message to the doctor peer) or directly to the HRC peer as necessary. All probability distributions were set following the pattern described earlier in the paper.

The simulation was run on a single computer, with all "locations" virtually present in the same environment. The results of a single simulation run are shown below. Naturally any simulation should be run a repeated number of times until the expected

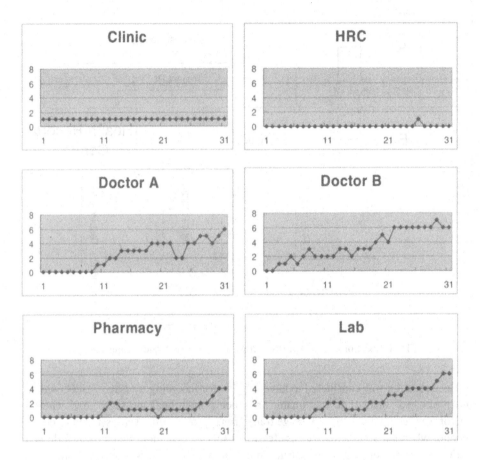

Fig. 5. Queue lengths over time for the different locations in the peer to peer system. X axis is time in minutes, while y axis is length of queue in messages.

error reaches a threshold level, however the mathematical analysis we shall describe in the next section fully explains the behavior of the system and makes such repeated simulations largely unnecessary. For the moment it is relevant to note that the peer simulation shows remarkably similar behavior to the agent system in that we see queues of increasing length at both doctors and at the lab and pharmacy.

Queueing theory (Allen, 1990) defines the traffic intensity (a) of a simple queueing system as the mean arrival rate (λ) divided by the mean service rate (μ), and states that the number of servers (c) must be greater than this ratio in order to avoid queues of ever increasing length, as shown in equation 7.

$$a = \frac{\lambda}{\mu} < c \tag{7}$$

If we make the plausible assumption that individual message transfer and processing times are trivial in comparison to professional service behavior the fundamental behavior of the system can be modeled in terms of individual doctors as a set of G/U/1 queuing systems. A G/U/1 queueing system has an unspecified inter-arrival time distribution (G or general), a Uniform service time distribution (U) and a single server (1). Patients in our system arrive with a deterministic or constant gap between arrivals (i.e. 1 minute), but they arrive wanting to see a particular doctor. Thus we can model the system as two queues, one for Dr. A and another for Dr. B. Given a sequence of patients wanting to see Dr. A we will eventually have a patient wanting to see Dr. B and so there is a gradually decreasing chance of longer inter-arrival times for each doctor. This amounts to a geometric distribution which counts as a general distribution in queueing theory.

Patients in the system are clearly processed in a Uniform amount of time (between 1 and 5 minutes), but it may not be so obvious how we can think in terms of a single server (the 1 in G/U/1). We can describe the system in terms of a single server because as we will show, the number of patients desiring to visit an individual doctor forms a bottleneck that makes any subsequent waiting times (e.g. at the lab or pharmacy) irrelevant in terms of the overall system behavior. Assuming for the moment that we accept the assertion that doctors create the system bottleneck it follows from our reasoning above that the two doctors should be considered as independent queues since patients have decided in advance which doctor they would like to see. As a result one doctor cannot process the others' patients, giving us effectively two independent G/U/1 type queues.

Let us consider the traffic intensity (a) for one doctor peer. We know that the service time distribution is normal and the arrival time distribution is geometric. The expected values of the service time ($E[s]$) and inter-arrival time ($E[\tau]$) are thus [min+max]/2 and [1-p/p]+1 respectively, where min is the minimum service time, max is the maximum service time and p is the probability of choosing one doctor over the other. The mean service time of each patient (μ) is the inverse of the expected service time (1/ $E[s]$) and the arrival rate of patients to each doctor (λ) is the inverse of the expected inter-arrival time (1/ $E[\tau]$). Given that min=1, max=5 and p = 0.5 we know the mean service time (μ) is 1/3 and the mean arrival rate (λ) is 1/2. Unfortunately for our patients this means that the traffic intensity as defined in equation 7 is 3/2 implying that a single doctor (and their patients) will always experience increasing queue lengths. Thus given that patients arrive at this rate, the only way for the system to function effectively is to have more than one doctor available for each patient. Assuming that patients had no choice as to which doctor they saw the system would still be unable to function, as although there are two doctors, the same analysis above applied to an inter-arrival time of 1 minute indicates that at least three doctors are required to ensure non-increasing queue lengths.

Thus the fundamental behavior of our computer implementation, simulation and previous mathematical analysis is explained by simple queueing theory. Our first reaction will likely be that the distributions specified for the simulations are not realistic, and that both patient arrival and service times are much more likely to be described by exponential distributions of some sort, and that it would be an uncommon health system that could always guarantee patients access to the doctor of their choice. Replacing the assumptions of the existing simulations with those found in real world settings would seems a logical next step, at which point it is likely that we would find the doctor bottleneck was removed and require a more comprehensive queueing model to explain system behaviour.

Fortunately Baskett et al. (1975) developed the BCMP Queuing network model that allows systems such as these to be modeled as a group of interconnected queues. This approach would become increasingly valuable for pinpointing particular system bottlenecks as simplifying assumptions, such as message processing time being trivial in comparison to professional service behavior, start to break down.

The particular advantage of a queuing analysis in general is that we can use it to predict precisely how many servers (doctors, labs, pharmacies, etc.) are required to support an operationally effective system rather than rely exclusively on a trial and error approach of making small changes and then repeating simulations or numerical analyses to see if the changes have had the expected effect.

5 Conclusion

In this work we have focused on the development of an agent-based mechanism to support the creation of a self-organizing electronic health record system. The method focuses on the problem of creating complete and consistent records using the strength of agent mobility. We have demonstrated that the agent system will behave as expected by employing both simulation techniques and mathematical modeling.

The second important strength of this type of modeling is that system behaviors such as the linear increase in patients at some of the sites in the health care system can be recognized and addressed before actual system implementation. This approach circumvents system problems by identifying them prior to implementation and allows for effective evaluation of mediating approaches. The approach demonstrates the advantages of test simulation and modeling in agent system design and development.

However our peer-to-peer model demonstrates that the ability to support a health record system with complete and consistent records does not explicitly require the use of mobile agents. Mobile agents are a powerful technology that has particular advantages over simple decentralized message passing systems in that they can transfer code and state along with simple message data. As described by Joseph & Kawamura (2001) there are only a limited set of circumstances in which the particular power of mobile agents can be used effectively, and we have not as yet demonstrated that the nature of the health care record maintenance challenge is one of them. We cannot rule out that as more complex health record behavior is manifested in such as system, mobile agent technology will be required. However in the absence of specific evidence and given that our somewhat simpler peer-to-peer system achieves exactly the same results as our mobile agent system, one has to ask the question of whether mobile agents are perhaps too powerful a technology to be employed for this particular application. Nonetheless we hope that our side by side comparison of an agent system implementation, a peer-to-peer simulation, a mathematical model of agents and queueing theory analysis will prove instructive for system designers in the medical informatics field.

Acknowledgments. The authors thank TRLabs and NSERC for their generous support of this project.

References

Allen, A.O.: Probability, Statistics and Queueing Theory with Computer Science Applications, 2nd edn. Academic Press, San Diego (1990)

Balakrishnan, H., Kaashoek, M.F., Karger, D., Morris, R., Stoica, I.: Looking Up Data in P2P Systems. Communications of the ACM 46(2), 43–48 (2003)

Baskett, F., Chandy, K., Muntz, R., Palacios, F.: Open, closed, and mixed networks of queues with different classes of customers. Journal of the ACM 22(2), 248–260 (1975)

Bonabeau, E., Dorigo, M., Theraulaz, G.: Swarm intelligence: from natural to artificial systems. Oxford University Press, New York (1999)

Collier, N.: Repast: the recursive porous agent simulation toolkit, [WWW document] (2003), http://repast.sourceforge.net

Dick, R.S., Steen, E.B.: The Computer Based Patient Record: An Essential Technology for Health Care. National Academy Press, Washington D.C (1991), http://www.nap.edu/books/0309055326/html/index.html

Gibbs, C.: TEEMA Reference Guide Version 1.0. Regina, TRLabs, Saskatchewan, Canada (2000)

Johns, M.L.: Information Management for Health Professionals, Delmar (1997)

Joseph, S., Kawamura, T.: Why Autonomy Makes the Agent. In: Liu, J., Zhong, N., Tang, Y.Y., Wang, P. (eds.) Agent Engineering, pp. 7–22. World Scientific Publishing, Singapore (2001)

Kotz, D., Gray, R., Rus, D.: Future directions for mobile-agent research. Technical Report TR2002-415, Dept. Computer Science, Dartmouth College (January 2002)

Lerman, K., Galstyan, A.: A methodology for mathematical analysis of multi-agent systems (University of California Information Sciences Technical Report ISI-TR-529). California, USA: University of California Information Sciences Institute (2001), http://www.isi.edu/~lerman/projects/task/

Lerman, K., Shehory, O.: Coalition formation for large-scale electronic markets [Electronic Version]. In: Proceedings of the Fourth International Conference on Multiagent Systems, Boston, MA, pp. 167–175 (2000)

Luna, F., Stefansson, B.: Economic simulations in Swarm: agent-based modelling and object programming. Kluwer Academic Publishers, Dordrecht (2000)

Martens, R.: TEEMA TRLabs Execution Environment for Mobile Agents. TRLabs, Regina, Saskatchewan, Canada (2001)

Minar, N., Burkhart, R., Langton, C., Askenazi, M.: The swarm simulation system, a toolkit for building multi-agent simulations (1996), http://www.santafe.edu/projects/swarm/overview/overview.html

Moreno, A.: Medical Applications of Multi-Agent Systems. In: Paper presented at the 2003 Intelligent and Adaptive Systems in Medicine Workshop, http://cyber.felk.cvut.cz/EUNITE03-BIO/pdf/Moreno.pdf

Nealon, J., Moreno, A.: Agent-based applications in health care. In: Paper presented at EU-LAT Workshop 2003 (2003), http://www.etse.urv.es/recerca/banzai/toni/MAS/papers.html

Raj, G.S.: A detailed comparison of CORBA, DCOM and Java/RMI, Tech. rep., Web Cornucopia, [WWW document] (1998), http://my.execpc.com/~gopalan/misc/compare.html

Smith, K., Paranjape, R., Benedicenti, L.: Agent behavior and agent models in unregulated markets [Electronic Version]. Association for Computing Machinery SIGAPP Applied Computing Review 9(3), 2–12 (2001)

Stone, P., Veloso, M.M.: Multiagent systems: A survey from a machine learning perspective. Autonomous Robots 8(3), 345–383 (2000)

Tecchia, F., Loscos, C., Conroy, R., Chrysanthou, Y.: Agent Behaviour Simulator (ABS): A Platform for Urban Behaviour Development. In: The First International Game Technology Conference and Idea Expo (GTEC 2001) in co-operation with ACM SIGGRAPH and EUROGRAPHICS, Hong Kong, pp. 17–21 (2001)

Tse, B., Paranjape, R.: Macroscopic Modeling of Information Flow in Agent-Based Electronic Health Record System, ch. 17. In: Lin, H. (ed.) Architectural Design of Multi-Agent Systems: Technologies and Techniques, Idea Group Publishing (2006)

Wei, H., Paranjape, R., Benedicenti, L.: Mobile agent network management system performance study in frame relay network. In: Proceedings of the 2002 Institute of Electrical and Electronics Engineers Canadian Conference on Electrical and Computer Engineering, Winnipeg, Manitoba, Canada, pp. 1499–1504 (2002)

Xu, D., Volz, R., Loerger, T., Yen, J.: Modeling and verifying multi-agent behaviors using predicate/transition nets. In: Association for Computing Machinery International Conference Proceeding Series, vol. 27, pp. 193–200 (2002)

Yang, Y., Paranjape, R., Benedicenti, L.: An examination of mobile agents system evolution in the course scheduling problem. In: Proceedings of the 2004 Institute of Electrical and Electronics Engineers Canadian Conference on Electrical and Computer Engineering, vol. 2, pp. 657–660 (2004)

Hybrid DHT Design for Mobile Environments

Stefan Zoels[1], Simon Schubert[1], Wolfgang Kellerer[2], and Zoran Despotovic[2]

[1] Institute of Communication Networks, Munich University of Technology, Germany
stefan.zoels@tum.de, corecode@fs.ei.tum.de
[2] Future Networking Lab, DoCoMo Communications Laboratories Europe, Germany
{kellerer, despotovic}@docomolab-euro.com

Abstract. In this paper we present a hybrid design concept for Distributed Hash Tables (DHTs), in order to increase the performance of DHTs in scenarios with mobile participants. By defining two classes of nodes (static and temporary) and assigning critical overlay networking tasks to reliable static nodes, our concept allows the disburdening of resource-constrained temporary nodes such as PDAs or mobile phones. Further we present an implementation of our system design, based on the Chord protocol, in the Network Simulator 2 (NS-2) and in the overlay simulator L7Sim and show simulation results that prove the significant advantages of our extension in comparison to conventional DHTs.

1 Introduction

Distributed Hash Tables (DHTs) are currently a major subject of research in the area of distributed computing and Peer-to-Peer (P2P) networks in particular. Their two key properties – hash table like lookup interface and extreme scalability – turn out to be sufficient for building large scale distributed applications. Additionally, in contrast to unstructured P2P networks, they avoid flooding of query messages, thus reducing the average number of search hops to $O(\log n)$ for a network with n nodes. As a result the signaling traffic in the overlay network decreases significantly.

However, the current mainstream research on P2P concentrates on fixed IP networks consisting of functionally equal nodes. As such, it usually neglects eventual heterogeneity among the participating computing devices. In this paper we focus on extending current DHTs to mobile environments. In order to do so, we have to be aware of the challenges resulting from this large heterogeneity of participating nodes, ranging from hard-wired work stations to GPRS-connected mobile phones:

- Limited resources of mobile devices (CPU power, RAM size, storage capacity) as well as low access data rates have to be addressed. Moreover, devices cannot be modeled as one class of nodes but their heterogeneity requires different consideration of different types of nodes.
- High costs for mobile data transfer lead to short online times of mobile participants. Resulting we face a highly dynamic environment, characterized by high churn rates.

S. Joseph et al. (Eds.): AP2PC 2006, LNAI 4461, pp. 19–30, 2008.

– The increased failure probability of mobile devices (due to wireless link breaks, discharged batteries...) can result in a high number of lost object references, which in turn may result in the (at least temporary) unavailability of shared objects.

In this paper we address these requirements by proposing a hybrid DHT design. We define two classes of nodes, which we call 'static' and 'temporary', and we assume that static nodes both perform routing tasks and maintain references to the available objects in the system, while temporary nodes only perform routing. In this way we disburden temporary nodes and avoid shifting object references when temporary nodes join or leave the system. The result is significantly decreased overall maintenance traffic.[1] Besides, we emphasize that this approach has another important advantage: It enables the low performance nodes (e.g. mobile terminals) to participate in a DHT based P2P network.

The work presented in this paper is an extension and a generalization of our previously proposed Hybrid Chord Protocol [1].

The paper is organized as follows. Section 2 gives an overview of distributed hash tables. Section 3 presents our hybrid DHT design in detail. In Section 4 we present an illustrative set of simulations we performed to test the performance of the proposed design. Section 4.1 illustrates the setup of simulation scenarios with our traffic generator, while Section 4.2 shows and discusses simulation results. Section 5 concludes this paper and gives an outlook to future work.

2 Distributed Hash Tables - Overview

The basic problem DHTs address is self-organized distribution of a set of objects among a set of peers, enabling their subsequent fast lookup. In a DHT peers collaboratively manage specific subsets of objects, identified by keys from a key space K, which depend on the set of all peers and the set of all objects available in the system. This is done by associating each peer with a key taken from K and also associating with this key a partition of the key space such that the peer becomes responsible to manage all objects identified by keys from the associated partition. Typically the key partition consists of all keys closest to the peer key in a suitable metric. Thus the key space K is equipped with a distance function d. To forward query requests peers form a routing network by taking into account the knowledge on the association of peers with key partitions.

In short, any DHT is equipped with a function $key : P \rightarrow K$ that associates peers with keys and, given $key(P)$, a function $partition : K \rightarrow 2^K$ associating peers with partitions of K, and a function $neighbors : K \rightarrow 2^P$ that associates each peer with a subset of other peers, making thus an overlay graph G [2].

Function key is a hash function mapping a peer's IP address or a randomly chosen string into a hash value. Please note that the set of all participating peers at any time can be considered as parameter of the function $partition$; the interpretation is that the objects must be assigned to the peers that are currently

---

[1] Throughout the remaining paper we use the term 'maintenance traffic' synonymously for the number of object references shifted to a joining node or from a leaving node.

present in the system. A side goal of using a hash function to map object keys to peers is balancing the load distribution: each peer should be responsible for approximately the same number of keys. The function *neighbors* is responsible for building the DHT routing graph. Using the metric of the key space, it normally enables peers to maintain short-range links to all peers with neighboring keys and in addition a small number of long-range links to some selected peers. Using thus established routing graph, peers forward query requests in a directed manner to other peers from their routing tables trying to greedily reduce the distance to the key that is being looked up. Most of DHTs achieve by virtue of this construction and routing algorithms lookup with a number of messages logarithmic in the size of network by using routing tables which are also logarithmic in the size of the network [3,4]. However, in recent few years there have been also some works that achieve constant outdegree graph topologies and consequently constant sized routing tables while retaining logarithmic routing [5,6]. To sum up, the specific designs of these structures depend on the choice of key space, distance function, key partitioning, and linking strategy. They have been subject of intensive research over the recent years and resulted in numerous designs of structured overlay networks.

However, the good properties related to the efficiency of routing do not come for free. For constructing and maintaining a structured P2P network peers have to deal in particular with the problem of node joins and failures. Since the freedom to choose neighbors in a structured P2P network is constrained by the conditions imposed by the function *neighbors*, maintenance algorithms are required to re-establish the consistency of routing tables in the presence of network dynamics. Depending on the type of guarantees given by the network different deterministic and probabilistic maintenance strategies have been developed. Maintenance actions can be triggered by various events, such as periodical node joins and leaves or routing failures due to inconsistent routing tables. The different maintenance strategies trade-off maintenance cost versus degree of consistency and thus failure resilience of the network.

3 Hybrid DHT Design

The main goal of our hybrid DHT design is to enable participation of mobile devices such as PDAs or mobile phones in a DHT based P2P lookup system. It sets up a hybrid overlay structure by extending a given conventional DHT protocol as to define two different types of nodes: static nodes and temporary nodes. Static nodes are reliable nodes in the overlay network that are characterized by long online times, low failure probabilities and good hardware resources (e.g. office computers with hard-wired connections to the Internet). All other, low-performance nodes in the overlay network (e.g. all mobile participants such as GSM mobile phones or WLAN PDAs) are temporary nodes.

We require a minor modification to the object mapping rules of the DHT: In contrast to the conventional DHT protocol, a reference to a shared object is stored on the closest *static* node of the object's key. (The term "closest" refers to the conventional DHT's distance metric: in Pastry it is the height of the smallest tree containing the two considered nodes, in Chord it is the simple difference of the nodes' identifiers.) In contrast, temporary nodes maintain only a pointer to their succeeding static node. Thus whenever a temporary node in the network receives an INSERT or QUERY request (due to its responsibility for the key given in the request) it simply forwards this request to its closest static node which in turn stores the according reference(s). Such hybrid structure can be realized by calling different JOIN and LEAVE procedures when nodes connect to or quit the overlay network, depending on the node class that this node belongs to (see pseudocode in Figure 1).

```
n.joinStatic()                          n.leaveStatic()
    setupRoutingTable();                    n = find_next_static(n.id);
    n = find_next_static(n.id);             transfer_references(n);
    transfer_matching_references(n);        inform_neighboring_nodes();
    start_timers();                         stop_timers();

n.joinTemporary()                       n.leaveTemporary()
    setupRoutingTable();                    inform_neighboring_nodes();
    n = find_next_static(n.id);             stop_timers();
    set_next_static(n);
    start_timers();
```

Fig. 1. Pseudocode for hybrid system structure setup

The differentiation between static and temporary nodes has three major advantages:

- The heterogeneity of the participating nodes that results from extending the overlay network to mobile environments is addressed.
- The maintenance traffic in the overlay network can be decreased significantly, as object references have to be shifted only when static nodes (which have long online times) join or leave the overlay network. Moreover, resource-constrained temporary nodes are prevented from storing and providing object references.
- Only reliable static nodes with low failure probability store references to shared objects. Resulting, the probability that an object is available in the system but the node(s) that is (are) responsible for storing a reference to it has failed is reduced. Consequently, the availability of provided content increases.

The extension we just presented assumes that there are two classes of nodes, static and temporary, defined independently of the current state of the system (i.e. the properties of the nodes available in the system). Thus any node can unambiguously determine to which class it belongs. In principle, it should be possible to make a step further and remove this constraint as to make a node class dependent on the system state at any time instant (a joining node might assess the current state of the system based on the properties of the nodes encountered in the joining process) and enable the total work division according to the nodes relative capabilities. We plan to investigate such extension in the future.

4   Simulations

In this section, we present the results from a series of simulations, in which we compare the conventional Chord protocol [4] and the Hybrid Chord Protocol (HCP), obtained by applying the above described modifications to Chord. The results show the significant advantages of HCP in scenarios with resource-constrained mobile participants.

4.1   Simulation Setup

To evaluate and compare the performance of conventional Chord and HCP we implemented both protocols in the Network Simulator 2 (NS-2) [7]. Since NS-2 simulates the complete packet flow through all layers of the ISO/OSI reference model, it requires a high amount of CPU power and Random Access Memory. Resulting, the size of the simulated overlay network is limited to only a few hundred nodes. In order to be able to simulate even larger overlay networks (typical for P2P networks) we modified the NS-2 implementation of both protocols so that only the overlay network is simulated. With this so-called L7Sim (Layer 7 Simulator), messages are exchanged directly between the P2P applications, without making use of the underlying layers of the ISO/OSI reference model. The delay of physical links is thereby represented by an equally distributed delay between 10 ms and 200 ms. The convergence of both approaches is shown in Section 4.2. To set up simulation scenarios we implemented a traffic generator that performs the following tasks:

- **Definition of different node classes.** For the simulated overlay networks, different classes of participating nodes can be defined. Appropriate parameters for node classes are the mean online time, the failure probability (i.e., the probability that a node leaves the overlay network without notifying other nodes), the number of shared objects, and the average query rate. For NS-2 simulations, also the data rate and the delay of the physical link to the core network can be defined.
- **Creation of an initial overlay network.** The traffic generator creates an initial Chord/HCP overlay structure with a given number of nodes, including the setting of predecessor pointer, successor list, finger table, next static pointer (for temporary HCP nodes) and provided content. For NS-2 simulations, it also connects the overlay nodes to the core network. The core network emulates the physical IP connections between the overlay nodes. It consists of 100 core nodes and is created with the BRITE [8] topology generator.
- **Generation of an eventfile.** The eventfile is created according to the specified parameters and is used as input for both network simulators.

Figure 2 shows the setup of an exemplary simulation scenario with the traffic generator using three node classes. In detail the simulation process runs as follows: Firstly, the traffic generator reads the scenario file and generates – according to the parameters given in the scenario file – an output file containing the initial

```
nodeclass WLAN_NOTEBOOK
        mean_online_time 3600s
        failure_probability 10%
        shared_objects 50
        query_rate 300s
        link datarate 1Mb delay 10ms
nodeclass UMTS_PHONE
        mean_online_time 1800s
        failure_probability 25%
        shared_objects 20
        query_rate 120s
        link datarate 384kb delay 120ms
nodeclass GPRS_PHONE
        mean_online_time 900s
        failure_probability 50%
        shared_objects 5
        query_rate 60s
        link datarate 100kb delay 400ms
initial
        100 WLAN_NOTEBOOK
        100 UMTS_PHONE
        100 GPRS_PHONE
simulation-duration 1h
```

Fig. 2. Scenario file for the setup of a simulation scenario

overlay network as well as simulation events. Simulation events are composed of NODE-JOIN, NODE-LEAVE, NODE-FAILURE and QUERY events. Secondly, the generated file is taken as input for the used network simulator, which in turn produces a tracing file that can be analyzed with appropriate evaluation tools.

4.2   Simulation Results

Based on multiple independent simulations, we evaluate HCP in comparison to the conventional Chord protocol. The focus of the following simulations is put onto the decreased maintenance traffic and the increased availability of provided content that can be achieved with HCP.

In a first simulation we set up a network with 100 overlay nodes which are connected randomly to the core network. The main goal of this simulation is to evaluate the differences between simulating the overlay network on top of a physical network using the complete protocol stack (NS-2) and simulating the overlay network independently, without considering the physical topology (L7Sim). Thus we want to determine the impact of lower-layer parameters such as queue length, packet loss or link latency on our simulations. Table 1 shows all relevant simulation parameters for this simulation scenario.

By varying the mean online time[2] of temporary nodes from 600 s to 1800 s, we create seven different independent eventfiles. We simulate each eventfile with

---

[2] The traffic generator determines the online time of each participating node following a negative-exponential distribution, with mean value given in the node class definition in the scenario file.

Table 1. Simulation parameters for scenario 1

Number of node classes:	2	
Node class:	*STATIC*	*TEMPORARY*
Mean online time:	1800 s (neg. exp. dist.)	600 s - 1800 s (neg. exp. dist.)
Number of shared objects:	10 per node	10 per node
Physical link:	1 Mb/s, 10 ms delay	100 kb/s, 100 ms delay
Mean number of nodes:	100	
Partitioning:	10 static, 90 temporary	
Simulation duration:	4 hours	

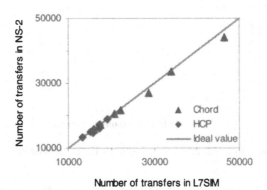

Fig. 3. Scenario 1: Maintenance traffic in both simulators

both protocols in NS-2 and in L7Sim, and compare the total number of transferred object references (i.e. the resulting maintenance traffic) in both simulators.

As we see from Figure 3, the measured numbers of transferred object references are nearly the same in both simulators. The marginal differences in NS-2 result from a negligible packet loss in the physical layer. Resulting we can state that simulating only the overlay network, without considering the underlying physical topology, is sufficient for our analysis.

The basic criterion for comparing maintenance traffic in HCP and in Chord is the ratio α of the mean online time of static nodes in HCP and the mean online time of all nodes in Chord:

$$\alpha = \frac{\text{Mean online time of static nodes}}{\text{Mean online time of all nodes}}$$

As stated in section 3, HCP stores object references only on static nodes. Therefore, the mean online time of static nodes is crucial for the maintenance traffic in HCP, as object references have to be shifted whenever a static node joins or leaves the overlay network. In contrast, Chord stores object references on all nodes in the overlay network, so the mean online time of all nodes is decisive for the maintenance traffic in Chord. By theoretical evaluation (see Appendix) we can show that the maintenance traffic in HCP is lowered by a factor of $1/\alpha$ in comparison to Chord.

In the above simulation scenario we obtain different values for the ratio α from the varying mean online time of temporary nodes. Figure 4 shows a comparison of the resulting maintenance traffic. It illustrates the percentage of transferred object references in HCP in comparison to Chord, depending on the ratio of mean online times α. The simulation results coincide with our theoretical evaluation that HCP reduces maintenance traffic by a factor of $1/\alpha$ compared to Chord.

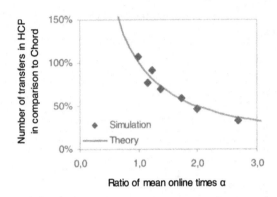

Fig. 4. Scenario 1: Maintenance traffic in HCP compared to Chord

Our next simulation aims at the verification of this theoretical evaluation in a large overlay network with a high percentage of mobile participants, and by a lot of different independent simulation runs. Therefore, we create multiple simulation scenarios according to the setup parameters given in Table 2. Please note that we vary the mean online time of static nodes from five to fifty minutes.

Table 2. Simulation parameters for scenario 2

Number of node classes:	2	
Node class:	*STATIC*	*MOBILE*
Mean online time:	300 s - 3000 s (neg. exp. dist.)	300 s (neg. exp. dist.)
Number of shared objects:	1 per node	1 per node
Mean number of nodes:	1000	
Partitioning:	100 static, 900 mobile	
Simulation duration:	2 hours	

Due to the high number of overlay nodes, and based on the findings of our first simulation we confine ourselves to simulate this scenario only in the overlay simulator L7Sim. We generate 56 different eventfiles with a ratio of mean online times α ranging from 0.99 to 8.93. The individual values for α result directly from the varying mean online time of all participating nodes in each scenario file. In Figure 5, the resulting maintenance traffic of all 56 simulation runs is depicted for both protocols. As expected, the total number of transferred object references in Chord nearly stays at a constant level, because the mean online time of all nodes in the overlay network only changes slightly (please note that 90% of the overlay network is formed by mobile nodes that have a constant mean online time of about 300 s). On the other hand the mean online time of static nodes rises from 300 s to 3000 s in average. Along with this increasing ratio α comes significantly decreased maintenance traffic in HCP. With this simulation we can prove our theoretical evaluation: As we can see in Figure 5, the amount of transferred object references in HCP decreases with $1/\alpha$, while it remains constantly high in Chord.

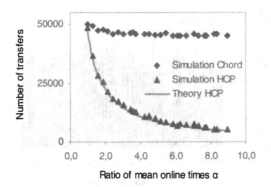

Fig. 5. Scenario 2: Maintenance traffic

So far, we have considered theoretical simulation scenarios with only two different node classes. To evaluate HCP in a more realistic scenario, we set up a heterogeneous overlay network with 2000 nodes, partitioned into five different node classes: 100 office computers, 700 DSL subscribers, 400 ISDN users, 400 PDAs, and 400 mobile phones. Table 3 illustrates the modeling of these nodes classes.

Table 3. Simulation parameters for scenario 3

Number of node classes:	5				
Node class:	*OFFICE*	*DSL*	*ISDN*	*PDA*	*PHONE*
Mean online time:	24 h	2 h	30 min	10 min	2 min
Failure probability:	0.1%	5%	10%	35%	50%
Number of shared objects:	0-30	0-30	0-15	0-8	0-5
Average query rate: 1 every...	10 min	8 min	5 min	1 min	20 s
Simulation duration:	1 hour				

Again, the mean online time and the average query rate of overlay nodes are negative exponentially distributed and the number of shared objects is distributed equally between the given minimum and maximum value. The simulated time is one hour. When simulating HCP, only nodes that belong to the node classes *OFFICE* and *DSL* are allowed to become static nodes, and thus to store references to shared objects. All following simulation results represent the average values calculated from 10 independent simulation runs.

Figure 6 shows the maintenance traffic of both protocols over time, simulated with L7Sim. Since a large part of the network consists of nodes with low mean online times, we notice a continuously high amount of transferred object references in Chord. In contrast, HCP offers significantly decreased maintenance traffic, as object references are stored only on static nodes (*OFFICE* and *DSL* nodes) which are characterized by long online times.

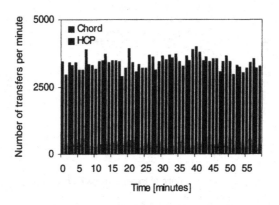

Fig. 6. Scenario 3: Maintenance traffic over time

In a second step we evaluate the content availability in both protocols, represented by the success rate of queries. We define the success rate λ of a query by dividing the number of providing hosts given in the query result by the real number of hosts currently providing the searched object. For example, when object X is shared by hosts A, B and C, and a query for X returns B and C as sharing hosts, the success rate of the query is $\lambda = 2/3 = 67\%$.

In Figure 7 the cumulative distribution of queries is plotted against the query success rate.[3] Chord can resolve 61.2% of all queries with 100% query success (i.e., the query result contains all providing hosts), but at the same time shows a sizeable fraction of non- or low-successful queries that return no or only a small number of currently providing hosts. These non- or low-successful queries result from failures of nodes that store the references to providing hosts, and from the fact that the providing hosts have not yet republished their shared objects. In contrast to Chord, HCP offers excellent query success rates. 95.5% of all queries in HCP return all currently providing hosts ($\lambda = 100\%$) and only 1.1% of all queries have a success rate less than 80%.

Thus, the above simulations prove the increased content availability in HCP that results from storing object references only on reliable static nodes. From

---

[3] An important parameter for this simulation is the refresh period for shared objects. It was set to 900 s, i.e. every shared object is republished by its owner every 15 minutes, in order to keep the object references in the system up-to-date.

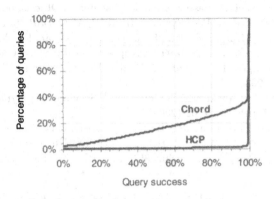

Fig. 7. Scenario 3: CDF of query success rates

our point of view, content availability is an important aspect when developing DHT-based services, as query success is a major criterion for user acceptance and hence the number of customers.

5 Conclusion

In this paper we presented a hybrid DHT design, which we applied to Chord to obtain the Hybrid Chord Protocol (HCP). We then evaluated its advantages in comparison to the conventional Chord algorithm. The introduced design aims primarily at the extension of structured DHT based P2P protocols to mobile environments, where a major part of the overlay network consists of resource-constrained mobile participants such as PDAs or mobile phones. By defining two different types of participating nodes, static and temporary nodes, the design allows disburdening of mobile participants, significantly decreased maintenance traffic and increased availability of provided content.

We performed multiple simulations of Chord and HCP in different scenarios. The simulations proved our theoretical analysis that HCP reduces the maintenance traffic by a factor of $1/\alpha$ in comparison to Chord, with α as the ratio of the mean online time of static nodes in HCP and the mean online time of all nodes in Chord. Moreover, our simulations verify the increased availability of provided content, and they show that it is sufficient for the evaluation of maintenance traffic to regard only the overlay network, without considering the underlying physical topology.

References

1. Zoels, S., Schollmeier, R., Kellerer, W., Tarlano, A.: The Hybrid Chord Protocol: A Peer-to-Peer Lookup Service for Context-Aware Mobile Applications. In: ICN 2005 (2005)
2. Aberer, K., Alima, L., Ghodsi, A., Girdzijauskas, S., Hauswirth, M., Haridi, S.: The Essence of P2P: A Reference Architecture for Overlay Networks. In: P2P 2005 (2005)

3. Rowstron, A., Druschel, P.: Pastry: Scalable, Distributed Object Location and Routing for Large-Scale Peer-to-Peer Systems. In: IFIP/ACM DSP 2001 (2001)
4. Stoica, I., Morris, R., Karger, D., Kaashoek, M., Balakrishnan, H.: Chord: A Scalable Peer-to-Peer Lookup Service for Internet Applications. In: SIG-COMM 2001 (2001)
5. Kaashoek, M., Karger, D.: Koorde: A Simple Degree-Optimal Distributed Hash Table. In: SODA 2004 (2004)
6. Malkhi, D., Naor, M., Ratajczak, D.: Viceroy: A Scalable and Dynamic Emulation of the Butterfly. In: PODC 2002 (2002)
7. NS-2, The Network Simulator NS-2 Homepage, http://www.isi.edu/nsnam/ns
8. Medina, A., Lakhina, A., Matta, I., Byers, J.: BRITE: Universal Topology Generation from a User's Perspective, Technical Report BU-CS-TR-2001-003 (2001)

Appendix: Theoretical Evaluation of Maintenance Traffic

Assume an overlay network with N nodes and a total number of R references to shared objects. In this case, each node is responsible for storing $r = R/N$ references in average. Thus r object references have to be shifted when a node joins or leaves the overlay network. The total number of join and leave events e in a simulation scenario is determined by the number of nodes, their mean online time T and the simulation duration D:

$$e = N \cdot (2/T) \cdot D$$

Resulting, the total number of object references transferred to a joining or from a leaving node during a simulation (i.e., the maintenance traffic) is given by

$$m = e \cdot r = 2 \cdot D \cdot R/T$$

From this equation we can now evaluate the reduced maintenance traffic in an HCP system. Since HCP stores object references only on static nodes with mean online time $T_{\text{HCP,static}}$, the total number of transferred references in an HCP simulation is

$$m_{\text{HCP}} = 2 \cdot D \cdot R/T_{\text{HCP,static}}$$

whereas Chord generates a total number of

$$m_{\text{Chord}} = 2 \cdot D \cdot R/T_{\text{Chord}}$$

transfers. The total number of references R and the simulation duration D remain constant in both cases. By definition, the mean online time of static HCP nodes is significantly higher than the mean online time of all nodes in a Chord system. Under the assumption that $T_{\text{HCP,static}} = \alpha \cdot T_{\text{Chord}}$ the generated maintenance traffic in HCP is decreased by a factor of

$$m_{\text{HCP}}/m_{\text{Chord}} = T_{\text{Chord}}/T_{\text{HCP,static}} = 1/\alpha$$

in comparison to the conventional Chord protocol.

DANTE: A Self-adapting Peer-to-Peer System

Luis Rodero Merino[1], Luis López[1], Antonio Fernández[1], and Vicent Cholvi[2]

[1] LADyR, Universidad Rey Juan Carlos,
28933, Móstoles, Spain
{lrodero,llopez,anto}@gsyc.escet.urjc.es
[2] Universitat Jaume I,
12071, Castellón, Spain
vcholvi@lsi.uji.es

Abstract. In this paper we introduce DANTE, an unstructured P2P system in which the topology of the underlying overlay network can be dynamically adapted to the system conditions. Such an adaption is performed by the peers in an autonomous manner. DANTE uses a simple search mechanism based on *random walks* that, combined with the topology adaptation, allows it to work in a very efficient way. We have evaluated how DANTE behaves in practice, showing that it successfully adapts to varying system load conditions.

1 Introduction

Peer-to-peer (P2P) systems [1] are one of the most important revolutions happening in the Internet today, offering new and richer communication opportunities for Internet users. P2P is a new communication paradigm in which *resources*, such as media files, services, data, etc., are *both* provided *and* consumed by all participants (also called *peers* or *network nodes*). This contrasts with the traditional client-server model, in which the role of each participant is restricted and well defined. In P2P systems, instead, each participant is at the same time a server, because it offers resources, and a client, because it demands them. Clear advantages of P2P systems, compared to classical systems, are their flexibility, scalability, and fault tolerance. These properties are mainly due to the lack of any central entity that coordinates or controls the peers. Nonetheless, the lack of a central coordinator has brought many new technical challenges to be solved.

One of the key issues that any P2P system has to face is how to efficiently locate resources. In most systems, to do so, peers that demand resources issue *queries* or *searches* that cause *search messages* to travel through the *overlay network*, looking for peers where those resources are offered. The *search mechanism* implemented by the P2P system dictates how search messages are routed through the overlay network. Roughly speaking, P2P systems and their search mechanisms can be classified as either *structured* or *unstructured*. Structured P2P networks (see [2] for examples) use specialized placement algorithms to assign responsibility for each resource to specific peers, as well as a "directed" search mechanism to efficiently locate resources. Directed search mechanisms

S. Joseph et al. (Eds.): AP2PC 2006, LNAI 4461, pp. 31–42, 2008.

are particularly efficient, because they efficiently route queries towards the peers responsible for a given resource. Additionally, they usually require few communication steps, generate little traffic, and do not produce false negatives (i.e., the search fails only if the demanded resource is not in the system).

In contrast, unstructured P2P networks (e.g., Gnutella [3]) have no precise control over the resource placement and generally use search mechanisms based on "flooding" or random walks. Search mechanisms based on flooding or random walks are usually less efficient than directed search mechanisms (queries are broadcast in a whole neighborhood or sent in random walks) and may yield false negatives. They have, however, very little management overhead, adapt well to the transient activity of P2P clients, take advantage of the spontaneous replication of popular content, and allow to perform queries by keyword in a simpler way than with directed search protocols. These properties seem to make unstructured P2P systems very suitable for mass-market distributed resource sharing. Flooding, nonetheless, presents the problem of scalability, as the network bandwidth consumed by search messages grows very quickly with the number of nodes and the scope of those messages. Thus, search mechanisms based on random walks have gained growing attention from the research community, which is looking for new ways to improve their efficiency. A new and promising technique to do so is the use of overlay networks with *dynamic topologies*.

In the next section we present DANTE[1], an unstructured P2P system in which the topology of the underlying overlay network is dynamically adapted to the system conditions. Furthermore, DANTE also uses a simple search mechanism based on *random walks*. In Section 3 we show how those features allow DANTE to work in an autonomous and efficient manner. Finally, Section 4 discusses other P2P systems that also use *random walks* along with *dynamic topologies*, and Section 5 concludes the paper.

2   DANTE

In this section, we describe DANTE, a P2P system that, as it has been said previously, uses a mechanism to form topologies that self-adapt depending on the network load conditions. Such an adaptation is performed by the peers without the need of global information, nor any central system to control their actions. To achieve this, each node runs a *reconnection mechanism* (described in detail in Section 2.2), that decides to which other peers it must connect to in the overlay network.

2.1   Resource Searches in DANTE

In DANTE, each node holds a set of resources and maintains an index of the resources held by its neighbors in the overlay network. Using this information, a node can explore its neighborhood at no communication cost. Clearly, in general, this also increases the success rate and reduces the network traffic, at a moderate storage cost increase.

---

[1] From Dynamic self-Adapting Network TopologiEs.

All peers can issue queries, which are performed by using *random walks*. Then, when a peer issues a query, it first locally checks if the searched resource is held by itself or by one of its neighbors. If this check succeeds, then the search finishes successfully. Otherwise, the node issues a TTL²-limited *Look For Resource* (*LFR*) message that is sent to a neighbor chosen uniformly at random. On the reception of that message, the receiving node operates in the same way as the first requesting node. The process ends when the resource is found, thus replying to the issuing peer with a *Resource Found* message (*RF*), or when the TTL expires, replying with a *Resource Not Found* (*RNF*) message.

2.2   DANTE Self-adaptation Mechanism

The self-adaptation mechanism used in DANTE is inspired on the results of Guimerà et al. [4] and of the algorithm proposed by Cholvi el al. [5]. Briefly, Guimerà et al., by means of using a combination of analytical and simulation techniques, were able to characterize the topologies that, given a search mechanism based on random walks and assuming that each node has information about the resources held by its first-order neighbors, minimize the average time needed to perform a search. Clearly, those topologies should be the topologies of choice in practical overlay networks. They found that, when the system is not congested, the topology that provides the best results is a star-like structure formed by a small number of central nodes with the rest of nodes connected to them. Furthermore, they also found that when the system is congested, the topology that provides the best results is a random-like one. But, perhaps more importantly, they reported that there is a sharp transition between these two topologies. However, the approach followed by Guimerà et al. assumes a global knowledge of the network, which is usually not available in a real P2P system. A practical topology adaptation mechanism that fits P2P systems should be run locally at the nodes, and should not need global knowledge.

In order to put these results to work, in [5], the authors proposed a mechanism that, depending on the current system load, makes nodes to locally change their connections so that the obtained topologies are random-like for high loads and star-like for low loads. To achieve this, they used a reconnection mechanism that assigns a value Π_i to each node i of the network. Such a value tries to capture the "willingness" of a node to accept new connections. Then, the destination of a changed connection is chosen using probabilities proportional to these values. Unfortunately, this mechanism cannot be directly applied to P2P systems, since although the value Π_i can be locally computed at node i, to choose the new neighbors of a node all values Π_i have to be known at the node.

In the rest of the section, we explain how the above mentioned problems are solved in DANTE. As said above, in DANTE each peer knows its own resources as well as the resources held by its neighbors. Based on this, it is easy to understand that nodes will be more interested on being connected to peers with many neighbors. Therefore, DANTE encourages peers to establish connections with

---

² Time-To-Live, the maximum number of links the message will traverse.

high degree nodes. However, this holds only as long as these highly connected nodes can handle all the incoming traffic. If the number of queries is high, a well- connected peer may receive more search messages that it can manage, thus becoming *congested*. To face this, the mechanism used in DANTE considers all congested nodes as the worst possible candidates, regardless of their degree.

Taking this into account, DANTE uses an algorithm that, when the network traffic is low, drives the network to a star-like overlay topology. Thus, searches could be answered in only one hop, since the central nodes will know all the resources in the system. In turn, when the number of searches increases, well-connected nodes will become congested and their neighbors will start to disconnect from them. Hence, this will drive the network to a random-like topology that although makes search messages to traverse longer paths to find some resource, will perform better than using a highly congested central node.

More specifically, in DANTE each node can establish connections to other nodes. We say that a connection is *native* for the establishing node and *foreign* for the accepting node. Nodes can change their native connections, but not their foreign ones. Furthermore, each node periodically runs a reconnection mechanism with which native connections are changed. This mechanism firstly obtains a list of potential candidates to which it can connect (this is described in Section 2.3). Then, it assigns a probability to each candidate, and chooses candidates at random using their respective probabilities. Finally, the peer reconnects its native connections to the chosen candidates.

The probability assigned to a candidate i is based on its "attractiveness", denoted as Π_i and defined as

$$\Pi_i = k_i^{\gamma_i}, \tag{1}$$

where k_i is the degree (number of neighbors) of peer i, and γ_i is computed as

$$\gamma_i = \begin{cases} 2 \text{ if node } i \text{ is not congested} \\ 0 \text{ otherwise.} \end{cases} \tag{2}$$

So, Π_i is set to 1 if peer i is congested, and to k_i^2 otherwise (note that the congestion of a node is a value that can be measured directly from the node's local state). Based on the values Π_j for each candidate j in a set C of candidates, we assign to peer i the probability p_i of being chosen as

$$p_i = \frac{\Pi_i}{\sum_{j \in C} \Pi_j}. \tag{3}$$

As it can be readily seen, nodes with higher attractiveness will be chosen with higher probability. Therefore, in DANTE there is a tendency to connect to nodes with high degree, unless those peers are congested.

The rationale behind the assignment of probabilities is as follows. First, note that it is known [6] that by assigning the same probability to each node, one obtains a random-like topology. This is achieved when all nodes are congested and so Π_i is set to 1 for all nodes. In turn, if no node is congested and the value of Π_i is set to k_i^2 for each node i, one obtains a star-like topology [6]. Consequently, the network will evolve towards a random-like topology when many nodes get congested and towards a star-like topology otherwise. Remember that this will provide us with the topologies of choice, both at low and high network loads.

2.3 Peer Sampling

In order to provide peers with sets of candidates (and their congestion level) to apply the heuristic presented in the previous section, DANTE uses a special message *Look For Nodes* (*LFN*) that is used for collecting information about the state of the network. This message traverses the network following a TTL-limited random walk, storing information about the nodes it visits. When the message TTL expires, a *Nodes Found* (*NF*) message is sent to the message's source node, carrying the information about the peers the *LFN* message visited. Then, the decision is taken considering only this information.

Clearly, if reconnections are not very frequent, this technique of sampling the peers has very small incidence on the network load. Furthermore, it has been shown [7, 8] that the sample obtained with this mechanism is a good sample of the overall network. Indeed, when the network has highly connected nodes or *hubs* (possibly due to low or medium loads), since the collecting message follows a random walk, these hubs will be reached with higher probability than poorly connected nodes. This is good since peers are mainly interested on hubs for reconnections. On the other hand, when the network is random (possibly due to high load), all nodes will have roughly the same degree, and then the chosen nodes will be representative of the whole network.

Other mechanisms than using random-walk messages could be considered for the purpose of collecting information. Gossiping, for example, could be used to spread information about peers, as in [9]. However, any peer sampling solution must fulfill some requirements. First, information about well connected, high capacity nodes should be more likely to be found. Second, it must be avoided to spread old information about peers state (that can get out of date quickly). Finally, a low communication overhead should be required by the sampling mechanism. Our experiments show empirically that random-walks are well suited to these requirements.

2.4 DANTE Robustness

Another interesting feature of DANTE is its robustness against node failures. This comes from the fact that when a peer enters or leaves the network, only its neighborhood is affected. Therefore, if the current network topology is random-like, a very small number of peers will notice the change. The same will happen if the current network topology is star-like and the node that leaves is not a central one. Even in the worst case, when a central node disappears, the system still will be able to keep working, since there are several central nodes (as many as the number of native connections of each peer). Furthermore, the DANTE adaptation mechanism also guarantees that some other node will quickly become central and replace the peer that disappeared.

3 DANTE at Work

A prototype of DANTE, as described above, has been implemented and used to evaluate the properties of the system. The prototype has been developed in Java and works over UDP[3]. Experiments performed with this implementation on a real network have confirmed that, as expected, the overlay network topology evolves as the load on the system changes, ranging from star-like topologies under low load to random-like topologies under high load. Moreover, our experiments also show that these topologies present the best performance for these load levels.

3.1 Experimental Setup

We start by describing the configuration we have used to run the experiments of DANTE's prototype. Our experiments have been executed with 42 peers, each with three native connections. (Initially, the network had a random topology.) Peers hosted disjoint sets of resources, all containing 5000 resources. (Note that there was no replication.) Every peer periodically issued a new query, in which the resource to search was chosen uniformly at random from the set of all resources in the system. The load in the system was controlled by the *query generation rate*, which was the number of queries per minute issued by every peer in the system. This rate was fixed for each experiment. We have run experiments with values of the query generation rate from 2 to 12 in steps of 2.

In the experiments conducted each query was issued with a TTL of 30. This value was empirically chosen in order to maintain a high success rate in searches (few false negatives). With this TTL value the rate of successful searches has been above 99% for all experiments, except when the topology was fully random, that had a 96% success rate.

In our experiments all peers had the same *real* processing power, since it was the same software running on similar hardware[4]. In each experiment, there was a global parameter named *capacity threshold* (or just *threshold*). This parameter intended to summarize the level of load every peer can take before being congested. In our prototype the threshold represents the maximum number of queries per minute a peer can handle: if a peer receives a number of queries per minute greater than this threshold, the node is considered to be *congested*. We have run experiments with 5 different threshold values, namely, 0, 10, 50, 100, and 1,000,000.

Each experiment has been run for 120 minutes, out of which we have analyzed only the queries started between minutes 16 and 75, both included (to avoid initial transient states and unfinished searches). During the experiments, DANTE's adaptation mechanism has been triggered periodically at each peer

---

[3] The source code of the prototype is available at http://ladyr.es/dante/.

[4] Although typical P2P systems have peers with different capacities, the resulting topologies in these heterogeneous systems under very low and very high loads would be similar to the ones obtained here. Furthermore, heterogeneity could improve the network performance, as the peers with higher capacity would become hubs, and hence the number of hops needed to find resources would be decreased.

every 30 seconds. Each time this happened, the peer changed its three native connections simultaneously.

3.2 Topology Adaptation

The first fact that can be observed from the experiments conducted is that the network topology actually adapts itself to the load in the system. This fact can be readily observed in Figure 1. This figure shows the network topologies obtained with the same threshold (of 10) under three different load levels. In Figure 1.(A) the system is lightly loaded. As expected, the network has evolved to a star-like topology. In Figure 1.(C) we see the overlay network obtained under high load, which forms a random-like topology.

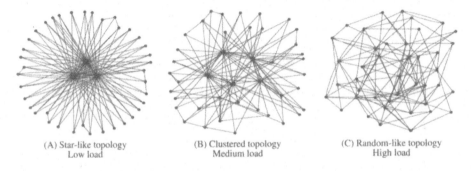

(A) Star-like topology   (B) Clustered topology   (C) Random-like topology
Low load   Medium load   High load

Fig. 1. Overlay topologies obtained in DANTE's prototype with (A) low, (B) medium, and (C) high load

It is interesting to observe the overlay network topology obtained under medium load, shown in Figure 1.(B). As it can be observed, the topology is somewhere in between a random-like and a star-like. In these networks obtained under medium load there are hubs that know many other peers. This, in general, will allow queries to finish in fewer hops than with a fully random topology.

Regarding topology adaptation, we have two especial sets of experiments in which no topology change is observed. The first set is the one done with a threshold value of 0. With this threshold all peers permanently consider themselves to be congested, and hence the resulting topology is always random-like, independently of the load. The second is the set of experiments done with a threshold value of 1,000,000. Since no peer ever receives that many queries per minute, then no peer ever considers itself congested. This makes the network to form a star-like topology regardless of the load on the system. These two sets of experiments have been run to have a reference on the performance of systems with pure random-like and star-like topologies.

3.3 Performance

We study now the search performance observed in our experiments under different topologies and loads. To measure the search performance we use the *mean search time*, which is computed as the average time taken to complete a query. A query is completed when either the issuing peer finds out the peer holding the resource or it receives a message indicating that the query failed. The values of the mean search time for all the experiments conducted are presented in Figure 2. The values that correspond to executions with the same threshold are connected.

A first look at Figure 2 allows to confirm the analytical results of Guimerà [4]. On the one hand, among those considered, the star-like topology (threshold 1,000,000) has the best performance under low load. The random-like topology (threshold 0), on the other hand, has the best performance under high load. Interestingly, the random-like topology has the worst performance under low load while the star-like topology has the worst performance under high load, justifying the interest on topology adaptation.

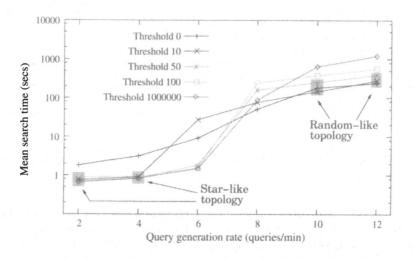

Fig. 2. Results of DANTE's prototype execution

A second conclusion that can be extracted from Figure 2 is that, when using a proper threshold, DANTE makes the network evolve to a topology with good performance given the system load. That is the objective of DANTE's adaptation mechanism: the network is able to self-adapt to the load conditions, trying to keep the topology close to optimal. Interestingly, the overall performance depends on tuning the threshold value properly. As it can be observed, while the three "reasonable" thresholds considered (10, 50, and 100) guarantee close to optimal performance under extreme load conditions, their performance at medium loads is not the same. For a query generation rate of 6 the experiments with threshold 10 show bad performance, because the threshold is too small and prevents the network to evolve to a star-like topology (which seems to be the optimal for this load).

3.4   Scalability

We now study how DANTE's performance changes as the number of peers increases. To do so, we fix a query generation rate and run experiments with systems of different sizes. Since the query generation rate is fixed, peers issue queries at the same rate, independently of the size. However, since most queries cannot be completed locally, the average load per peer (number of queries processed by the peer) will grow with the size (even in a star-like topology). This means that we cannot expect to observe that the mean search time remains constant as the network size grows (which is a classical definition of scalability).

In order to evaluate systems with thousands of peers we have developed a simulator of DANTE[5], which captures the essence of both DANTE and its prototype. Then, we have run simulations under similar conditions as the experiments done with the prototype. We performed simulations with five different network sizes, namely, 30, 100, 300, 1000, and 3000, and three different threshold values, namely, 0, 100, and 1,000,000. In all cases the query generation rate was fixed to one query every 100 seconds. In order to guarantee a high success rate[6] we set the TTL for query messages to $n \log n$ for a system with n peers (this estimation is based on results in [10]), and fixed the TTL of *LFN* messages to 25 (which empirically provided a good peer sample, even for 3,000 peers).

The results obtained from the simulations are presented in Figure 3. There it can be seen that the star-like topology (threshold value of 1,000,000) shows very good performance for networks with few peers. However, as the number of peers increases, the central nodes get congested and the performance degrades quickly.

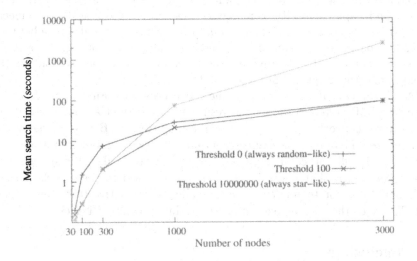

Fig. 3. Results of DANTE scalability simulations

---

[5] We could not run those experiments in a real network since this requires having an infrastructure formed with thousands on peers.

[6] All completed searches were successful.

On the other hand, the random-like topology (threshold value of 0) shows a comparatively bad performance for low number of peers, but its relative performance improves as the number of peers increases. As expected, the experiments with threshold 100 present the very desirable feature that for small networks show a performance close to that of the star-like topology, while a performance close to that of a random-like topology for large networks. Interestingly, for medium size networks (1000 peers) this threshold shows better performance than both the star-like and the random-like topologies.

4   Related Work

There are mainly two proposed systems that are directly related with DANTE. Both works already propose to combine dynamic topologies with random walks to improve the performance of the P2P system. First, Lv *et al.* [11] have introduced a P2P system in which nodes avoid congestion by means of a flow control mechanism that changes the topology, trying to make messages to traverse nodes with higher capacities. To do so, every node checks periodically its load. When the node is overloaded, it redirects its most active neighbor (the one sending most queries) to some of its neighbors with spare capacity. Thus, higher capacity nodes tend to have more connections, and so manage more queries.

Then, Chawathe *et al.* [12] have proposed **Gia**, a system that tries to avoid overloading nodes by explicitly accounting for their capacity constraints. In Gia, queries are forwarded to high capacity nodes, which should be more able to handle them. An active flow control mechanism avoids overloading hot spots: each node notifies its neighbors the number of queries they can send to it, which depends on its spare capacity. Topology is also adapted dynamically by a mechanism based on nodes *level of satisfaction*, which measures the distance between a node's capacity to the sum of its neighbors capacities, normalized by their degrees. This parameter determines whether or not each node will adapt the topology, and the frequency of these adaptations.

DANTE differs substantially from these two proposals. First of all, DANTE is the first P2P system to apply the results of Guimerà et al. on the relationship between network topologies and search performance. Based on that work, DANTE's self-adaptation mechanism continuously tries to configure the network topology to an efficient configuration depending on the load on the system. Another difference, is that nodes in DANTE do not need to keep track of their neighbors state, nor to implement any explicit flow control technique. Thus, DANTE avoids the communication overhead due to those activities.

5   Conclusions

P2P systems are a promising new paradigm, specially suited to situations where there is not a hierarchy among system participants. However, the lack of central entities in the system demands innovative solutions to new problems. For example, users do not have a central repository to ask for the location of resources. To face this problem, new search techniques must be devised.

Recent research has shown the key importance of the overlay network topology on search efficiency. With DANTE we propose a self-adapting mechanism that makes the network change its topology aiming always to an optimal configuration that depends on the system load. This mechanism envisions the P2P system as a community where, from the individual work of participants, a global behavior emerges making the system able to adapt to changing conditions.

The first results obtained with this approach seem promising. However, much work remains to be done in order to improve the efficiency of these techniques. For example new heuristics can be developed that make the overlay network topology to evolve more smoothly depending on the peer congestion, avoiding sharp changes.

Acknowledgments

This work was partially supported by the Spanish Ministry of Science and Technology under Grant No. TSI2004-02940 and TIN2005-09198-C02-01, by Bancaixa under Grant No. P1-1B2003-37 and by the Comunidad de Madrid under grant S-0505/TIC/0285.

References

1. Androutsellis-Theotokis, S., Spinellis, D.: A survey of peer-to-peer content distribution technologies. ACM Comput. Surv. 36, 335–371 (2004)
2. Balakrishnan, H., Kaashoek, M.F., Karger, D.R., Morris, R., Stoica, I.: Looking up data in P2P systems. Communications of the ACM 46, 43–48 (2003)
3. Gnutella.com: (The gnutella website), http://www.gnutella.com
4. Guimerà, R., Díaz-Guilera, A., Vega-Redondo, F., Cabrales, A., Arenas, A.: Optimal network topologies for local search with congestion. Physical Review Letters 89 (2002)
5. Cholvi, V., Laderas, V., López, L., Fernández, A.: Self-adapting network topologies in congested scenarios. Physical Review E 71, 35–103 (2005)
6. Krapivsky, P.L., Redner, S., Leyvraz, F.: Connectivity of growing random networks. Physical Review Letters 85, 4629–4632 (2000)
7. Gkantsidis, C., Mihail, M., Saberi, A.: Random walks in peer-to-peer networks. In: INFOCOM (2004)
8. Newman, M.E.J.: A measure of betweenness centrality based on random walks. Social Networks 27, 39–54 (2005)
9. Jelasity, M., Guerraoui, R., Kermarrec, A.M., van Steen, M.: The peer sampling service: Experimental evaluation of unstructured gossip-based implementations. In: Jacobsen, H.-A. (ed.) Middleware 2004. LNCS, vol. 3231, pp. 79–98. Springer, Heidelberg (2004)
10. Cooper, C., Frieze, A.: The cover time of sparse random graphs. In: Proceedings of the fourteenth annual ACM-SIAM symposium on discrete algorithms, Society for Industrial and Applied Mathematics, pp. 140–147 (2003)

11. Lv, Q., Ratnasamy, S., Shenker, S.: Can heterogeneity make Gnutella scalable? In: Revised Papers from the First International Workshop on Peer-to-Peer Systems, Cambridge, United States, pp. 94–103 (2002)
12. Chawathe, Y., Ratnasamy, S., Lanham, N., Shenker, S.: Making Gnutella-like P2P systems scalable. In: Proceedings of the 2003 conference on applications, technologies, architectures, and protocols for computer communications (SIGCOMM 2003), Karlsruhe, Germany, pp. 407–418 (2003)

The Exclusion of Malicious Routing Peers in Structured P2P Systems

Bong-Soo Roh, O-Hoon Kwon, Sung Je Hong, and Jong Kim

Dept. of Computer Science and Engineering,
Pohang University of Science and Technology
{saintroh,dolphin,sjhong,jkim}@postech.ac.kr

Abstract. We propose a scheme which excludes malicious routing peers from the normal routing process of structured P2P systems such as Chord. This scheme prevents continuous routing overheads from malicious peers. Simulation results show that the proposed scheme reduces the average routing length compared with the routing algorithm only using the alternate lookup path.

1 Introduction

Structured peer-to-peer (P2P) systems such as Chord [1], CAN [2], and Pastry [3] provide good characteristics such as load balance, decentralization, scalability and availability when their algorithms are executed correctly. The routing algorithms are especially important because the peers place and lookup data deterministically using robust routing algorithms. Therefore, *incorrect lookup routing* is a serious problem in structured P2P systems. It means that malicious peers deliver query messages to incorrect or non-existing nodes. Even a small number of malicious peers can prevent correct message delivery and cause large overheads. Existing approaches for solving *incorrect lookup routing* are based on the concept of *secure message forwarding*. It is to deliver the message to good peers who are responsible with the query message in the presence of malicious peers. For example, there are techniques such as the iterative routing [4], the redundant routing [5] and the alternate lookup path [6]. However, even though these techniques securely delivere messages at once, malicious peers can participate again in the routing protocols. Therefore, lookups would continue to be routed to the malicious peers, which would increase the routing overheads.

In this paper, we propose a scheme which excludes the malicious routing peers from the normal routing process of structured P2P systems. This scheme prevents continuous routing overheads from existing malicious nodes. The proposed scheme has four characteristics. First, it is a fully distributed scheme to exclude malicious routing peers. Second, it makes the system work well even in the high ratio of malicious peers in the overlay. Third, it allows the arbitrary behavior of malicious routing peers. Fourth, it uses *the alternate lookup path* [6] and *the query observation* [4].

The rest of this paper is organized as follows. In Section 2, related works and their differences with our work are discussed. In Section 3 and 4, the adversary model and the characteristics of the proposed system are described. Section 5 describes the exclusion routing protocol. Section 6 shows the simulation results. Finally, we summarize this paper and discuss concluding remarks in Section 7.

S. Joseph et al. (Eds.): AP2PC 2006, LNAI 4461, pp. 43–50, 2008.

2   Related Works

In this section, we briefly discuss the previous works which deal with *incorrect lookup routing* in structured P2P systems.

Sit and Morris [4] proposed the *iterative routing* using a query observation to defend against incorrect lookup routing. At each hop, the querier checks if the lookup gets closer to the key identifier. If an incorrect lookup is detected, the querier might recover by backtracking to the last good hop and asking for an alternative step that offers less progress. However, they had no experimental data to prove their claim. Castro et al. [5] proposed *redundant routing* using a routing failure test for secure routing in structured P2P Systems. The redundant routing technique is invoked when the failure test returns positive. The idea is simply to route copies of the message over multiple routes towards each of the destination key's replica roots. Their techniques allow P2P systems to tolerate up to 25% malicious nodes while providing good performance when the fraction of malicious nodes is small. Srivatsa and Liu [6] emphasized the importance of multiple *alternate lookup paths* for secure routing in structured P2P Systems. If the query originator detects an incorrect lookup using the query observation [4], it can choose an alternative (possibly sub-optimal) lookup path towards the destination identifier. Even though the above techniques can support secure message forwarding, malicious peers can continuously cause routing errors and routing overheads. Therefore, we will propose a scheme which excludes malicious routing peers from the normal routing process.

3   Adversary Model

In this paper, adversaries refer to those peers, which do not follow the routing protocol of the system and mislead good peers by providing them with incorrect routing information or no response.

We assume that most of peers can be malicious nodes in the overlay. In the worst case, almost all of the routing entries will be incorrect paths. As a result, the routing overheads such as the lookup failure, path re-computation and network bandwidth wastage can be increased, but the routing operation will work correctly. Generally, a malicious node behavior is assumed to be consistent. But, we assume that malicious nodes can perform arbitrary behaviors. We consider that malicious nodes may intentionally upgrade their trustworthiness by performing normal routing from time to time. However, if their behavior is accumulated, their trustworthiness will be evaluated accordingly.

We also assume that the malicious nodes cannot collude. Since general P2P architectures guarantee anonymity, the collusion attack by malicious nodes is a very complex problem. Although many research groups have worked on this problem, a complete solution has not been proposed. This problem is related to the authentication for P2P nodes. We assume that the underlying network layer is secure. That is, an adversary node can only access the packets that have been addressed to it. If the packet is not encrypted, the malicious node may modify it. Also, the domain name service, the network routers, and the related networking infrastructure are completely secure. Therefore, we assume that these infrastructures cannot be compromised by malicious nodes.

4 Characteristics of the System

In this section, we describe the characteristics of the system extended from general structure P2P systems in order to support the proposed exclusion scheme. The proposed scheme can be applied to all DHT-based P2P systems, but we will explain it for Chord [1].

4.1 Extended Routing Table

In structured P2P systems, each node uses the per-node routing tables for routing the query message. The routing table consists of references to other neighbors. In Chord [1], it is called the finger table. The k-th finger node is the first node that succeeds the current node by at least 2^{k-1}, where $1 \leq k \leq m$ and the identifier is a m-bit number. The finger table is used for efficient routing. In order to exclude malicious routing peers from the finger table, we add one column to each row. The column represents the ratio of how much incorrect routing the corresponding neighbor had done. The column is called the TCR (Total Claim Ratio). In our system, every peer forwards the query message to a peer with the minimum TCR value.

4.2 TCR(Total Claim Ratio)

The claim ratio (CR) is a ratio of the claim count (CC) to the forwarding count (FC). FC increases when the query is forwarded to each routing entry. CC increases when a peer receives the claim. Periodically, CR is reseted at every time interval of TCR. By doing so, the system is not influenced by unintentional routing failures such as malicious claims or short-term path errors.

The total claim ratio (TCR) reflects the node's historic behavior. The proposed scheme assumes that malicious peers can fabricate their CR. For example, if malicious nodes have normal behaviors in many routing steps initially, their FC increases enough for malicious behaviors to have no effect on their CR later on. Therefore, recent malicious behavior has a stronger influence on TCR that the old behaviors.

$$TCR = \sum_{k=1}^{n} \alpha_n * CR = \alpha_1 * CR_1 + \ldots + \alpha_n * CR_n \qquad (1)$$

where $\alpha_1 + \alpha_2 + \ldots + \alpha_n = 1$ and $\alpha_n > \alpha_{n-1} > \cdots > \alpha_2 > \alpha_1$. CR_n is the most recent CR and CR_1 is the oldest CR, where n is the number of time interval.

4.3 Query Observation and Alternate Lookup Path

In the proposed scheme, the query originator checks if the lookup is correct by using the query observation [4] at each hop. Thus, each step of query process must be visible to the querier. In our system, the receivers of the query report *the identifier of the current node* and *the identifier of the next node* to the query originator at each hop. Using this information, the query originator can check for incorrect routing because the lookup is always supposed to get closer to the key identifier in the clockwise motion. Therefore, if an incorrect lookup is detected, the query originator can recover the lookup by backtracking to the last good hop for another path.

Upon detecting an incorrect routing by using the query observation, the query originator asks the previous good node along the lookup path for an alternate lookup path toward the destination identifier [6]. Due to the characteristics of the finger table in Chord [1], it is likely that the alternate lookup path proceeds only by half the distance along the identifier circle compared to the original path.

5   The Exclusion Routing Protocol

In this section, we describe the exclusion routing protocol against malicious routing peers. The exclusion routing protocol consists of the claim process and the verification process.

5.1   Claim Process

A misrouting node (MRN) is a node which misroutes a message intentionally or unintentionally. A previous good node (PGN) is a good node which delivers a message to a MRN. If the query originator detects an incorrect lookup routing, it gives a notice to MRNs and PGNs, which is called a *claim*. The purpose of this process is to leave the history table on the neighbors' routing trustworthiness as a column of the extended routing table. The *claim* includes the following information.

- the identifier and the IP address of the querier
- the identifier of a target node for the claim
- the destination key identifier

The claim process is as follows.

1. When the querier receives a wrong routing result, the querier gives a claim message to MRN and PGN, respectively.
2. PGN delivers the query through the minimal TCR path.
3. Using the verification process, PGN verifies if the claim is correct or not.
4. If the claim is correct, the receivers of the claim reflect the TCR value.
5. If MRN is a good node, MRN also does the steps 3) and 4).

As a result of the above claim process, nodes with the higher TCR value are excluded in each node's routing entries. Each node always forwards the query to the minimal TCR node among available paths. If more than two TCR values are the same, a PGN forwards the query to the neighbor which is closer to the key identifier. If a node with the minimal TCR value is malicious, a PGN forwards the query to the next minimal TCR node.

Fig. 1 is an example of the claim process. We assumed that N8 is the querier and N51 is the malicious node. N8 learns its query trace by using the query observation.

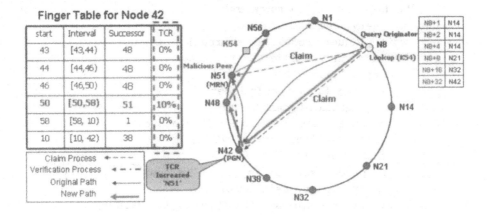

Fig. 1. An Example for the Claim Process

Pseudo Code of ALP_{basic}**(query_result)**

```
if (query_result is false) {
  while !(query_result is correct) {
    current_node = PN;
    Decrease finger_table_index by 1;
    Send a query using current_node[finger_table_index];
  }
}
```

Fig. 2. The Algorithm of Alternate Lookup Path

If N51 incorrectly routes to N1, N8 detects the malicious node (N51) using the query observation. Then, N8 sends the claim to N42 (PGN) and N51 (MRN). N42 verifies a claim message using the verification process. If the claim message is verified to be correct, N42 reflects a TCR value for N51 (MRN).

This algorithm is based on the query observation. The observation of queries can inform the querier on where the message is currently arriving from. Using this mechanism, the querier can go back to the last good node. Then, the querier selects the sub-optimal path within the routing entries. However, this algorithm has a problem. It has not considered another querier who will pass by this location. Therefore, many of them go through the same situation.

Fig. 2 shows the pseudo code of the alternate lookup path (ALP). Fig. 3 shows the pseudo code of finding an alternate lookup path using TCR values. These algorithms are based on the query observation [6]. Unlike the alternate lookup path, the proposed algorithm checks a routing history column to determine the routing path. Using this accumulated data, every P2P node forwards the query message to a minimum TCR node. This procedure means that all of the P2P nodes exclude the higher TCR nodes from the normal routing process.

Pseudo Code of ALP_{TCR}**(query_result)**

```
if (query_result is false) {
 while !(query_result is correct) {
   MRN = current_node;
   current_node = PGN;
   Decrease finger_table_index
     by next_minimum_TCR_entry;
   if (next_minimum_TCR_entry does not exist)
     Increase finger_table_index;
   Send a query;
   if (predecessor of key is malicious)
     Send a query using replica;
   verification_process(faulty_node,key_value);
   if (verification_process is correct)
     Increase TCR_of_faulty_node;
 }
}
```

Fig. 3. Algorithm for finding an Alternate Lookup Path Using TCR values

5.2 Verification Process

Since the query originator can also be malicious, the receivers of the claim need to verify the claim before reflecting it to their TCR column. If PGN receives the claim, they send the same query to a MRN using the identifier of the target and the destination key identifier. Then, if PGN receives the same claim from the querier, it updates its TCR column. Since malicious nodes do not know whether the query is the PGN's message or not, it is impossible for MRN to selectively perform different routings.

5.3 Replication

In Chord [1], all lookup queries for a key pass only through the predecessor of the responsible node for the key. If the predecessor node is malicious, all lookups for the key will always fail. Therefore, all data should be replicated on several nodes. There are some research works on replication schemes [7,8]. They used neighbors of the responsible peer as the replication nodes. In our case, when there are 2^r replication nodes for a key k in m-bit identifier space, the data are replicated on the successors of the following keys: $\{(k + 2^{m-r}), (k + 2^{m-(r-1)}), \cdots, (k + 2^{m-2}), (k + 2^{m-1})\}$ (mod 2^m).

If the query receiver finds the responsible node in the routing entry but the query cannot be forwarded to the node, the query originator forwards the query towards the next responsible node of the replication group.

6 Simulation Results

We have performed experiments to show that the proposed scheme reduce the average routing length even when the rate of malicious nodes is high. We simulated the alternate

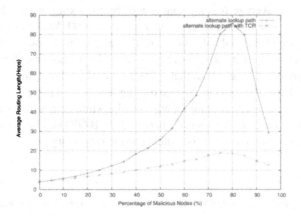

Fig. 4. Alternate Lookup Path Vs. TCR (B=5, Q=1000)

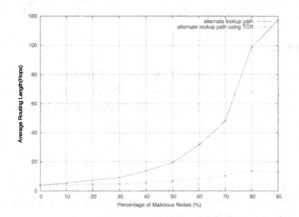

Fig. 5. Alternate Lookup Path Vs TCR (B=5, Q=1000000)

lookup path and the proposed scheme on a Chord system with 1024 nodes. The identifier of the nodes is 0 to 1023. The average routing length is 4 hop when there are no
malicious nodes. The location of malicious nodes and the query originator is randomly
selected.

Malicious nodes mislead good nodes to false successors. Therefore, if good nodes go
through malicious nodes, the average routing length increases because they should find
an alternate lookup path. When the querier can find the responsible node for a desired
key in the routing entry, the routing successfully ends, while other cases are failures.
Also, for a simple adversary model, we assumed that $\alpha = 1$ and $n = 1$.

If a ratio of malicious nodes increases, the number of nodes with false routing information in their routing table also increases. If all nodes in the routing entries are
malicious, the querier cannot forward the query properly. To solve this problem, our
system backtracks to a PGN and restarts the routing. Naturally, the average routing
length increases, but the lookup failure rate decreases.

Fig. 4 shows the average routing length with backtracking, where the number of backtracking(B) is 5 and the number of queries(Q) is 1000. We can observe that the average routing length is doubled. The more the ratio of malicious nodes increases, the more the count of backtracking increases. Thus, the average routing length in the backtracking protocol is longer than that in the non-backtracking protocol. This result shows that our scheme reduces the average routing length even more by backtracking.

Fig. 5 shows the average routing length with backtracking, where the number of backtracking(B) is 5 and the number of queries(Q) is 1000000. This result shows that our scheme is more effective when the number of queries is large.

7 Conclusion

In this paper, we proposed a scheme which excludes malicious routing peers using TCR in a structured P2P system. Because our scheme excludes malicious nodes, the intermediate nodes along the routing path do not select a false routing path. The simulation results showed that the proposed scheme reduces the average routing length compared to the secure routing scheme which only uses the alternate lookup path.

Acknowledgments

This research was supported by the MIC(Ministry of Information and Communication), Korea, under the Chung-Ang University HNRC-ITRC(Home Network Research Center) support program supervised by the IITA(Institute of Information Technology Assessment).

References

1. Stoica, I., Morris, R., Liben-Nowell, D., Karger, D.R., Kaashoek, M.F., Dabek, F., Balakrishnan, H.: Chord: A scalable peer-to-peer lookup protocol for internet applications. IEEE/ACM Transactions on Networking (February 2003)
2. Ratnasamy, S., Francis, P., Handley, M., Karp, R.: A scalable content addressable network. In: Proceedings of ACM SIGCOMM 2001 Techinical Conference (August 2001)
3. Rowstron, A., Druschel, P.: Pastry: Scalable, distributed object location and routing for large-scale peer-to-peer systems. In: Proceedings of the 18th IFIP/ACM International Conference on Distributed Systems Platforms (November 2001)
4. Sit, E., Morris, R.: Security considerations for peer-to-peer distributed hash tables. In: Druschel, P., Kaashoek, M.F., Rowstron, A. (eds.) IPTPS 2002. LNCS, vol. 2429, Springer, Heidelberg (2002)
5. Castro, M., Druschel, P., Ganesh, A., Rowstron, A., Wallach, D.S.: Secure routing for structured peer-to-peer overlay networks. In: Proceedings of the 5th Usenix Symposium on Operating Systems Design and Implementation (OSDI) (December 2002)
6. Srivatsa, M., Liu, L.: Vulnerabilities and security threats in structured overlay networks: A quantitative analysis. In: Proceedings of the 20th Annual Computer Security Applications Conference (ACSAC) (December 2004)
7. Maymounkov, Kademlia: A peer to peer inforamtion system based on the xor metric. In: Proceeding of 1st International Workshop on Peer-to-Peer Systems (March 2002)
8. Ratnasamy, Fancis: A scalable content addressable network. In: Proceeding of the ACM 2001 SIGCOMM Conference (August 2001)

Cooperative CBR System for Peer Agent Committee Formation

Hager Karoui, Rushed Kanawati, and Laure Petrucci

LIPN, CNRS UMR 7030, Université Paris XIII
99, avenue Jean-Baptiste Clément
F-93430 Villetaneuse, France
{hager.karoui,rushed.kanawati,laure.petrucci}@lipn.univ-paris13.fr

Abstract. This paper deals with the problem of peer agent selection in
an unstructured P2P recommendation system. The problem is studied
in the context of a collaborative P2P bibliographical data management
and recommendation system. In this system, each user is assisted with a
personal software agent that helps her/him in managing bibliographical
data and recommending new bibliographical references that are known
by peer agents. One key issue is to define the set of peer agents that can
provide the most relevant recommendations. Here, we treat this problem
by using CBR methodology. We aim at enhancing the system overall
performances by reducing network load (i.e. number of contacted peers,
avoiding redundancy) and enhancing the relevance of computed recommendations by reducing the number of *noisy* recommendations. The peer
selection learning cycle is described in detail. Experimental results are
also provided and discussed.

1 Introduction

In [7], we have proposed a peer-to-peer (P2P hereafter) collaborative system for
bibliographical references management and recommendation. The system, called
COBRAS (standing for COoperative Bibliography Recommendation Agent System) aims at: providing help for users to manage their local bibliographical
databases and to allow exchanging bibliographical data among like-minded group
of users in an *implicit* (i.e. without user request) and *intelligent* (i.e. exchanging relevant data) way. Each user is associated with a personal software agent
helping her/him at filling bibliographical records, verifying the correctness of the
information entered and more importantly, recommending the user with relevant
bibliographical references.

  In order to compute relevant recommendations, personal agents collaborate
one with each other. A key issue is to define the set of peer agents that can provide
the most relevant recommendations. One simple strategy can be to request help
from all available agents. However, such a strategy can be expensive or slow if the
set of available agents is large, and it is not obvious that it gives the best results
in all situations [8]. In this paper, we propose a case-based reasoning (CBR)
system for committee recommendation. CBR is a problem solving methodology

S. Joseph et al. (Eds.): AP2PC 2006, LNAI 4461, pp. 51–62, 2008.

[3]. A new problem is solved by finding a similar previous case, and reusing it in the new problem situation. An important feature is that CBR is an approach to incremental, sustained learning since a new experience is retained each time a problem has been solved, making it immediately available for future problems. Our idea is to have a set of interesting peer agents with which the initiator agent will collaborate in a given context. In this system, the initiator agent applies a CBR cycle in order to form a committee. A committee is a set of peer agents supposed to be interesting for a given interest topic. The committee formation is computed when the initiator agent detects some *hot topics* of the associated user. For each detected topic, the agent searchs in his interaction history with other agents in order to choose a subset of peers that are likely to provide relevant references . A CBR-based approach is used for this purpose.

The structure of the paper is as follows. First, we give a global peer-to-peer system overview in section 2. Then, we focus on the committee formation policy in section 3. We give some experimentations in section 4. In section 5, we discuss related work. In section 6, we conclude and we give some directions for future work.

2   System Overview

In COBRAS system, each user is assisted by a personal agent that helps in managing her/his own bibliographical database. Different services are provided by the local assistant such as references edition, references correctness verification and recommendation. We focus on this later service which aims at sharing bibliographic knowledge among the users and taking advantage of past experiences of a single user or even a group of users for recommending more relevant references [7]. Each reference is described by a record containing the following information:

- Bibliographical data: these are the classical data describing a reference such as the type (e.g. Article, In Proceedings, etc), authors, title, etc.
- Keywords: this is a list of keywords describing the reference. The keywords are defined by the user.
- Topics: this is a list of topics the reference is related to. The same topic hierarchy is shared by all users. It has a tree structure and is based on the ACM hierarchy [1] related to the Computer Science domain.

The personal assistant suggests various and interesting recommendations to the associated user according to her/his current activity. The user can either accept or refuse the proposed recommendations. The recommendation computation is made as follows:

- First, the agent applies a simple algorithm described in [7], in order to determine topics from the structure hierarchy that are of current interest to the user. The degree of interest is function of the user activity (i.e. her/his actions on the database).

- For each found topic, the agent sends a recommendation request to a committee of peers. A committee is a set of peer agents that are likely to have references related to the current interesting topic. A recommendation request message is given by: $R = \langle A, T, KL \rangle$ where:
  - A is the sender agent identifier,
  - T is a target topic,
  - KL is a list of keywords that is computed from the set of keywords lists describing references related, directly or indirectly to the topic T.
  A reference is indirectly related to a topic T if it is related to a topic T' more specific than T. In this paper, we focus on this functionnality: the committee formation approach.
- Upon receiving a recommendation request, each agent computes a list of references to recommend.
- The agent merges the received results and proposes the best references to its associated user [7].

3   Committee Formation

The goal of the committee is to enhance the system overall performances by reducing network load and to enhance the relevance of computed recommendations by reducing the number of *noisy* recommendations. The goal consists also to take advantage of the knowledge and experience of other peers. We propose to use a CBR approach in order to exploit history interaction of each agent with others and to learn to find an appropriate committee for each request type. The CBR uses a case base containing relevant evaluated cases. Generally, a case is composed of two parts: the problem part and the solution part (*Case = (Problem, Solution)*). A target problem is a problem to which we search for a solution. It involves a type of recommendation request (in our case, it is the current interesting topic), which presents a part of the user's interests. A case has the following structure: *Case = (T, C)* where:

- *Problem* = T is a current interesting topic,
- *Solution* = C is a committee composed of recommended agent to contact according to the topic T.

A CBR cycle is computed for each recommendation request. We describe here the different phases of the CBR cycle for committee formation.

The search phase. Receiving a target problem (a topic T of the computed interesting topic list), the agent selects cases that are similar to the target problem. The committee search is based on a topic similarity which compares the target problem to cases stored in the agent's case base. If the similarity value is above a given threshold σ_t, then the case will be recalled. At the beginning, since the committee case base is empty, the initiator agent sends the recommendation request to all available agents. The topic similarity function is as follows:

$$Sim_{Topics}(T_1, T_2) = 1 - \frac{path(T_1, MSCA(T_1, T_2)) + path(T_2, MSCA(T_1, T_2))}{path(T_1, root) + path(T_2, root)} \quad (1)$$

where:

- $path(a, b)$ returns the path length between nodes a and b,
- $root$ is the topic's tree root,
- $MSCA(a, b)$ returns the most specific common ancestor of nodes a and b in the topic tree.

The same topic map is used by all users. However, we stress that the same hierarchy will be used differently by different users. That's to say the same reference can be related to different topics by different users. For example one may index all CBR-related papers to the same topic, let's say CBR, while another user may index the same papers differently: some related to memory organization in CBR systems and others for CBR case maintenance. A third may index the same references as all related to lazy learning. The topic similarity measure uses the topics underlying hierarchical structure. The applied heuristic is the following: the similarity between two topics depends on the length of the path that links the two topics and on the depth of the topics in the hierarchy. Moreover, a match with specific nodes closer to leaf nodes results in a higher similarity than nodes matching at higher levels of the tree. The heuristic is to return the most specific topics which concentrate a given level of the user's focus.

Reuse Phase. This phase aims at finding a solution to the target problem from a set of source cases found in the previous phase. The solution presents an interesting peer agents committee, to which the recommendation request will be forwarded. The solution committee contains a set of agents computed from the different committees of the source cases found on the previous phase. The *target case = (T, C)*, is such that: T is the initial topic, $C = \cup C_i$, where C_i is the solution of the source case i. The recommendation request will be broadcasted to all peer agents composing the committee C.

Revision Phase. The computed solution is then evaluated by the initiator agent according to the user's evaluation of the recommended references. If the user is interested by a set of recommended references (e.g. the user adds some references to her/his local base). Then, their associated cases and agents will be well evaluated.

Learning Phase. This step consists of adding new cases to the local agent case base. It is the most important step in the CBR cycle. In fact, the selection of retained agents for futur similar problems is done at this stage. As we have explained before, the peer selection is done in a manner to reduce committee size while preserving result quality. The elaboration of a case must be accurate in order to store the relevant information. This phase is based on the agent addition strategy, i.e. the criteria used in order to decide if a given responding agent will be added to the new formed committee or not. A natural idea is to choose all agents which propose some relevant references. Although this simple strategy gives encouraging preliminary results, it does not optimize the committee size. In order to reduce the number of contacted agents, we define criteria which evaluate each agent contribution within the selected committee. We define two criteria-based strategies: heuristics 1 and heuristics 2.

1. **Heuristics 1:** consists of retaining only agents with a local recall value greater than or equal to the average recall value of the references recommending agents. The recall represents the rate of good recommended references among the good existing references ($Recall = \frac{Good\_recommended\_references}{Good\_references}$). Good references are references that are well evaluated by the user. The local recall presents the recall of each agent.

2. **Heuristics 2:** consists of retaining only agents with a local precision value greater than or equal to the average precision value of the recommended references. The precision represents the rate of good recommended references among all the recommended ones ($Precision = \frac{Good\_recommended\_references}{All\_recommended\_references}$). The local precision is the precision of each agent.

4 Experimentation

Experiment settings: n agents which have the same references but they are distributed differently and randomly among the topics of the topic tree. We fix a hot topic, which is considered as a query and we apply our strategy in order to find appropriate agents. We vary each time the number of interesting agents in the system and we compute the recall and the precision. We propose interesting agent term which means agent having good references. In this experiment, we produce the interesting agent as agent having at least x% of the references associated to the current interesting topic. To evaluate our committee formation strategy, we considered three evaluation criteria (recall, precision and committee size). These criteria are of two types :

- Quality criteria: presented by the recall and the precision measures (described in 3).
- Performance criteria: presented in this experiment by the committee size.

The simulation is performed with three different settings:

- *All*: we use a naive approach where the recommendation request is broadcasted to all available agents.
- *Random*: we apply a simple peer selection algorithm, which randomly selects m agents knowing that m corresponds to the number of interesting agents at each time (m varies from 1 to n).
- *Committee*: we apply the CBR-based selection natural approach as described in section 3.

In our experiments, we fixed the number of agent to 10, the used topic similarity threshold σ_t has the value of 0.7. We suppose that an interesting agent is an agent disposing of at least 70% of the reference set associated with the hot topic. A single simulation consists of fixing the minimum number of good references for the interesting agents. Interesting agents do not necessarily have

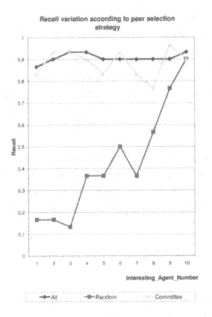

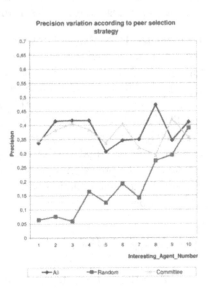

Fig. 1. Recall variation

Fig. 2. Precision variation

the same set of good references. The set is chosen randomly. The other references are dispersed among the other topics in a random manner.

Figure 1 shows the recall variation according to the number of interesting agents. We notice that the recall for the *committee* strategy is very close to the *all* strategy and clearly better than the *random* strategy. The recall is often improved by the increase of the number of interesting agents when we randomly choose the agents.

The precision variation is described in figure 2 for the three settings. The *all* and *committee* strategies present more or less similar results, which are better than the naive approach based on random peer selection. However, the precision value is fairly weak with an average of 0.364.

Then, in order to evaluate the performance of the system using the proposed committee formation strategy, figure 3 shows the number of contacted agents among these ten available agents. We notice that the number of contacted agents is reduced. For example in the case of one interesting agent, we solicit 5 agents instead of 10, for 5 and 7 interesting agents, we solicit 8 agents.

Finally, we can say that our natural committee strategy improves the system performance by reducing the number of contacted agents, while it gives similar quality results (i.e. recall and precision) as when all available agents are contacted. However, these results are not satisfactory because we do not want to solicit non interesting agents (without good references), or those which are interesting, but propose the same references as the other agents. In order to improve the results obtained, we studied the effect of applying Heuristics 1 and Heuristics 2 for agents selection (see 3). The results are described in figures 4, 5

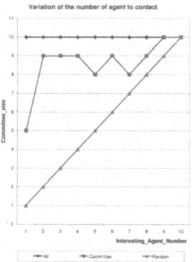

Fig. 3. Committee Size

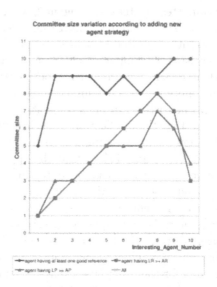

Fig. 4. Committee size variation

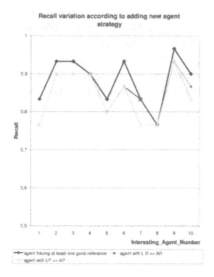

Fig. 5. Recall variation

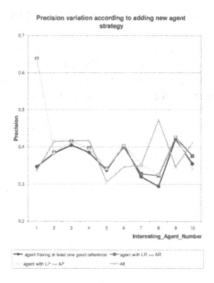

Fig. 6. Precision variation

and 6. Figure 4 shows a clear improvement of the system performance since for both cases (i.e. heuristics 1 and 2), the system solicits at worst all interesting agents. The system contacts even less agents when there is a quite important number of interesting agents. For example, for 6 and 7 interesting agents, the system contacts 6 and 7 agents according to heuristics 1 and respectively 5 and 5 agents according to heuristics 2, compared to 9 and 8 agents for the simple committee strategy (i.e. agent having at least one good reference). The same holds for the 9 and 10 interesting agents, the system solicits respectively 7 and 3 agents according to heuristics 1 and respectively 6 and 4 agents according to heuristics 2, compared to 10 and 10 agents for the simple committee strategy. Heuristics 2 gives, in general, better results than heuristics 1 mainly when there is a quite important number of agents. For example, in the 7 interesting agents case, heuristics 2 retains 5 agents while heuristics 1 retains 7 agents. We conclude that the application of such heuristics gives better system performances. We now examine its impact on the quality criteria (i.e. recall and precision).

Figures 5 and 6 show that the application of the two heuristics gives a recall value similar to the case of contacting all available agents or all agents composing the committee. We also note an improvement of the system precision since we solicit all agents proposing an acceptable contribution (in terms of recall and precision). For example, the precision is improved in the 1, 5, 6 and 9 interesting agents cases. The two heuristics based methods present identical results at the begining, i.e. when the number of interesting agents is lower than 6, and similar results for the other cases. These results show that, even when applying simple heuristics, we succeed in reducing the number of agents to solicit while we keep a very similar result quality, and moreover, we notice an improvement of the precision criterion.

In our experiments, we supposed that an interesting agent is an agent disposing of at least $x\%$ of the reference set associated with the hot topic. We varied the x and we studied its effect on the committee formation evaluation criteria. The experimental results are described in figures 7, 8 and 9. These results are obtained by adding heuristics 2 to the simple committee formation strategy. We note that, for the different values of x, the curves have the same trend. We remark

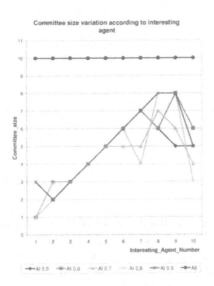

Fig. 7. Committee size variation

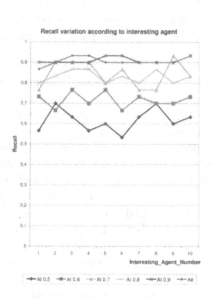

Fig. 8. Recall variation

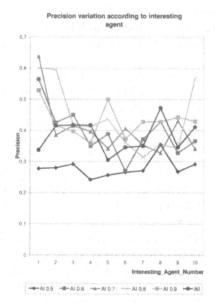

Fig. 9. Precision variation

also that, in all cases, the number of retained agents is reduced while maintaining similar result quality (i.e. recall and precision) or even an improvement. Although the results obtained are acceptable and encouraging, we think that the results (mainly the precision which is quite low) presented will be improved by introducing some constraints in the committee formation process such as:

- using better reference similarity taking into account semantic criteria (e.g. same authors, same conference, etc). This will improve the quality of recommendation and the precision of the system.
- handling the redundancy problem between agents results. In many cases, some of the references proposed by interesting agents are the same. So it is useful to verify this before contacting all possibly interesting agents.
- proposing an appropriate cooperative approach to up to date committee according to the changing user's interests in a dynamic network. This constitues our present work.

5 Related Work

Different committee formation approaches are proposed in the literature. Some are based on the notion of agent reputation [5] or agent expertise [4]. Others propose to apply automatic learning techniques in order to enable each agent to determine if it needs to increase the committee of peers and, if it is the case, which peer agent to invite [8]. For our purposes, the idea consists of providing each peer agent with the capacity of selecting a subset of peer agents having good results according to a given recommendation request type (in our case, the recommendation of bibliographical references). The goal is to improve the performance of the whole system by reducing the network and the agents charge.

- Bibster system (standing for Semantic-Based Bibliographic Peer-to-Peer System)[4], has a peer-to-peer architecture and aims at sharing bibliographic data between researchers. The peer selection is based on the *expertise* notion [6]. The expertise is a set of ACM topics. All system peers share a common ontology for publishing semantic descriptions of their expertise in a peer-to-peer network. This knowledge about the other peers expertise forms the semantic topology, which is independent of the underlying network topology. When a peer receives a request, it decides to forward the query to peers whose expertise is similar to the subject of the query. Peers decide autonomously to whom advertisements should be sent and which advertisements to accept. This decision is based on the semantic similarity between expertise descriptions. This strategy gives good results compared to broadcasting the query to all or to a random set of peers but does not exploit past experience to learn and improve the formed semantic topology.
- Gupta et. al. [5] propose a reputation system for decentralized unstructured P2P networks like Gnutella [2] for searching and information sharing. The peer selection strategy is based on the agent *reputation* notion. The reputation system uses objective criteria to track each peer's contribution in the system and allows peers to store their reputations locally. They propose two alternate computation mechanisms for a reputation system that objectively map each peer's activity in the P2P network to a dynamically updated reputation score. The two mechanisms are the debit-credit reputation computation (DCRC) and the credit-only reputation computation (CORC). The first mechanism (DCRC), credits peer reputation scores for serving content and debits for downloading. The second one (CORC), credits peer reputation scores for serving content but offers no debits. The expiration on the scores instead serves as a debit. A reputation score is intended to give a general idea of the peer's level of participation in the system. Reputation scores are based on two essential factors: the peer capability and its behavior. The capability of a peer depends on its processing capacity, memory, storage capacity, and bandwith. The behavior of a peer is determined by the level of contribution offered by it for the common good of the P2P network. Peers are free to enroll in the reputation computation or not. A reputation computation agent (RCA) is used for enrolling peers who wish to enroll in reputation computations and for updating peer reputations in a secure, light-weight, and partially distributed manner. Having reliable reputation information about peers can form the basis of an incentive system and can guide peers in taking decisions.
- Ontañón and Plaza [8] propose another strategy of selection of the agents that join a committee for solving a problem in the classification tasks. The basic reason of the incentive of agents to cooperate in the form of a committee is that they can improve their performmance in solving problems. The

committee organization improves (in general) the classification accuracy with respect to individual agents. It is a learning framework that unifies both the when and the who issues. In fact, the agent learns to assess the likelihood that the current committee will provide a correct solution. If the likelihood is not high, the agent has to invite a new agent and has to decide which agent to invite. The agent learns to form a committee in a dynamic way and to take decisions such as whether it is better to invite a new member to join a committee, when to individually solve a problem, when it is better to convene a committee.

We have chosen to propose a new strategy of committee formation which will be dynamic, extensible and adaptable. The proposed strategy exploits as much as possible past experiences and will be adaptable with the new real constraints. To ensure this, our strategy relies on a case-based reasoning system. It aims at computing committee's recommendations. In fact, when an agent detects a hot topic, it applies a CBR cycle to find some committee recommendation associated with the request type. The reference recommendation request will then be forwarded to peer agents composing the recommended committee.

6 Conclusion

We have presented a cooperative CBR approach for peer committee recommendation in a bibliographical references recommendation system COBRAS. The agents cooperate with each other in order to share their knowledge and their past experience to improve their efficiency.

We proposed a strategy allowing an agent to determine peer agents committee for a given recommendation request. This strategy uses a CBR technique in a cooperative way allowing for reusing and sharing of knowledge and experience.

The results obtained are encouraging. Different tracks however should be explored in order to improve both the quality and the performance criteria: handling the problem of agent redundancy in a commitee; proposing a strategy to maintain the agent case base and ensuring up-to-dated committee according to user's interest changing. These perspectives are the subject of our present work.

References

1. Acm, http://www.acm.org/
2. Gnutella, http://gnutella.wego.com/
3. Aamodt, A., Plaza, E.: Case-based reasoning: Foundational issues, methodological variations, and system approaches. AI Communications 7(1), 39–59 (1994)
4. Broekstra, J., Ehrig, M., Haase, P., Harmelen, F., Menken, M., Mika, P., Schnizler, B., Siebes, R.: Bibster -a semantics-based bibliographic peer-to-peer system. In: Proceedings of SemPGRID 2004, 2nd Workshop on Semantics in Peer-to-Peer and Grid Computing, New York, USA, May 2004, pp. 3–22 (2004)
5. Gupta, M., Judge, P., Ammar, M.: A reputation system for peer-to-peer networks. In: Proceedings of ACM Networks and Operating System Support for Digital And Video NOSSDAV 2003, Monterey, CA (2003)

6. Haase, P., Siebes, R., Harmelen, F.: Peer selection in peer-to-peer networks with semantic topologies. In: International Conference on Semantics of a Networked World: Semantics for Grid Databases, Paris (2004)
7. Karoui, H.: Agent RàPC pour la gestion coopérative de bases bibliographiques personnelles. In: Plate-forme AFIA 2005, 13 ème atelier de Raisonnement à Partir de Cas, Nice, France (May 2005)
8. Ontanón, S., Plaza, E.: Learning to form dynamic committees. In: Proceedings of the second International joint Conference on Autonomous Agents and Multiagent Systems, Melbourne, Australia, pp. 504–511. ACM Press, New York, USA (2003)

Mobile Agent-Based Approach for Resource Discovery in Peer-to-Peer Networks

Jaafar Gaber and Mohamed Bakhouya

Universite de Technologie de Belfort-Montbeliard
Laboratoire SeT
90010 Belfort cedex, France
{gaber,bakhouya}@utbm.fr

Abstract. Peer-to-peer networks are distributed computing infrastructures that can provide globally available network resources. Their size and complexity continue to increase and permit an almost ubiquitous availability of resources. Therefore, new discovery approaches are required and need to be highly flexible in order to cope with a dynamically changing environment. In this paper, a distributed agent-based approach for resource discovery in peer-to-peer network is proposed. This approach is based on the mobile agent paradigm and uses random walks to allow dynamic and adaptive resource discovery. We analyze this approach through three distributed resource discovery scenarios by NS2 simulator.

1 Introduction

Resource discovery is an important issue in peer-to-peer network; given a user request, a resource discovery mechanism should locate and return a set of peer addresses that match the description of the requested resources. Resources can be divided into two basic categories [1], [2]: system resources and application resources. System resources are bound to specific hosts, representing hardware devises (e.g. disk) or logical system objects. Application resources are software entities managed by an application. In this paper, a service is considered to be composed by a set of resources that users need to discover and select [3], [4], [5]. These resources could be interfaced by web services. Web services are applications that permit to describe software components; in particular they define identification and accessing methods that enable the discovery and the use of these components (i.e., the resources). For example, for a punctual need, a user peer who would like to open video files or create video CD might need the following resources: a video player, format transcoding software, the MPEG-4 codec (for his wireless laptop), video effect or edge detection algorithms, etc.

In peer-to-peer networks, centralized discovery architecture cannot meet the requirements of both scalability and adaptability simultaneously. Issues are that network resource discovery systems must be able to scale and able to adapt to dynamic conditions in the network.

In this paper, we will use both random walks and a cloning mobile agent-based approach for resource discovery in unstructured peer-to-peer networks. The rest

S. Joseph et al. (Eds.): AP2PC 2006, LNAI 4461, pp. 63–73, 2008.

of the paper is organized as follows. Section 2 presents the related work. In section 3, the proposed approach is presented. Section 4 presents the simulation results. Conclusion is given in section 5.

2   Related Work

Resource discovery systems proposed in the literature can be classified into three categories as depicted in figure 1: structured systems, unstructured systems and self-organization systems [4], [6]. Structured systems can be classified also into indexation-based architectures and hashing-based architectures. In indexation-based architectures, there are two subcategories: centralized and decentralized systems. In centralized indexation-based systems, typical resource discovery architectures consists of three entities: resource providers that create and publish resources, resource brokers that maintain repositories of published resources to support their discovery, and resources requesters that search in the resource broker's repositories. Centralized approaches, such as Napster [7], scale poorly and have a single point of failure. To overcome the scalability problem, decentralized approaches adopt traditionally a hierarchical architecture consisting of multiple repositories that synchronize periodically [1], [8], [9]. In a large-scale P2P network, hierarchical architecture cannot meet the requirements of both scalability and adaptability simultaneously. More precisely, the way in which they have typically been constructed is often very inflexible due to the risk of bottlenecks and the difficulty of repositories updating [1], [10], [11]. Also, peer-to-peer network is a dynamic environment where the location and availability of resources are constantly changing; some resources could be disconnected from the network and new ones may join it at any time.

Therefore, a resource discovery system should be decentralized to avoid bottlenecks and guarantee scalability and adaptability. Most of structured systems that implement non hierarchical and decentralized infrastructures use Distributed Hash Tables (DHTs) to locate and assign resources to specific peers. Hashing-based architectures such as Chord [12], Pastry [13], and Tapestry [14] allow the implementation of direct routing search algorithms to efficiently locate files [15]. However, a Hashing-based architectures require overlay networks between peers that are generally hard to maintain.

In contrast, unstructured systems [7] have no precise control over resources emplacements. Therefore, the most typical localization method is the flooding technique, wherein the request is broadcasted to all neighbors within a certain radius with TTL mechanism (TTL for Time To Live) [15]. More precisely, in order to find resources on the network, search queries are flooded to neighbor peers for bounded number of hops. Each query has an attached TTL to control the number of hops that a query can be propagated to away in the network. On receiving a query, a peer decrements its TTL, and if the TTL is greater than 0, it forwards the query to neighbor peers. When a TTL reaches 0, the query was no longer forwarded. However, it is not possible to guarantee the success or failure of a query. In other words, a resource may not be found even though it does exist in the network. To overcome this disadvantage, the mechanism of dynamic TTL based on the expanding ring technique is proposed in [16]. The principe of expanding ring is the following: a peer starts a flood with small TTL, and waits to see if the search is successful. If it is, then the peer stops the flooding. Otherwise, the peer increases the TTL and restarts another flood. This process is repeated until finding the required resource or covering all the network. According to [15], [16], unlike regular flooding with a fixed TTL, the expanding ring technique guaranties that if a required resource is present in the network it will be located. However, if expanding ring technique solves the TTL selection problem, it does not address the message duplication problem that could generate large loads on the network [15], [16].

Random walk-based search mechanism, which forwards a query message (i.e., walker) to a randomly chosen neighbor at each step until the service is found, is a well-known technique that can avoid the message duplication problem. Using one walker, it cuts down the message overhead significantly, but it could increase the delay of successful searches [15], [16]. To decrease the delay, a requesting peer could send k parallel query messages, and each query message takes its own random walk. However, it is difficult to determine a priori a suitable number k of walkers. More precisely, if this number is big enough, the message traffic could increase significantly [15]. Replication mechanisms, such as caching some objects along the reverse path of queries, are proposed in [16], in order to reduce the lookup length and decrease the message traffic. However, in dynamic and distributed setting, it is difficult to maintain the coherence of duplicated objects.

Both structured and unstructured systems present some drawbacks. Structured systems use repositories or DHT overlay networks between peers that are generally hard to maintain. In particular, peer join/leave operations could incur huge overheads [16]. In contrast, unstructured systems allow the peer to enter and leave the systems without overheads. However, mechanisms used in the request resolution can generate large traffic loads on the network.

Recently, new alternatives paradigms to the traditional Client/Server paradigm have been proposed in [3] and [17] for ubiquitous and pervasive computing. These new paradigms require that discovery systems should have self-organizing and self-adaptive capabilities. An approach inspired by the human immune system to carry out these alternatives paradigms has been presented in [3], [5], [4]. This approach operates as follows: unlike the classical Client/Server approach,, each user request is considered as an attack launched against the global network. The immune networking middleware reacts like an immune system against pathogens that have entered the body. It detects the infection (i.e., user request) and delivers a response to eliminate it (i.e., satisfy the user request) [3], [17]. This approach can be classified in the third category of self-organization discovery systems (see Figure 1). More precisely, peers (i.e., servers) are organized into communities by the creation of affinity relationships, like the idiotypic network [18] created by human immune cells (i.e., peers) against foreign antigens (i.e., user requests). The establishment of relationship affinities between peers allows to solve, by collaboration, user requests. A reinforcement learning mechanism is used to adjust and reinforce dynamically relationship affinity values according to delivered responses. This reinforcement mechanism permits to cope with dynamic changes in the network, the services availability and the user requests. In other words, new communities may be created or others may be modified according to dynamic environment changes. Peers may acquire new memberships to new communities or drop themselves from current ones through establishing or deleting affinity relationships [5], [4].

In this paper, a cloning approach based on mobile agent for resource discovery in unstructured peer-to-peer network together with random walks technique is presented, as depicted in the figure 1. Within this approach, peers might dynamically and unpredictably join/leave the network, such that any complete knowledge of these changes and modifications is difficult even impossible to obtain.

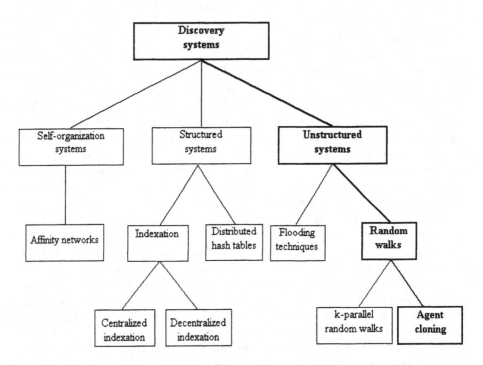

Fig. 1. Classification of service discovery systems according to their architectures and their operating modes. Cloning approach presented in this paper is indicated by bold lines.

3   The Resource Discovery Approach

Unstructured peer-to-peer network can be viewed as an indirect connected graph $G = (S, V)$, where S is the set of peers ($|S| = n$) and V the set of links ($|V| = m$) connecting the peers. A peer p_i is considered to be connected to a peer p_j, if there is a link between p_i and p_j. In this section, the possibility of embedding the mobile agent paradigm and the random walk approach in designing distributed algorithm for resource discovery in unstructured peer-to-peer network is analyzed. A mobile agent is a software entity which may move from location to location to meet other agents or to access resources provided at each location [19], [20]. A random walk on a graph is a stochastic process that iteratively visits the vertices of the graph. From a given peer, the walk process moves at the next step to an adjacent peer chosen uniformly at random [21], [22].

To use mobile agents for resource discovery, let us consider the following three scenarios. The first scenario associates a unique agent to each peer request while the second scenario involves multiple agents for each request. The third scenario uses cloning operation to clone an agent during its random walk.

In the first scenario, to locate a service, the requester peer (origin of the request) creates a mobile agent, called request agent, and gives it the service to be located. A service can be composed of one or a set of resources. The mobile agent starts from a requester peer and then uses links within it to get access to other peers. The mobile agent chooses randomly between these peers, determines the IP address of the chosen one and moves to the corresponding peer. The mobile agent repeats this process with the new peers reached until it find the required resources. Upon mobile agent termination (i.e. success or fail) it starts a backtracking phase. During this phase, the agent comes back using the path computed between the peer holding the last remaining resource to collect (i.e., an end point of walk) and the requester peer. It should be noted that compared to client/server approach, in this scenario, the single mobile agent eliminates the transfer of intermediate results across the network and thus reduces the end-to-end latency [20]. However, the time to resolve the request could be unreasonable in large scale network where peers have no preexisting knowledge of where resources are located so searching for them could require steps. More precisely, steps are required for a mobile agent to cover a given graph with n nodes i.e., the mobile agent visits all nodes of the graph [23].

To reduce this latency problem, multiple mobile agents and mobile agent cloning scenarios could be more suitable scenarios for the resolution request process. In the multiple agents' scenario, an initial population of mobile agents is initially created and dispatched randomly for resource discovery. This scenario should allow the agents to resolve request in a reasonable amount of time compared to the single mobile agent scenario. However, it is difficult to determine the initial mobile agent population size. When this number is big enough, the agents traffic increases significantly, but the delay of successful searches is decreased. Also, the use of very small number decreases the agents traffic and increases delay of successful searches.

In the mobile agent cloning scenario, a mobile agent starts, at its first step, on its requester peer. At each hop, mobile agent determines the IP address of randomly chosen neighboring peers, creates replication (i.e. clone) to itself, passes tasks to this clones that move to further peers. This scenario should allow mobiles agents to cover a much wide area of network peers in a reasonable amount of time compared to the single mobile agent scenario and the multiple mobile agents' scenario. It's worth noting that in multiple mobile agents' scenario, initial population size does not change at each step but in mobile agent cloning scenario, it evolves during the random walks.

More precisely, the algorithm of mobile agent cloning scenario is as follows. The peer willing to locate a service creates a mobile agent, called request agent. This agent initiates a random walk in the network until it meets appropriate peers that can resolves the request or it terminates its random walk. At each hop, the mobile agent can clones itself. The request discovery process is made in two phase: forwarding phase and backtracking phase. During the forwarding phase, request agents seek peers that can provide the required resources. When the all required resources are discovered, a request agent stops cloning itself, send results to the requester, and starts the backtracking phase. In this phase, mobile agent travels back to its initial peer following back the founded path. The role of this backtracking phase is to perform a reinforcement learning mechanism on links between peers [24]. More precisely, the objective of this backtracking phase is to permit for peers to learn from mobile agents satisfactions on past requests to carry out biased random walk in order to improve performance of future requests.

During its random walk, a request agent stores the list of the visited peers. Based on this stored list, called service path, the agent chooses moving to peers that are not visited yet. However, mobile agents require a mechanism to terminate their walks. To this aim, a mobile agent starts with an initial TTL. If the required service is found, it stops the search and starts the backtracking phase. Otherwise, the agent checks if the requester has already get the service from another clone. If it is the case, the agent is killed. If not, the requester could assign a new initial TTL to the agent and initiates a new random walk.

It is worth noting that, in the agent cloning scenario, the increasing of the agent population size with cloning operation will increase resource demands in the network which will affect the overall performance. Amin and Mikler have proposed in [25] a regulation algorithm to control the number of clones spawned in the network (AM algorithm). This algorithm is inspired by stigmergetic propriety of "ant colony" to facilitate coordination between mobile agents. More precisely, mobiles agents with minimum cognitive capabilities communicate with each other using pheromones that assist them to select an appropriate action. The intensity of pheromones deposited by agents at each node visited is determined by the equation $e^{-\lambda \Delta t}$, where Δt is the time since the deposition of pheromone and λ is a constant value fixed between 0 and 1. The controller of each agent contains the action selection algorithm that is defined as follows. An agent visiting a node at time t_b extracts the value of the pheromone that was deposited at time t_a $(t_a \leq t_b)$ using the equation $e^{-\lambda(t_b - t_a)}$. If this value is above a certain termination threshold Max, the agent kills itself. On the other hand, if the pheromone value reduces below a cloning threshold Min, the agent clones itself. But, if the pheromone is comprised between the termination and cloning threshold, the agent neither clones nor kills itself. In this case, it migrates to another peer node.

Bakhouya and Gaber have proposed in [26], [27] a self-adaptive and distributed regulation algorithm inspired by the "human immune system" to regulate dynamically the agents population size in a network, without using any global or constant threshold parameters (BG algorithm). The immune system has emergent properties to make self-regulating and self-adapting in dynamically changing environment [27], [5]. In this algorithm, each mobile agent selects locally an appropriate behavior to its environment state from the following ones: death, moving or cloning without using any global information [27].

It should be noted that with AM algorithm, the number of agents in the network converges to a constant number that depends only on the threshold parameters that should be determined a priori with empirical simulations for example. With the BG algorithm however, the number of agents in the network converges to a value that is adjusted dynamically according to the changes in the network. Therefore, BG algorithm is a distributed self-regulation algorithm.

The Figure 2 shows an example of how request resolution process works with cloning scenario. Peer P_1 possesses the resource R_1 and desires locate a service $S = (R_1, R_2, R_3, R_4)$ To locate this service, P_1 creates a request, initiates one mobile agent MA_1 and gives it the list of resources to be located, the IP address and the initial TTL. The agent add the peer P_1 to its visited peers list (i.e., service path) and moves to the peer P_2 chosen randomly. Since, this peer provides the required resource R_2, it is added to the visited peers list. At this step, MA_1 residing in peer P_2 creates another agent MA_2 that walk to peer P_6. These agents repeat the same process until they find the required service or their TTL is expired (i.e., TTL becomes equal to 0). The visited peers of request forwarding phase of the two mobile agents are shown with thicker arrows. The mobile agent (MA_2) with service path (P_1, P_2, P_6, P_5) fails, while the second mobile agent (MA_1) with service path (P_1, P_2, P_3, P_4) terminates with a successful research. During the backtracking phase, the mobile agents goes back from the last peer visited, via the intermediate peers on the founded service path, to the initial peer. The backtracking phase is started for this two mobile agents on the reverse path shown in figure 2 with dotted arrows. It should be noted that we can use a reinforcement learning mechanism to adjust and reinforce dynamically relationship affinity values between peers according to the delivered responses as pointed out in [24].

4   Simulation Results

Simulations are implemented by NS2 [28]. The objective of the simulations is to compare these three mobile agent-based scenarios. A network of 100 peers is generated randomly with BRITE generator [29]. Each peer provides one resource among ten kinds of resources. The simulation abstracts any considerations about networking issues such as bandwidth constraints and time processing. Recall that the objective of the resource discovery system is to discover and select peers that can resolve user requests.

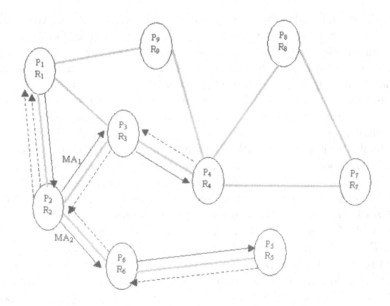

Fig. 2. Request forwarding and backtracking phases to locate the service ($R_1, R_2, R_3,$ R_4) with the mobile agents cloning scenario

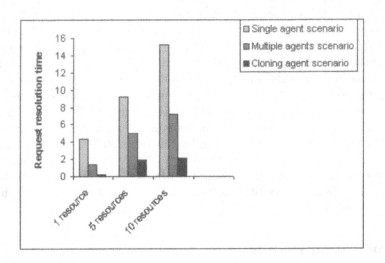

Fig. 3. Resolution request time for mobile agent scenarios

In figure 3, the cloning mobile agent scenario shows a request resolution time better than that of single and multiple mobile agents scenarios independent of searched service (one, five or ten resources). This is due to the number of agents launched by cloning operation for the request discovery. More precisely, mobile agents may be cloned and dispatched in different directions. Therefore, this end allows mobiles agents to cover a much wide area of network peers and resolve requests in a shorter time. In multiple mobile agent scenario, a requester peer creates a fixed number of mobile agents (5 mobile agents in this simulation) and dispatch them in different directions. This scenario allows mobile agents to work in parallel, but shows a running time greater than that of a mobile agent cloning scenario as shown in figure 3.

5   Conclusion

This paper analyzes three scenarios for resource discovery in unstructured peer-to-peer network based on a mobile agent-based approach together with random walks technique. From the simulation, the agent-based approach with cloning scenario outperforms the single agent scenario and the multiple agent scenario.

Future work will address additional simulations with ns2 to evaluate the approach performance when storage and bandwidth communication are considered and compare it with other approaches proposed in the literature. In this paper, we have concentrated our effort first to demonstrate the viability of the proposed agent based approach with three scenarios together with ns2 simulations. Further investigation will address also the specification issue and the performance evaluation of the approach with various biased random walks schemes.

References

1. Krauter, K., Buyya, R., Maheswaran, M.: A taxonomy and survey of grid resource management systems for distributed computing. Software Practice and Experience 32, 135–164 (2002)
2. Gidron, Y., Holder, O., Ben-Shaul, I., Aridor, Y.: A taxonomy and survey of grid resource manage-ment systems for distributed computing. Software Practice and Experience 13, 5–21 (2001)
3. Gaber, J.: New paradigms for ubiquitous and pervasive computing. Technical Report RR-09-00, Universite de Technologie de Belfort-Montbeliard (2000)
4. Bakhouya, M., Gaber, J.: Adaptive approches for ubiquitous computing. In: Lobiod, H. (ed.) Mobile networks and wireless sensor networks, Hemes-Lavoisier, pp. 129–163 (2006), ISBN 2-7462-1292-7
5. Bakhouya, M.: Self-adaptive approach based on mobile agent and inspired by human immune system for service discovery in large scale networks. Phd thesis, Universite de Technologie de Belfort-Montbeliard, Belfort CEDEX, 90010 France (2005)
6. Bakhouya, M., Gaber, J.: Self-adaptive and self-organizing approaches to design ubiquitous and pervasive applications. In: Encyclopedia in Mobile Computing and Commerce (EMCC) (to appear, 2007)
7. Saroiu, S., Gummadi, P.K., Gribble, S.D.: Measuring and analyzing the characteristics of napster and gnutella hosts. ACM Multimedia Systems Journal 9, 170–1840 (2003)
8. Czerwinski, S., Zhao, B., Hodes, T., Joseph, A., Katz, R.: An architecture for a secure service discovery service. In: ACM MobiCom 1999, Atlanta, USA, ACM, New York (1999)

9. Xu, D., Nahrstedt, K., Wichadakul, D.: Qos-aware discovery of wide-area distributed services. In: First IEEE/ACM International Symposium on Cluster Computing and the Grid (CCGrid), IEEE/ACM (2001)

10. Iamnitchi, A., Foster, I., Nurmi, D.: A peer-to-peer approach to resource discovery in grid environments. In: High Performance Distributed Computing (HPDC 2002), Edinbourgh, UK, IEEE, Los Alamitos (2002)

11. Talia, D., Trunfio, P.: Web services for peer-to-peer resource discovery on the grid. In: High Performance Distributed Computing (HPDC 2002) (2002), www.grid.it/

12. Stoicay, I., Morrisz, R., Liben-Nowellz, D., Kargerz, D., Kaashoekz, M.F., Dabekz, F., Balakrishnanz, H.: Chord: A scalable peer-to-peer lookup protocol for internet applicationss. In: Proceedings of the 2001 ACM SIGCOMM Conference, California, USA, pp. 149–160. ACM, New York (2001)

13. Rowstron, A., Druschel, P.: Pastry: Scalable, decentralized object location, and routing for large-scale peer-to-peer systems. In: Guerraoui, R. (ed.) Middleware 2001. LNCS, vol. 2218, pp. 329–350. Springer, Heidelberg (2001)

14. Zhao, B., Kubiatowicz, J., Joseph, A.: Tapestry: An infrastructure for fault-tolerant wide-area location and routing. Technical Report UCB/CSD-01-1141, UC Berkeley (2001)

15. Wang, C., Li, B.: Peer-to-peer overlay networks: A survey. Technical Report TR-P2P, Department of Computer Science, HKUST (2003)

16. Lv, Q., Cao, P., Cohen, E., Li, K., Shenker, S.: Search and replication in unstructured peer-to-peer network. In: 16th ACM International Conference on Supercomputing (ICS 2002), pp. 329–350. ACM, New York (2002)

17. Gaber, J.: New paradigms for ubiquitous and pervasive applications. In: Proc. of the First Workshop on Software Engineering Challenges for Ubiquitous Computing SEUC 2006, Lancaster, UK (2006)

18. Jerne, N.: Towards a network theory of the immune system. Ann. Immunol (Inst. Pasteur) 125, 373–389 (1974)

19. Carzaniga, A., Picco, G., Vigna, G.: Designing distributed applications with mobile code paradigms. In: 19th International Conference on Software Engineering, Boston, MA (1997)

20. Straber, M., Schwehm, M.: A performance model for mobile agent systems. In: Parallel and Distributed Processing Techniques and Application (PDPTA 1997), Las Vegas, USA, pp. 1132–1140 (1997)

21. Broder, A.Z., Karlin, A., Raghavan, P., Upfal, E.: Trading space for time in undirected s-t connectivity. In: ACM STOC 1989, pp. 543–549 (1989)

22. Baala, H., Flauzac, O., Gaber, J., Buid, M., El-Ghazawi, T.: A self-stabilizing distributed algorithm for spanning tree construction in wireless ad hoc networks. Journal of Parallel and Distributed Computing (JPDC) 63, 97–104 (2003)

23. Broder, A., Karlin, A.: Bounds on the cover time. Journal of Theoretical Probability 2, 101–120 (1989)

24. Bakhouya, M., Gaber, J.: A reinforcement learning of link affinities and user requests for self-adaptive graph emergence from an arbitrary graph. Technical Report RR-03-07, Universite de Technologie de Belfort-Montbeliard, UTBM (2003)

25. Amin, K., Mikler, A.: Dynamic agent population in agent-based distance vector routing. In: Second International Workshop on Intelligent Systems Design and Applications, Atlanta, USA, pp. 543–549 (2002)

26. Bakhouya, M., Gaber, J.: Distributed autoregulation approach of a mobile agent population in a network. Technical Report RR-02-12, Universite de Technologie de Belfort-Montbeliard (2002)

27. Bakhouya, M., Gaber, J.: Adaptive approach for the regulation of a mobile agent population in a distributed network. In: International Symposium on Parallel and Distributed Computing (ISPDC 2006), Timisoara, Romania, pp. 1132–1140. IEEE, Los Alamitos (1997)
28. Wittner, O.: Nework simulator patch. In: Faculty of Information Technology, Mathematics and Electrical Engineering, Department of Telematics (2000)
29. Medina, A., Lakhina, A., Matta, I., Byers, J.: Brite: An approach to universal topology generation. In: Proceedings of the International Workshop on Modeling, Analysis and Simulation of Computer and Telecommunications Systems (MASCOTS 2001), Cincinnati, Ohio (2001)

CHORA: Expert-Based P2P Web Search

Halldor Isak Gylfason, Omar Khan, and Grant Schoenebeck

Electrical Engineering and Computer Science
University of California, Berkeley
{halldor,omar,grant}@cs.berkeley.edu

Abstract. We present CHORA, a P2P web search engine which complements, not replaces, traditional web search by using peers' web viewing history to recommend useful web sites to queriers. CHORA is designed around a two-step paradigm. First, CHORA determines which peers to query and then it executes a query across these peers. Each peer uses a desktop search engine to query their local web history and retrieve results ordered by relevance. To determine which peers to query, a small sketch of the information available from each peer is stored in a DHT. Peers with sketches indicating that they may have relevant information are queried. The query is dispersed through an ad hoc network connecting only those machines in the query and is optimized for getting good results as quickly as possible.

1 Introduction

While P2P Web search is not a new technique, most of the previous work in this area focuses on creating a P2P network which searches the *entire* Web [1,2,3,4]. Previous P2P Web search efforts have grown out of two observations: (1) even the largest centralized search engines probably cannot index the entire web and (2) Distributed Hash Tables (DHTs) [5,6] provide an efficient way to index large amounts of data in a distributed manner. However, there are problems with these observations and the systems built upon them. One simple proof that there is something wrong is that these systems, some of which have been deployed commercially, have not been very successful.

We believe that one crucial observation is missing: you cannot replace a web search engine solely with promises of the future. With all P2P systems you need a bootstrapping mechanism: a way to grow the system until it reaches a sufficient number of users to sustain itself. None of the previous systems describe an effective bootstrapping mechanism. The added benefits that these systems claim, such as resistance to censorship and ability to search over a larger database, exist only in the future, and until these systems have many users, they are essentially an incomplete reproduction of a centrally hosted search engine.

By recognizing the extra observation above, we designed CHORA not to replace centralized Web search engines, but rather to use P2P search in the areas of Web search where it can offer the most improvement. The design of CHORA was motivated by a few scenarios where additional peer information could potentially improve search:

S. Joseph et al. (Eds.): AP2PC 2006, LNAI 4461, pp. 74–85, 2008.

1. You find a new band that you like, say, *Arcade Fire*. You want to find out more about this band: who else likes their music and what they enjoy about it?
2. You need to concatenate two `pdf` files but do not know how.

In the first case, there is a group of people, *experts*, who will be able to answer the query well. If you could find and directly contact these experts for advice, they would be able to show you the results they found most useful. In the second case, you are seeking the same item which a large group of people has already sought and found. If you can identify these pages, you could use their experience to expedite your own search.

P2P search is a natural way to aggregate the experiences of individual users. P2P search interacts directly with user nodes, which contain a user's full browsing experience, along with many other facets of their computing history. On the other hand, web search engines, for the most part, only have access to result clicks, and suppositions inferred from those clicks.

CHORA, facilitated by using a two-phase query, provides a means of aggregating a user's rich computing history. In the first phase, *sketch query*, it queries a database stored in a Distributed Hash Table (DHT) to obtain a list of peers which are most likely to have relevant information. This DHT contains a sketch of what is on each computer, each sketch being a collection of the most important keywords for each user. From this query CHORA builds a *target list* of peers to query. During the second phase, *peer query*, CHORA delivers a query to each of these peers and aggregates the results.

Our two-phase execution works by limiting the number of peers queried by first identifying who is likely to be able to give relevant information. This necessity is born out of two limitations: it is infeasible to query every peer as has been seen in P2P applications such as Gnutella [7,8,9]. On the other hand, users are weary about the privacy of their web-browsing history. With a full index, in a centralized server or on a DHT, this information has to leave the user's computer wholesale. In CHORA the only information that needs to leave the peer's computer is a small sketch, which the user can filter.

There are two major contributions of this work: the observation that much of a single user's browsing history (along with all their computer interactions) is readily available to help supplement the web search results of *all users*; and a method that generates a sufficient description of the content of each user's computer, in order to efficiently direct queries to users likely to have good results. For the method presented in this paper, we use a user's browsing history and behavior as available in desktop search products like Google Desktop [10] to concisely capture their expertise. The main abstraction used is the concept of a click graph, which helps organize a user's web pages based on connectivity implied by their clicks and summary statistics describing their interaction with each page.

Previous work has not fully explored the method of first locating peers using sketches. Many have thought that it would simply be too difficult to find information stored in this way. A contribution of this paper is a study on how feasible it is. An additional contribution is the design and implementation of CHORA which efficiently routes queries, in order to receive good results as quickly as possible.

The paper is organized as follows: Section 2 explains the systems related details of the implementation. Section 3 explains how CHORA generates sketches and aggregates query results, while Section 4 contains an evaluation of CHORA. Finally, Section 5 briefly surveys relevant previous work and Section 6 concludes.

2   System Architecture

In this section we describe the architecture of CHORA. Our implementation uses the Python programming language, the OpenDHT Distributed Hash table [11] and Google Desktop.

2.1   Query Setup

Initially, when a user joins CHORA, the user's set of keywords is computed, as described in Section 3, and subsequently each keyword is registered in OpenDHT under the SHA1 hash of the keyword. Each registered keyword contains meta-data such as the URL of the computer, location/bandwidth parameters, and a set of related keywords on that computer. This is done to optimize queries involving multiple query terms, where we wish to find computers containing all of those keywords. Finally, every computer registers under a common fixed key, so the system can optionally flood queries to all participants – an option clearly feasible in the first stages of deployment.

2.2   Phase 1 - Sketch Query

When a user issues a query to CHORA, the system attempts to locate computers that are likely to have good results, based on each machine's list of keywords. This list of peers is referred to as the *target list*. Conceptually, a *Get* is performed to OpenDHT on each word in the query, and the peers whose sketches contain the most keywords are computed and prioritized. This can be optimized by using the meta-data that stores a set of other keywords for that computer, or by a mechanism embedded in the DHT such as PIER's in-network joins [12]. Once a target list has been constructed, the system moves to the peer query phase.

2.3   Phase 2 - Peer Query

At this stage, the query needs to be distributed to all the nodes in the target list. Since in the OpenDHT model, the nodes are not participants in the DHT routing, they must build a routing mechanism external to the DHT. In this model each node has greater control over the routing than it would have if the routing were embedded in a multicast enabled DHT. In particular, queries can first be sent to the nodes most likely to have good results.

For a large P2P network, it is likely infeasible for the issuing node to send the query directly to all of the related peers, so a query dissemination tree is constructed with the issuing node as the root. Each node in the tree receives the query from its parent, along with a list of computers which will become that node's descendants. The node then selects some of the descendant nodes from that list to become its children, divides the rest of the list among them, and forwards the query. Then the node executes the query locally using Google Desktop, and sends the local query results upstream. For fault tolerance, a list of ancestors can be maintained, so single node failures will not break the tree.

When constructing the tree it is important to be aware of the location of the nodes. Clearly, when selecting children it is important that the latency is as low as possible; a node in North America should not distribute its query to China, when it can choose other nearby nodes. Furthermore, nearby nodes are not equal. Some have access to more bandwidth, are more likely to have relevant information, have longer up-times and are more reliable. This observation has lead to a super-node architecture (e.g. Gnutella ultrapeers). The super-node architecture contains two types of nodes: *leaf-nodes* and *super-nodes*. The main tree is composed solely of super-nodes and the leaf-nodes are leaves of a super-node in the tree. In particular, only super-nodes have children. One advantage of this model is that slow nodes can be placed near the root of the tree without negatively affecting the time it takes results from other nodes to return.

Detecting near-by nodes can be done in various ways. In CHORA, query trees are short lived so we do not want to do any costly probing of individual machines at the time of the query. Thus, we opted for a network coordinate system to compute the latency [13]. Every node stores its Internet coordinates in the keyword meta-data. The state in the DHT is soft, so this registration is continuously updated to reflect changes in the coordinates.

We implemented 3 different methods of constructing the query tree:

1. **Random:** Here each node selects its children randomly, while respecting some system-configured fan out.
2. **Location based:** In this model each node selects the children to be the closest nodes according to the network coordinates, again respecting some system-configured fan out.
3. **Location based with super-nodes:** In the super-node model each node selects two types of children: super-children and leaf-children. Thus if a super-node is sufficiently close it will be selected as a super-child, despite the fact that some other nodes may be slightly closer. The primary goal when selecting leaf-children is to select nodes with data relevant to the query, in order for the user to more quickly receive good results. Each node decides for itself if it is a super-node, and may include metrics such as bandwidth, uptime or be statically configured. This indicator is stored in the DHT meta-data.

We have simulated these three approaches and results indicate that with the super-node approach we are successful in getting more results in early, and since the tree is constructed with nodes near the root that are likely to have good results, the user will notice considerable improvement.

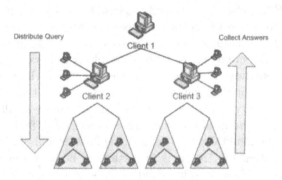

Fig. 1. Query Execution with super-nodes

3   Search Quality

3.1   Sketches

CHORA's two-step query relies on good sketches in order to locate peers who have information relevant to the query. Because the DHT can only look up keywords, we are restricted to describing users by a list of searchable keywords (assuming a user population large enough to render flooding impractical).

Recall the goal behind these sketches: each user wants to advertise topics for which they have already done extensive research so that other users can leverage that research. For example, CHORA can leverage users that might have no long-term interest in a topic like "DVD players," but who are marked as an expert on "DVD players" because they recently performed extensive research on DVD players in preparation for a purchase. We observe that the users who share similar interests are only good users to query if the query is related to their shared interests. Therefore, characterizations of peers that are not query sensitive (i.e. bookmarks) are insufficient for our purpose.

Because these sketches are stored on another system, privacy is a concern. Mechanisms can be added to allow the user to filter the keywords in sketches published by his computer or to disallow certain queries from being accepted by his computer. Another way to ensure privacy is to obfuscate the results from each peer. For example, each peer could be made to contain a few results that the user did not browse. In this way the user could deny having actively viewed any results issuing from his machine.

Clustering. To make a sketch, we attempt to cluster related web pages in the user's browsing history. The keywords from the best clusters will constitute our sketch. Clustering has three parts: generating click graphs, merging click graphs, and extracting keywords.

Generating Click Graphs. We can divide web viewing into sessions. Each viewing session is initiated by the user opening the web-browser or actively entering data

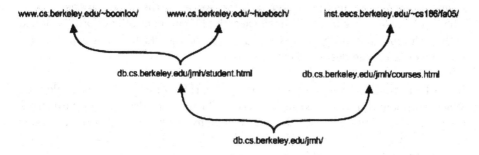

Fig. 2. A Click Graph

into the web browser (e.g. entering a URL or executing a web search query). Within each session the user navigates by clicking links. For each session we can define a *click graph* $G = (V, E)$, where V is the set of web pages visited during the session and there is a directed edge between web pages p_1 and p_2 if the user clicked a link leading to the web page p_2 from the web page p_1 (see figure 2). We assume each page is labeled by its URL. In addition, there are other summary statistics associated with a page: the amount of time the user spent on the page, the number of times the user visited the page, etc..

Merging Click Graphs. We combine click graphs that pertain to sessions on related subjects. For example, when users are researching a subject, they often perform multiple queries on that subject. All these queries induce distinct click graphs, however all these graphs are related and should be combined and treated as one.

Click graphs generated from chronologically contiguous sessions are more likely to be on the same topic. Additionally, click graphs that share URLs or have many common words are likely to be on the same topic. CHORA uses these three criteria: time, word commonalities, and link commonalities, to help identify and merge click graphs that are on the same topic.

Keyword Extraction. We now show how CHORA computes a vector v which contains word-score pairs $(w, s(w))$ for each word w that appears on a page in the session using a variant of TF-IDF. We can associate a duration t_p with each vertex $p \in V$ which indicates the time the user spent on that page. Let $f_p(w) = \{\text{\# of times w appears on p}\}/\{\text{\# of words on p}\}$ be the frequency of word w on page $p \in V$.[1] We define the score of word w for session i as $\hat{s}^{(i)}(w) = \sum_p f_p(w)t_p/T$ where $T = \sum_{p \in V} t_p$ is the total time spent in this cluster. It can easily be verified that $\sum_w \hat{s}_{(i)}(w) = 1$.

Finally, in order to get the words that best describe a cluster we normalize across all clusters. Let $\mathcal{I}$ be the set of clusters. $s^{(i)}(w) = \hat{s}^{(i)}(w) - \frac{1}{|\mathcal{I}|-1} \sum_{j \in \mathcal{I}, j \neq i} \hat{s}^{(i)}(w)$. Note that not all of the $s^{(i)}(w)$s will be positive. We then score each cluster based on a combination of the time the user

---

[1] In computing f_p we also take other factors into account, e.g. capitalization.

spent viewing pages in the cluster and the scores of the words in the cluster. The top k clusters are included in the sketch. The number of keywords included with each cluster is proportional to the score of the cluster. k is a parameter that depends on the desired sketch size.

Size of Sketch. Currently, CHORA limits its DHT entries to at most 1 kilobyte. When each keyword is stored in the DHT, CHORA includes the keyword itself, the meta-data of the user's machine and as many other keywords from the same cluster as will fit. Priority is given to the most important keywords and this number tends to be around 30 in practice.

By using the estimations from [14] that each participating node in the DHT can store 1 GB, and estimating that 10% of the the users of CHORA participate in the DHT, each user can store $100,000$ keywords. In our opinion that is larger than is needed for CHORA.

Keyword Shortfalls. One issue with keywords is that there are situations where it is not desirable to search over individual keywords, for example when searching for a quote. The query "It was the best of times, it was the worst of times" would almost certainly fail if we use the keyword mechanism described above.

This problem can be mitigated by asking the user to separate their query into a topic ("Charles Dickens") and a subquery (the quote mentioned above). Then CHORA would use "Dickens" as a keyword (to identify a target list of machines), but locally search each machine with the subquery. Some users might not be able to connect a quote like this with the context ("Dickens"), but we note that centralized search engines already perform exceedingly well on this type of search.

Another issue is that the DHT can only support exact matches amongst keywords. If one machine is an expert on "UC Berkeley", but a user searches for "University of California, Berkeley" the first machine may not be included in the target list.

Two ways to alleviate this problem include searching over URLs and automatically generating keywords synonyms. Sometimes a URL describes a topic better than any word. In the aforementioned example, there are many ways to describe UC Berkeley as exact keywords, but it has only one homepage: www.berkeley.edu. Furthermore, additional keywords can be generated on the fly, for example, by looking at the words the appear in the snippets – the 2 or 3 line query-sensitive summaries of each result – of a centralized web search.

3.2 Ranking and Aggregation

In each of the two phases, sketch query and peer query, the results must be ranked. The order of the sketch query rank is used to decide which machines to query if too many positive results come back. It is also used in the super-node model to decide where peers should be in the query tree.

Sketch query ranking. CHORA ranks the machines based on three criteria:

1. The number of query words that the keyword list contains.
2. Where the query words appear in the keyword list (keywords at the front of the keyword list are assumed to be more important).
3. How closely related the keywords are in the peer. (For example, if all the keywords are found in the same DHT entry, they must all be keywords for the same cluster or topic).

Peer query ranking. Locally, each computer uses a desktop search application to locate the relevant web sites from their browser history. Unfortunately, desktop search systems still have poor relevancy ranking algorithms. We attempt to improve the ranking by considering the time the user spent on the page (if they spent very little time, the page is likely bad) and the number of times the user visits the page. When aggregating these results, CHORA takes two things into account: the number of peers that recommend a particular site and the rank that each recommending peer gives the site (relative to their other recommendations).

The results are updated on the fly, so when CHORA receives more complete responses that reorder or add additional results, these updates are immediately conveyed to the user. Ideally these results would be used to rerank typical web search engine results. In our current implementation we place the CHORA results beside the web search engine results.

4 Evaluation

Keyword Coverage. Consider k users, each with a set D_i documents. Suppose we have a query q. Clearly if we issued q against a full-text index which indexed every word for each document $d \in D_1 \cup D_2 \cup \ldots \cup D_k$ then we would be absolutely sure that the results $R_f(q)$ (f for full) cover every possible document. In our setting, the DHT acts as a *partial-text-index*. If $R_p(q)$ (p for partial) is the results for querying q against our partial text index, then we are interested in maximizing the coverage ratio, $C(q) = |R_p(q)|/|R_f(q)|$. Coverage ratio is a relaxed definition of recall: it says that the set of relevant documents *is* $R_f(q)$. In this relaxed setting, precision is trivially 1.

One way of growing $R_p(q)$ is to just store more keywords for each document. In the limit, we approach a full-text index. However, we tradeoff increasing keywords with the increased storage and communication overhead.

One observation is that as long as we use a partial-text index, one will always be able to construct a query q that makes $C(q)$ small [2]. However, in reality, it is only important that $C(q)$ be large for *reasonable* queries. For a given topic, like "Peer to Peer Networks," we would expect a reasonable query to be something like "Gnutella Ultrapeers," whereas there are a huge number of unreasonable

---

[2] Note that this analysis does not apply if we assume that users will change their querying behavior to first specify a topic (e.g. "Charles Dickens") that is used to get a list of machines, and then specify a query.

queries. Our ultimate goal is to cover a high percentage of the reasonable queries for all topics with a small number of keywords for each cluster in the sketch.

To test our system, we hand-generated 10 topics. You can see one such topic in Table 1. The table contains a set of training and test queries for the popular topic, "Harry Potter." Each topic has 15 training queries that describe the topic, and at least 5 test queries.

When users index the Google results for training queries like "Harry Potter" and "Professor Snape," we expect that one or more of their partial text indices would be able to answer test queries like "Ron Weasley."

Given this, we now create a set of fictional users. Each user u chooses a topic from their topic distribution T_u, and then from within that topic they choose k queries from the training set. They then take m of the results for each query from Google as their own pages. At this point, each user has km webpages.

We then build a full-text-index over all the documents, as well as the CHORA keyword-list sketches. For each topic set, we run the test queries against each index and compute the coverage for each query.

The coverage percentages in Table 1 indicate that for the training queries, the coverage is perfect, which is not surprising. The test query coverages are indicative of a trend across all the topics: we found that queries either had full coverage ($R_p = R_f$), or no coverage at all ($R_p = 0$). The keyword generation mechanism, while good in some instances, nevertheless fails for many queries we consider to be reasonable extensions of the training sets.[3]

Table 1. Training and Test Queries for the topic Harry Potter, along with their coverage

Harry Potter	
Training Queries	**Percent Coverage**
Harry Potter	100 %
Harry Potter and the Sorcerer's Stone	100 %
Professor Snape	100 %
Professor McGonagall	100 %
Albus Dumbledore	100 %
. . .	
Test Queries	**Percent Coverage**
Hogwarts School of Magic	100 %
Phoenix hair wand	100 %
Ron Weasley	0 %
Daniel Radcliffe	0 %

To understand the coverage across topics, Figure 3 was generated by taking the average coverage over each topic and then placing each average in the indicated bins. While it's encouraging that on all topics most test queries are hit, there clearly remains room for improvement.

---

[3] Again note that if the query here were topic = "Harry Potter", subquery = "Ron Weasley" we would do much better.

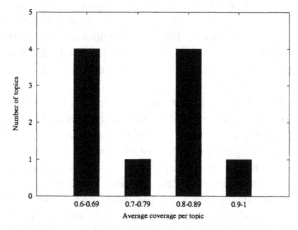

Fig. 3. Average Topic Coverage for Test Queries (each user has at most 1000 keywords per topic)

Because we ran this experiment on hand-picked data and did not actually browse the web pages, it does not make sense to talk about a relevant set of documents that is a subset of $R_f(q)$. We first hope to improve the coverage ratio and then run our algorithms on real user data where users can describe a relevant set of documents for the query, and hence we can generate true precision and recall numbers.

5   Related Work

While several P2P Web search engines have been created to search the entire web, [1,2,3] and to a lesser extent [4], CHORA is more closely related to [2,15].

Similar to CHORA, [2] proposes a two-phase paradigm. However, these two phases are significantly different to CHORA's. The first phase looks for peers by searching for both query terms and the user's bookmarks in a full inverted index. It then uses the KL divergence over the distribution of words to prune the list of candidates. At query time, the query is sent point-to-point to all peers discovered during step 1. In contrast, CHORA exploits the user's full web viewing history and habits to generate (and prune) the keywords which summarize the data on the computer, and distributes the query through an optimized query tree. In addition, CHORA uses the peers' web viewing history to recommend documents.

Other approaches have been proposed for finding peers with related content in P2P systems. In [16], the authors of the Minerva system analyze multiple algorithms that can be used to compare a query to a peer's local database. Unlike CHORA, the Minerva analysis does not divide the database of documents into clusters or click graphs, but instead looks at global statistics of terms when choosing the best peer to query. However, like CHORA, Minerva generates lists of the best peers to query by storing term-to-peer mappings in a DHT [17]. In [18], the system routes queries to peers using an implicit, distributed index, rather than an explicit index as in CHORA. For each neighbor, a node stores a summary of the content available at that neighbor and all nodes within a small number of hops of that neighbor. A query is routed to the neighbor with the most related summary.

Coopeer is similar to CHORA in the sense that it does not necessarily attempt to replicate and improve the centralized web search, but, initially, at least, to complement it. It can be seen as a web-search generalization of Gnutella. While it uses local flooding for queries, it attempts to learn a good network on which to do this flooding. It is also similar to CHORA in two significant ways. 1) Limited information, besides query results, are removed from a users' computer. 2) It attempts to use information from the users' web favorites to answer the query. However, CHORA differs from Coopeer significantly in that CHORA uses a two-step query while Coopeer floods the network. Also, while Coopeer only use favorites, CHORA makes full use of the web browsing history, and attempts to organize it according to topics.

As previously mentioned, CHORA uses some techniques developed in the Gnutella setting, such as the concept of ultrapeers [19,20] when building the query tree (see Section 2 for details). Another similarity is that CHORA's two-phase query processing can be seen as a dynamic version of semantic overlays [21], which limit the flood plain of queries in Gnutella. Each semantic overlay clusters users around a particular topic and when a file is looked for, only the relevant semantic overlays are flooded.

6   Conclusions

We have presented CHORA, a P2P Web Search engine that complements, not replaces, traditional web search engines. The execution of a query in CHORA involves a two-step paradigm, where first a set of peers is selected to query based on summary sketches, and then the query is executed on these peers in an ad-hoc query dissemination tree. The sketches are created using a sketch generation algorithm which employs the novel use of a click graph.

CHORA could be further improved by integrating techniques from the IR community into the sketch generation algorithm. Also, it could be augmented by using learning techniques. For example, CHORA could be customized to each peer by weighting the advice of peers that it has, in the past, found helpful. Another example is that keywords which are commonly searched for could be pinned into the list of keywords for a user and unused keywords could be replaced by other relevant words. We hope to explore these areas in future work.

Acknowledgements. We would like to thank Joseph Hellerstein and Timothy Roscoe for their helpful conversations and support.

References

1. Festa, P.: Search project prepares to challenge google. C-net News (2001)
2. Bender, M., Michel, S., Weikum, G., Zimmer, C.: Bookmark-driven query routing in peer-to-peer web search. In: Workshop on Peer-to-Peer Information Retrieval (2004)
3. Christen, M.: (Yacy - distributed p2p-based web indexing), http://www.yacy.net/yacy/
4. Suel, T., Mathur, C., Wu, J.W., Zhang, J., Delis, A., Kharrazi, M., Long, X., Shanmugasundaram, K.: Odissea: A peer-to-peer architecture for scalable web search and information retrieval (2003)
5. Stoica, I., Morris, R., Karger, D., Kaashoek, F., Balakrishnan, H.: Chord: A scalable Peer-To-Peer lookup service for internet applications. In: Proceedings of the 2001 ACM SIGCOMM Conference, pp. 149–160 (2001)
6. Ratnasamy, S., Francis, P., Handley, M., Karp, R., Shenker, S.: A scalable content addressable network. Technical Report TR-00-010, Berkeley, CA (2000)
7. Ratnasamy, S., Francis, P., Handley, M., Karp, R., Shenker, S.: CLIP2: Gnutella Protocol Specification v 0.4 (2001)
8. Loo, B.T., Huebsch, R., Stoica, I., Hellerstein, J.M.: The case for a hybrid p2p search infrastructure. Technical report, Intel Research (2003)
9. Loo, B.T., Huebsch, R., Stoica, I., Hellerstein, J.M.: (Gnutella proposals for dynamic querying.), http://www9.limewire.com/developer/dynamic_query.html
10. Loo, B.T., Huebsch, R., Stoica, I., Hellerstein, J.M.: (Google desktop), http://desktop.google.com
11. Rhea, S., Godfrey, B., Karp, B., Kubiatowicz, J., Ratnasamy, S., Shenker, S., Stoica, I., Yu, H.: Opendht: A public dht service and its uses. In: Proceedings of ACM SIGCOMM 2005 (2005)
12. Huebsch, R., Hellerstein, J.M., Boon, N.L., Loo, T., Shenker, S., Stoica, I.: Querying the internet with pier. In: Proceedings of 29th International Conference on Very Large Databases (VLDB) (2003)
13. Dabek, F., Cox, R., Kaashoek, F., Morris, R.: Vivaldi: A decentralized network coordinate system (2004)
14. Li, J., Loo, B.T., Hellerstein, J.M., Kaashoek, M.F., Karger, D.R., Morris, R.: On the feasibility of peer-to-peer web indexing and search. In: 2nd International Workshop on Peer-to-Peer Systems (2003)
15. Zhou, J., Li, K., Tang, L.: Toward a fully distributed p2p web search engine. In: Proceedings of the 10th IEEE International Workshop on Future Trends of Distributed Computing Systems
16. Chernov, S., Serdyukov, P., Bender, M., Michel, S., Weikum, G., Zimmer, C.: Database selection and result merging in p2p web search. In: Third International Workshop on Databases, Information Systems and Peer-to-Peer Computing (2005)
17. Bender, M., Michel, S., Triantafillou, P., Weikum, G., Zimmer, C.: Minerva: Collaborative p2p search (demo). In: Proceedings of the 31st International Conference on Very Large Databases (VLDB) (2005)
18. Petrakis, Y., Koloniari, G., Pitoura, E.: On using histograms as routing indexes in peer-to-peer systems. In: Ng, W.S., Ooi, B.-C., Ouksel, A.M., Sartori, C. (eds.) DBISP2P 2004. LNCS, vol. 3367, pp. 16–30. Springer, Heidelberg (2005)
19. Petrakis, Y., Koloniari, G., Pitoura, E.: (Gnutella ultrapeers), http://rfc-gnutella.sourceforge.net/Proposals/Ultrapeer/Ultrapeers.htm
20. Petrakis, Y., Koloniari, G., Pitoura, E.: (Gnutella), http://gnutella.wego.com
21. Crespo, A., Carcia-Molina, H.: Semantic overlay networks for p2p systems. Technical report (2002)

K-link: A Peer-to-Peer Solution for Organizational Knowledge Management

Giuseppe Pirro'[1], Domenico Talia[1,3], and Massimo Ruffolo[2,3]

[1] Department of Electronics, Computer Science and Systems, University of Calabria
Via Pietro Bucci, Cubo 41C, I-87036 Rende (CS), Italy
{gpirro,talia}@deis.unical.it
[2] ICAR-CNR, Via Pietro Bucci, Cubo 41C, I-87036 Rende, Italy
ruffolo@icar.cnr.it
[3] EXEURA s.rl, Rende (CS), Italy

Abstract. In the latest years knowledge management received more and more attention as a source of competitive advantage for enterprises and organizations, therefore becomes important to understand how computer science solutions should be designed to efficiently manage knowledge. Most of the current knowledge management systems use technological architectures that are in contradiction with the social processes concerning the creation of new knowledge, slowing down organizational innovation. Actually, most of those systems use centralized architectures filtering knowledge from any form of personal and contextual interpretation. Recently a new paradigm supporting cooperative and dynamic aspects of knowledge management (KM) has been proposed: Distributed Knowledge Management (DKM). In particular, peer to peer (P2P) architectures seem to naturally fulfil the requirements of this new model. Nevertheless, current P2P architectures suffer from heavy limitations due to the lack of semantic supports for handling knowledge. To overcome these limitations, the scientific community is appraising the possibility of using ontologies as a semantic support in KM processes. This paper presents an ontology based P2P system for DKM named *K-link*. The system design and its implementation are described. Moreover an ad hoc ontology framework for supporting organizational KM is also presented.

1 Introduction

In the nineties a new organizational paradigm has been proposed [1]. This paradigm points out knowledge as a key resource for organizations and aims at establishing paths to be followed for better exploiting organizational knowledge. Earlier organizational models [2] saw the organization like a box with the aim to maximize the output given an input or like something that can be scientifically and rigorously managed. With Simon's theories about the bounded rationality [3]the theme of the KM becomes more important and the role of the organization in the KM processes notably changes. The organization becomes a way to connect the knowledge of many subjects into a more complete understanding of the

S. Joseph et al. (Eds.): AP2PC 2006, LNAI 4461, pp. 86–97, 2008.
© Springer-Verlag Berlin Heidelberg 2008

reality. The technologies' role also changes: they become a way to increase people's rationality by allowing memory and computational increase and knowledge exchange. Along the years several other theories about knowledge have been proposed. A generally accepted classification proposed by Polanyi [4,5] and extended by Nonaka [6] identifies from one side: "tacit knowledge" as the knowledge resulting from personal learning within an organization. Form the other side, the "explicit knowledge" is a generally shared and publicly accessible form of knowledge. This kind of knowledge is typically stored. Explicit knowledge can also be classified on the basis of the following forms: "structured" (available in database), "semi-structured" (generally available in Web sites: HTML pages, XML documents, etc.) and "unstructured" (available as textual documents: project documents, procedures, white papers, templates, etc.). More recently, new importance has been given to social processes and to the communities of practice as sources of knowledge. Through communities of practice the individual could learn from the community, but also the same community can innovate and create new knowledge. "Community is the social dimension of the practice", which is the ideal context for creating knowledge, a virtual space where the individuals learn, putting personal experiences and social competences in relation and having the possibility of acting on the same social competences through sharing [7]. According to this vision, organizations must become a community of communities, offering spaces for the creation of autonomous communities, that are connected one another . The different types of KM solutions are related to the image of the corresponding social interactions in KM processes. According to this consideration, technological systems for KM can be classified and inserted in a scheme according to the adopted social model. Therefore, on one hand we have centralized systems that are practically identified with the Enterprise Knowledge Portal (EKP) and, on the other hand, we have distributed KM systems. In this paper we describe *K-link*, a JXTA based P2P system coherent with the vision of distributed knowledge management (DKM). K-link provide users with an environment allowing a work activities management in a semantic way. For example projects users are involved in, are in K-link represented by workspaces. A workspace is a community of peers endowed with a set of tools (such a Calendar, File Sharing, etc.) enabling distributed and real-time interactions. For example the File Sharing tool allows users to search documents inside a workspace on a semantic basis (selecting an ontology concept and forwarding the query to the network, all the documents classified by the workspace members under that concept will be given back). Indeed, P2P systems seem particularly suitable to implement the two core principles of DKM, namely the principle of autonomy - communities of knowledge should be granted the highest possible degree of semantic autonomy to manage their local knowledge - and the principle of coordination - the collaboration between autonomous entities must be achieved through a process of semantic coordination, rather than through a process of semantic homogenization-. In K-link, each knowledge entity (or Knowledge Link Node - KLN) is represented by a peer, and the two principles mentioned above are implemented in a direct way:

- each KLN (peer) is endowed with a set of services for creating and organizing its own local knowledge (autonomy), and
- ii) defining cooperating structures (peer groups) and an ad hoc ontology framework in order to achieve semantic interoperability (e.g., classifying and searching documents on a semantic basis).

The paper is organized as follows. Section 2 presents the K-link architecture and its implementation in JXTA explaining how it provides a useful support to DKM. Section 3 presents the ontology framework supporting the system, developed by a Disjunctive Programming Language (DLP+). Section 4 presents the implemented system. Finally,sections 5 and 6 outline some related works in the DKM field, draw some conclusions and sketch future work.

2   K-link Architecture

K-link is a P2P system which allows a collection of subjects (individuals, groups, or whole organizations) to manage and search for knowledge on a semantic basis through the ontology support. Because of its decentralized model, K-link doesn't impose a single model to classify knowledge. Furthermore, through K-link it is possible to integrate knowledge stored in pre-existing systems (such as servers, knowledge bases, etc.) if based on our ontology framework. In the next sections we describe the K-link high-layer and low-layer architecture. For both layers we analyze the main components and the services that allow the system to support users and communities in managing distributed organizational knowledge. The following figure shows the system architecture.

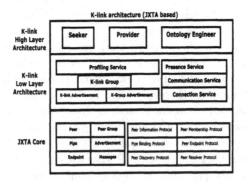

Fig. 1. K-link low level architecture

2.1   K-link Low-Level Architecture

The K-link low-layer architecture contains services built by the JXTA framework. JXTA (http://www.jxta.org) is a set of protocols, through which P2P ad-hoc networks can be carried out. JXTA also allows the autonomous peer group creation. By the peer group abstraction, the communities of practice can be formed. In a specific group it will be possible to create a set of services only for the members of the group. Moreover, this framework allows various device set (server, PC, PDA, etc.) to communicate within a peer group independently from the transport protocol. The common format for exchanging information inside JXTA is the advertisement. An Advertisement is an XML document containing information about each network resource (peer, peer group, services, etc.). A certain resource (to be used), must be first "announced" to the network. In JXTA there is a wide number of protocols; each of them devoted to an activity. For example, the Pipe Binding Protocol handles the creation of pipes, namely communications channels. Furthermore, the Peer Rendezvous Protocol handles the message exchanging within the network of JXTA rendezvous peers . A Rendezvous peer, or "super peer", represents a generic peer provided with message routing capabilities. From this point of view, JXTA allows to overcome the limits of pure P2P architectures.

2.2   K-link Services

K-link services created on the top of the JXTA architecture, allow KLN to implement all the requirements of DKM as discussed before. In the following we give a brief description of each service.

- **Profiling Service:** This service is close in meaning with the profile concept. A profile represents a semantic description of each KLN within a K-link group. Each profile contains useful information about the KLN (name, email address, skills, etc.). Moreover, the Profiling Service guarantees the profile consistency with respect to any change. If any change is detected the profile will be republished within the group.
- **Connection Service:** The Connection Service is responsible for all the operations concerning the JXTA network setting up. This service creates the super group K-link within the JXTA NetPeerGroup. This service also deals with the creation of the other subgroup of the super group. All the services (Discovery Service, Rendezvous Service etc.) will be inherited from this group. Moreover, this service provides all the operations for joining the K-link groups.
- **Communication Service:** The Communication Service deals with the information exchanging operations through the Jnutella protocol. Jnutella is a JXTA-based implementation of Gnutella. It is composed by a set of descriptors designed using the JXTA messages. Moreover, Jnutella adds two new kinds of descriptors (i.e. profile request and profile reply) for exchanging profile information. Jnutella messages are not forwarded to all KLNs, but only to a subset of those (contained in a buddylist) the KLN has chosen to deal with. In this way, the network traffic is reduced and messages will not propagate blindly.

– **Presence service:** The Presence Service provides a mechanism for exchanging presence information. Through this service, each KLN lookups the current status of the other KLNs (contained in its buddylist). In fact, this service on a regular basis manages message exchanging in a ping/pong style.

2.3   K-link High-Level Architecture

This layer implements the following K-link roles: *seeker*, *provider* and *ontology engineer*. The architecture of each KLN is shown in figure 2.

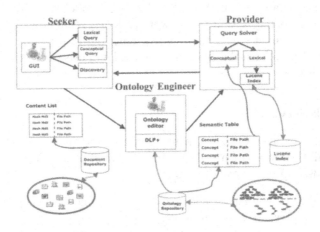

Fig. 2. K-link high level architecture

2.4   K-link Node

A K-link node (KLN) represents a knowledge entity that able to produce, store and exchange knowledge. In general, a KLN could be a PC, a server, or also a community of entities that exchange information in a P2P way. A KLN will be able to play the role of Seeker when it searches for knowledge, or the role of Provider when it publishes its own knowledge. Furthermore, a third role (ontology engineer) leads the processes of ontology personalization. In K-link system ontologies are represented by DLP+ [9]. In the following we illustrate the main components of this layer.

2.5   K-link Main Components

– **Document Repository:** A Document Repository is the place where each KLN stores its own knowledge. Thus, this repository can be viewed as a private space in which each KLN holds its own documents and data according to a local scheme (e.g., a file system, a database, etc.). This repository contains knowledge that through other system components will be annotated, indexed, and shared. It is important to guarantee the consistency of that repository since it will assure the "quality" of the answers to the others KLNs.

- **Ontology Repository:** This repository contains the DLP+ implementation of the ontology framework described in section 3. The DLP+ ontology language is an extension of the Disjunctive Logic Programming (DLP) that extends Datalog allowing disjunction in the rules' head. The presence of disjunction in the heads of the rules makes DLP inherently non-monotonic. The ontology repository contains also the contexts (i.e. personal concepts networks) created from the Upper Ontology. A context represents a vision about a piece of knowledge. From this point of view, the application gives autonomy to a user to specialize its context as her/him prefers. The only tie is that the basic concept (the root of the hierarchy) must be a core ontology concept. Documents stored in the document repository will be semantically annotated to the context concepts, allowing to assign a semantic meaning to their contents.

- **Lucene Index:** This repository contains the Lucene index allowing to search for information inside user documents. This index is permanently stored on the disk. Nevertheless, Lucene (http://lucene.apache.org) doesn't provide any mechanism for checking index consistency. In fact, in case of a document removal or changing the index should be updated manually. In the K-link system the index consistency is assured through a cyclical control checking of the contained documents.

- **Content List:** This list contains pairs *(Hash Md5, File Path)* used for managing the Lucene index consistency. Through the cyclical control of such list, the system can know which files currently owns. The file paths are obtained from the document repository, while md5 hashes are obtained trough the JXTA API. From the modifications of the Md5 value, file changes will be noticed and the system can proceed to the new indexization or deletion inside the index.

- **Semantic Table:** This table stores permanently the file-to-concepts associations on disk as pairs *(Concept Id, File Path)*. In the current K-link implementation it is possible to associate one file to more than one concept by creating different views for it. The role played by the semantic table is essential for conceptual querying. In fact, by specifying the name of a concept and issuing a remote query, all the contents classified from other KLNs under that concept will be returned.

2.6   K-link Main Roles

Each KLN can play three roles: seeker, provider and ontology engineer. Here we describe them in detail.

1. **Seeker.** A KLN plays the seeker role when it searches for knowledge inside a group. Moreover, the Seeker role includes the mechanisms allowing the discover of both KLNs and K-link groups. A KLN can issue two kinds of query (conceptual and keyword based) forwarding requests to its "buddylist" that contains the others KLNs chosen to deal with. For each query, a

handling process will be activated. with the aim to gather the responses and to send back them. The seeker component of the receiver can group these results on query type and KLN sender basis. When the results are shown, a KLN can activate a download request handled by the JXTA CMS service (http://cms.jxta.org).

2. **Provider.** In the Provider role, a KLN should deal with queries coming from other KLNs. Also in this case, for each query (identified a timestamp) a handling process will be activated. This process queries the local indexes for the requested information. If any result is found, the KLN sends back replies to the remote peers. The handling process will be different depending on the query type.

   - Keyword query: for this type of query, the KLN looks at its local Lucene index, obtaining the documents containing the requested keyword. The results composed by pairs (file path, content id), will be sent back to the requester and then locally handled through its query handler process. The content id allows the requester peer to identify the last file version.
   - Conceptual query: When a conceptual query is issued, a KLN in the provider role will check its own semantic table giving back all the documents associated to the concept expressed in the query. Also in this case it is important to send back the content id in order to obtain the last file version.

3. **Ontology engineer.** In the Ontology Engineer role, a KLN peer can deal with the context creation operations. A context represents a proper view on a part of the domain of interest. In fact, each KLN can specialize this part of knowledge on a personal basis rising from real use cases. Moreover, this role deals with all the core ontology modification operations. In this version of K-link, those operations are carried out manually, but in a future release they will be handled through a distributed mechanism.

3   The K-link Ontology Scenario

Recently KM tools using ontologies as semantic support for describing contents have been designed. Mainly two classes of tools can be identified:

- Tools that through standardized ontologies aim at working out all the comprehension problems deriving from their use in dynamic environments.
- Tools that don't accept any layer of standardization, and allow users to define ontologies (in this case would be more appropriate to speak of contexts) according to the needs and the abilities of everyone. In this case, all the processes of meaning negotiation are totally trusted to automatic mechanisms with no (or almost) involvement from the users.

In an organizational environment both those classes of tools cannot be properly used. An intermediate solution provided with a time-changing basic ontology could represent an effective trade-off between the demand of common models and the demand of individuals (people or organizations) of defining local concepts in their models. Our approach, through the basic ontology and the user's feedbacks tries to build a shared conceptualization. Moreover, K-link goes beyond the classification of information, taking into account all the resources and the cognitive legacy of an organization (business processes, human resources, etc.) through their accurate definition. Through an intensive use of Ontologies, the work of organizing, understanding and looking for information will result more accurate, simple and efficient. The proposed ontology-based framework [8] is organized as in two layer as shown in figure 3. The first ontology layer contains the Upper Ontology (UO) that contains concepts characterizing the organizational background knowledge. These concepts are used for annotating Core Organizational Knowledge Entities (COKE) contained in the second ontology layer. Our framework gives an abstract representation of COKE allowing handling of semantic knowledge objects (e.g. semantic search and retrieval, semantic process management, etc.). In particular, the framework provides a uniform abstract representation of static (concepts) and dynamic (processes) organizational knowledge handled by users. All peers are initially provided with this framework in which the upper ontology contains basic organizational knowledge. Each peer can extend the upper ontology with own relevant concepts. In the following the framework structure is explained more in detail.

3.1   The Upper Ontology

The UO defines concepts characterizing the typical organizational knowledge background. It specifies explicitly organizational topic (i.e. declarative knowledge concerning the concepts characterizing an application domain). For example an IT enterprise background is founded on concepts coming from computer science such as databases, programming languages, architectures, etc. The UO provides COKE ontologies with concepts to formally annotate their contents.

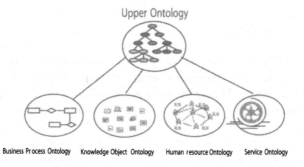

Fig. 3. K-link ontology framework

3.2   The COKE Ontologies

COKE Ontologies contain the formal representation of human resources and their organization in groups, processes and their activities, knowledge objects constituting elements produced or used in business processes, services in term of instruments used during business process execution. The **Human Resource Ontology** defines individuals working in the organization (knowledge workers) and social groups they are involved in. For each individual, a profile in term of skills, topics of interest, organizational role, group membership is defined. For each group (community of practice, project team, organizational group, etc.), a group profile in term of topics of interest, required services is defined. The **Business Processes Ontology** contains procedural knowledge related to the managerial and operational processes. The business process ontology exploits an interesting capability of DLP+ language allowing the expression of taxonomic and non-taxonomic relations between classes enabling the representation of process meta-model, process schemas and process instances. Therefore, each process is described in terms of a three layer structure. The meta-model layer allows the definition of process elements (i.e. activities, sub-processes, transition states and conditions, involved actors, treated topics). The schema layer allows the definition of a single process in term of process elements. The instance layer allows the definition and acquisition of process instances. The **Knowledge Objects** Ontology maps the structure of logical objects (e. g. textual documents, web pages, process activities, blog and chat sessions, e-mail, etc.). These are used in the business processes and handled by the human resources through services. Semantic knowledge objects management and handling (e.g. search and retrieval) is facilitated by the annotation on the UO concepts. The **Services Ontology** identifies the tools by which knowledge objects are created, acquired, stored and retrieved. The execution of a query on the UO can be executed using a specific tool able to retrieve all the elements related with a specific concept. Element can be filtered to obtain a specific COKE related to the query. For example, a query result can contain info about people knowing a given concept or knowledge objects related to some concepts.

4   K-link in a Nutshell

Figure 4 shows the main GUI from which a user can create new workspaces, open existing workspaces, deleting existing workspaces, and also deal with all the Personal Knowledge Management tasks (local document indexing, semantic and full text search, etc.). Furthermore is also possible to invite contacts to the created workspaces.

The Figure 4 shows also the contacts view trough which is possible to search and add new contact to our contact list. Moreover from the contact view is also possible to start a one to one chat session.

Figure 5 shows the K-link *Personal Knowledge Management* environment.

From the *Personal Knowledge Management* GUI is possible to query local knowledge. Currently there are two kinds of queries, the first (keyword based)

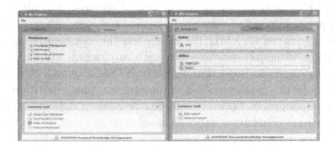

Fig. 4. K-link main GUI

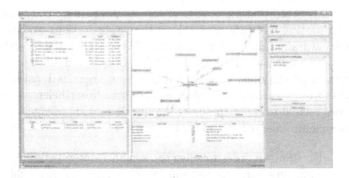

Fig. 5. K-link Personal Knowledge Management GUI

uses the Lucene index and show the results in a *JTable* as can be viewed in the left side of the figure. From this table is possible to open directly the content. Is also possible to associate file to concepts by dragging the file on the left hand side to the ontology representation in the center. The figure shows also the the semantic table represented also in this case by a *JTable*. From this table is possible to erase semantic associations and to check the semantic table consistency with respect to the ontology (e.g in the case of a concept deletion).

5   Related Works

To the best of our knowledge, recently only two P2P KM systems have been proposed: SWAP and KEEx. SWAP (Semantic Web and Peer to Peer) is a research project started in 2002, aiming at combining ontologies and P2P for KM purposes. SWAP allows local KM by a component called LR (Local node repository), which gathers knowledge from several source and represents it in RDF-Schema. Moreover, SWAP allows to search for knowledge using a language called SeRQL an evolution of RQL [10]. KEEx [7] is a P2P architecture that aims to combine both semantic and P2P technologies. This system implemented in JXTA allows a set of K-nodes to exchange information on a semantic basis.

Semantic in KEEx is achieved by the notion of context. A context in KEEx, represents a personal point of view about reality and is represented using a proprietary language called CTXML [12]. KEEx lets the user completely free about context creation without providing him with any organizational background. For the reasons discussed in section 3 we argue that although this approach is innovative, due to the presence of an automatic mapping algorithm which aim is to find correspondences between concepts present in different contexts, this complete autonomy could turn into isolation.

6   Conclusions and Research Issues

In this paper we argued that technological and social architectures must be consistent for supporting KM processes. Along the paper sections we discussed as P2P systems naturally fulfill this requirement. We designed a P2P architecture called K-link and implemented it by using JXTA, Lucene and other technologies. K-link addresses all the main needs emerging in an organizational distributed KM scenario through an ad-hoc ontology framework. Nevertheless, a number of research issues related to the mapping of the distributed knowledge into technological requirements emerged. Two of them are:

- Mapping algorithm: In order to solve the semantic interoperability problem we are designing an algorithm that aims at discovering the potential semantic relations among concepts in different contexts in a semi-automatic way. This algorithm uses all the expressiveness of the DLP+ and *Wordnet* as source of knowledge about the word.
- Automatic classifier: Based on the rules definition related to the concepts of Upper Ontology we are developing a semiautomatic classification system supported by the Hylex [11] system.

References

1. Nonaka, I., Takeuchi, H.: The Knowledge-Creating Company. How Japanese Companies Create the Dynamics of Innovation. Oxford University Press, New York, USA (1995)
2. Taylor, F.W.: The Principles of Scientific Management. Harper and Row, New York, USA (1911)
3. Simon, H.A.: Theories of bounded rationality. In: McGuire, C.B., Radner, R. (eds.) Decision and organization: A volume in honor of Jacob Marschak (Ch. 8), Amsterdam, Olanda (1972)
4. Polanyi, M.: The tacit dimension. Routledge and Kegan Paul, London, England (1966)
5. Polanyi, M.: Tacit Knowledge. Ch.7 In: Prusak, L. (ed.) in Knowledge in Organizations, Butterworth-Heinemann, Boston, USA (1997)
6. Nonaka, I.: A Dynamic Theory of Organizational Knowledge Creation. In: Organization Science, vol. 5 (1994)

7. Bonifacio, M., Nori, M., Bouquet, P., Busetta, P., Danieli, A., Don, A., Mameli, G.: KEEx: A Peer-to-Peer Tool for Distributed Knowledge Management. In: Proc. P2PKM 2004, Boston, MA (2004)
8. Ruffolo, M., Gualtieri, A.: An Ontology-Based Framework for Representing Organizational Knowledge. In: Proc. I-Know - International Conference on Knowledge Management, Graz, Austria (June 2005)
9. Eiter, T., Leone, N., Mateis, C., Pfeifer, G., Scarcello, F.: A Deductive System for Non-Monotonic Reasoning. In: Fuhrbach, U., Dix, J., Nerode, A. (eds.) LPNMR 1997. LNCS, vol. 1265, pp. 364–375. Springer, Heidelberg (1997)
10. SWAP:Ontology-based Knowledge Management with Peer-to-Peer Technology Marc Ehrig Christoph Tempich, Jeen Broekstra Frank van Harmelen, Marta Sabou, Ronny Siebes, Steffen Staab, Heiner Stuckenschmidt
11. Ruffolo, M., Leone, N., Manna, M., Sacc, D., Zavatto, A.: Esploiting ASP for Semantic Information Extraction. In: The ASP 2005 workshop - Answer Set Programming: Advances in Theory and Implementation, University of Bath, Bath, UK, July 27th–29th (2005)
12. Bouquet, P., Serafini, L., Zanobini, S.: Semantic coordination: A new approach and an application. In: Fensel, D., Sycara, K.P., Mylopoulos, J. (eds.) ISWC 2003. LNCS, vol. 2870, pp. 130–145. Springer, Heidelberg (2003)

An Analysis of Interest-Community Facilitated Peer-to-Peer Search

Elth Ogston

Vrije Universiteit Amsterdam
De Boelelaan 1081A, 1081 HV, Amsterdam, The Netherlands

Abstract. We study the effect of semantic overlay structure on the performance of decentralized search. Semantic overlays create communities of nodes that share particular interests. In peer-to-peer systems these communities can be designed to improve the recall of search algorithms. Such communities also play a role in balancing load between agents. An examination of these two performance metrics on some basic semantic overlay topologies shows that the choice of the best decentralized search algorithm can be influenced by differing design goals. We present an extensive experimental evaluation using data sets from eDonkey and Movielens. We find that, in general, these data sets do not exhibit obvious semantic clusters of nodes. For this reason, using a best-neighbors overlay, in which nodes individually choose their neighbors, to implement search produces better recall values than using an overlay that specifically clusters nodes into groups. Using best-neighbors overlays, on the other hand, can lead to highly unbalanced load distributions, a problem avoided in clustered overlays. We also find that forwarding search queries to "friends" in best-neighbors overlays does little to improve recall while further unbalancing load distributions.

1 Introduction

At first glance, peer-to-peer systems and decentralized multi-agent systems appear to be the same subject with different names. "Peers" in the former case may be renamed "autonomous agents" in the latter, but the underlying issues associated with decentralization are similar in each type of system. For instance, the problem of optimizing search, whether for files or for joint-task partners, is about how to organize information. However, although the basic problems encountered in decentralized systems may often be identical, the differing objectives of the two system types can have a large influence on appropriate design choices.

We use the example of improving decentralized search by creating interest communities among nodes to explore the concept of how system design can depend on system objectives. Search efficiency in unstructured peer-to-peer systems is often improved by making use of a semantic overlay, a virtual network in which a node's location is based on its semantic similarity to other nodes. This idea, of creating virtual organizations of similar nodes to limit the scope of tasks that might otherwise need to be carried out over the entire set of nodes, is common to both peer-to-peer and multi-agent systems. The type of semantic overlay preferred in each system, however, differs. Multi-agent systems research is concerned with decentralizing coordination among complex autonomous agents. Multi-agent systems thus often favor creating well-defined groups, or

S. Joseph et al. (Eds.): AP2PC 2006, LNAI 4461, pp. 98–110, 2008.

clusters, of nodes, allowing for a high degree of cooperation among agents in a group. Peer-to-peer systems research, on the other hand, is focused on designing simple decentralized algorithms among peers with minimal abilities. Peer-to-peer systems therefore tend to favor looser, more easily created organizations in which each node maintains a number of neighbors, and neighbors usually have other neighbors in common, but no specific group boundaries are defined.

Both of these approaches, creating interest neighborhoods and specific interest clusters are valid methods of organizing a decentralized search network. Which is better for a particular application is, however, not well understood. One reason for this is that search performance in such networks depends on how suited the overlay structure is to the actual semantic structure of the data being searched. To investigate further the exact difference between the two approaches, we compare the theoretical performance of several basic search methods on typical file-sharing data sets taken from the eDonkey [1] and Movielens [2] systems.

Three common forms of semantic overlay search are compared: (1) direct-neighbor search in a best-neighbors overlay with large neighbor caches, (2) friends-of-friends limited-radius flooding search in a best-neighbors overlay with small neighbor caches, and (3) group-based search in a clustered overlay. The basic case where there is no known item classification that can be used to guide the semantic overlay structure is used to test the three overlay search approaches. We consider two measures: an estimate of the hit rate that nodes would achieve for searches in their overlay neighborhood, and an estimate of the query load that would be seen by each node in comparison to the number of queries it makes itself.

For the data sets studied, we find that, although clusters that perform better than random groupings can be devised, obvious semantic clusters of nodes do not exist. Therefore, search methods based on the idea that nodes can be classified do not always improve search recall as much as could be hoped. A simple search of a node's best neighbors (overlay approach 1) produces the best hit rates. However, we also observed that because the distribution of files over the nodes, as well as the distribution of the popularity of files, is highly uneven, best-neighbors networks can result in fairly imbalanced query-load distributions. A small number of nodes may contribute much more to the system than they recieve, and a large percentage of nodes can contribute very little while benefiting from the system. Although this may be acceptable in peer-to-peer file sharing, such imbalances may be less acceptable in multi-agent systems where replying to a query for a service often involves more resources than those required to simply transfer a file. Clustered-overlay based search (overlay approach 3) removes the query-load distribution problem, but only produces hit rates comparable to best-neighbors search (overlay approach 1) when item replication is high. Friends-of-friends search (overlay approach 2) appears to be ill suited for both of the data sets studied because a node's neighbor's neighbors do not tend to contribute much to improving hit rates, while this form of routing further unbalances query loads

2   Related Work

Search in peer-to-peer systems, at a bird's eye level, can be seen as an attempt to find items in a collection of data spread out over a collection of nodes. Since strict peer-to-peer systems exclude the use of central directories, optimizing search involves organizing the placement of data. In the absence of a name space that can be used as the basis for a placement scheme, data content, or "semantics'" can used. Items that are determined to have similar content should thus be grouped together.

One way of using semantics is to directly organize the placement of data items on nodes, either by moving or replicating items [3], or by creating indices to guide query routing [4]. If, however, the nodes themselves can be categorized, for instance due to the behavior or preferences of the users who own them, semantic organizations built between nodes should also reflect an organization of the data.

There are a number of systems that have explored rearranging a peer-to-peer overlay to reflect the semantic similarity of nodes. In general they consider nodes to be similar based on the co-placement of items. Node similarity is measured either directly by examining the contents of nodes, or indirectly by considering which nodes answer each other's queries. Two basic forms of overlay arrangement can be created based on these similarities. First, links can be placed between nodes based on their pairwise similarity [5,6,7,8]. Second, an overlay can be built in which an attempt is made to divide nodes into groups [9,10,11,12,13].

In a best-neighbors overlay each node maintains a list of the other nodes that it believes are most similar to itself. Search queries are first made to these neighbors since they are more likely to be able to provide replies than an average node. Queries are often also forward to neighbor's neighbors on the assumption that these nodes will also exhibit higher than average similarity to the requester. Usually, to maintain search coverage, queries that fail in the best-neighbors overlay are directed to an alternative non-semantic overlay. Sripanidkulchai et al. [6] propose adding "interest-based shortcuts" between nodes. They perform experiments that show that shortcuts based on observing network traffic in a Gnutella-like random network improve the performance of query-forwarding searches. They also observe that with shortcuts queries are often resolved in a single hop. Cholvi et al. [5] study a similar system in which peers maintain links to "acquaintances". They focus on solutions to the load-balancing problem that arises when some peers are more popular acquaintances than others. Yang et al. [8] consider "non-forwarding search", in which peers directly query other peers chosen according to some policy. Their "most results" policy, which they conclude produces the best results, is a measure of the semantic similarity of peers. They also note issues with load-balancing. Voulgaris and Van Steen [7] explore the active creation of semantic relationships between peers. They propose to gossip information among peers to allow for more complex similarity comparisons, rather than basing semantic links on observations of query traffic.

An alternative to nodes maintaining purely independent similar-neighbors caches is to create an overlay that defines groups of similar nodes. Nodes belong to one or more of these groups, and queries are sent to the most appropriate group for their subject. The Associative Overlay design in [9] defines a set of "guide rules", or groups of peers that satisfy some predicate. Predicates based on "possession rules", which ask if a peer contains a particular item, are studied. Nodes classify their queries based on which guide rules have provided answers in the past. In [10] nodes are grouped in "Semantic Overlay Networks" (SONs) corresponding to categories in a predefined classification hierarchy.

This classification hierarchy determines in which SON a query should be made. The notion of grouping similar nodes is also used to optimize super-peer networks [12,11]. Super-peers are nodes with extra capabilities that act as servers to sets of weak peers. Such networks can be designed so that each super-peer groups together a set of similar weaker peers, thus limiting the set of super-peers to which a query must be forwarded. In [12] these groups are determined by a pre-defined topic ontology or set of query characteristics. In [11] weak peers associate themselves with the super-peers that have answered their past queries. The abstract problem of clustering data in a peer-to-peer manner is considered in [13].

The networks structures examined in this study represent the basic methods of re-arranging overlays explored in the above system designs. Best-neighbors overlays represent designs in which only the pairwise semantic relationship between nodes is considered when building the overlay. We consider direct-neighbor, or one hop search, and "friends-of-friends" or multi-hop search on this form of network. A clustered-overlay structure tests the assumption that distinct semantic groups of nodes, which define the best set of nodes in which to perform a search, can be identified. For these network structures we examine the two main issues identified in previous work: the query hit rate obtained in the semantic overlay and load-balancing among peers.

3 Experimental Setup and Methodology

As the literature review above shows, there are several ways of performing search based on semantic overlays, and there are good arguments for using each one. Which is best for a given data set is, however, unclear. The purpose of this work is to do some initial investigation into guidelines for choosing a form of semantic search when building a peer-to-peer system. Because many of the systems proposed so far are still in the development phase, rather than comparing particular implementations we choose to study the underlying properties of several abstract versions of semantic overlay search. To make this comparison, we estimate the theoretically best performance that could be obtained by each on a given data set.

3.1 Overlay Structures and Search Methods

Semantic overlays can be divided into two general forms: those where nodes are positioned based entirely on individual information, and those where some form of local coordination is used to discover node groupings. We shall call the first of these *best-neighbors networks*. In a best-neighbors network nodes are modeled as each having an individual *neighbor cache*, which stores links to a set of nodes, chosen according to some distance function. Nodes each individually fill their caches with the neighbors that are the best for their purposes. In the simplest form, a node's *search neighborhood* consists of the nodes in its neighbor cache. We will call this form of search *direct best-neighbors search*. Alternatively, a node can expand its search space by asking its neighbors to forward a query on to their neighbors, or "friends". We will call this *friends-of-friends search*, parameterized by a radius variable, r, which defines how many times each query will be forwarded.

Best-neighbors networks are simple to build since they require no joint decision making. They do not, however, necessarily result in clearly defined groups of nodes. This is due to a chaining problem; Node A may perceive itself to be similar to Node B, and Node B may think itself similar to Node C, but this does not always mean that Nodes A and C are similar to each other. Thus for group operations, such as search, it is difficult to determine where the boundaries of a group should be placed. In addition, there is the risk that some nodes will be vastly more popular as neighbors than others, creating an unfair query load distribution. These problem becomes especially prevalent for high dimensional data.

A solution to this problem is to build a more complex form of overlay network in which nodes are divided into clusters, based on some local inter-node agreement on where to place group boundaries. We shall call this a *clustered-overlay network*, and consider a node's search neighborhood in this network to be all the members of its cluster. Clustered-overlays balance the search load by limiting how many nodes can have any particular node in their search neighborhood. This form of search will, however, only be effective if a good clustering of the nodes exists, and can be identified.

3.2   Experimental Design

When evaluating decentralized search algorithms the most important factor is that they find the requested data. Considering systems in which evaluating queries can be costly, such as multi-agent systems, along with peer-to-peer systems places a further priority of balancing query loads between peers. In the following experiments we compare abstract search methods by analyzing their expected performance on data measured from actual systems. In order to make this comparison we first need to devise measures that estimate how often queries can be expected to find the data they require and how evenly query load is divided between nodes.

Unfortunately, the data sets that have been collected to date on peer-to-peer search give only a partial view of the data that might be available in a real system (see Section 3.3). For the data sets we study, only the file replicas stored in nodes at a given time are recorded. A set of queries made by those nodes is unavailable. It is fairly reasonable to assume that file replicas are the result of earlier queries. Thus in other work such data sets are divided into a training set of replicas that are actually placed in the nodes and a test set of replicas which are used to represent queries. Given the already sparse nature of the data sets, however, experimental methods that further reduce the file sets, making similarity less apparent and files harder to find, are probably too pessimistic. We instead opt to build our semantic overlays using all of the data, and to measure average search hit rates and loads for all nodes in these overlays. Overlays are built so as to maximize hit rates, thus giving us estimates of the *best possible* performance that a search implementation could achieve on the given data sets.

Best-neighbors overlays are built by placing the nodes with which a node has the most file replicas in common in its neighbor cache. If a node shares the same number of replicas with two other nodes, the one with the smaller file cache is considered to be better. Neighbors are chosen independently of each other, no account is taken of files already available to a node through previously chosen neighbors. Note that neighbor caches are not necessarily filled. For large neighbor cache sizes, nodes can run out of neighbors with which they have any files at all in common. Clustered-overlays are built using a clustering algorithm to divide nodes into groups. Clusterings are based on the same measure of similarity between nodes, the number of replicas they have in common, as used for the best-neighbors overlays. The exact method of determining clusters is discussed in Section 4.3.

For a given overlay structure we define the *average hit rate* for a search method to be the number of replicas a node has in common with any other node in its search neighborhood divided by the number of replicas a node holds in its item cache, averaged over all the nodes. This measure is roughly equivalent to treating a single replica as the test set for search and averaging hit rates over all possible test sets, thus giving the overall fraction of files that can be found in an overlay.

We define the *load ratio* for a node, under a search method, to be the number of replicas a node potentially has to serve divided by the number of useful replicas a node finds in its search neighborhood. Nodes can often find several copies of an item for which they are searching. How often a particular replica is downloaded thus depends on how popular it is, and the method nodes use for choosing which of several replicas to download. Rather than defining which copy a node will choose when estimating query loads, we simply consider that all queries received for items nodes hold replicas of might potentially need to be answered. Thus we measure the highest possible number of replicas a node may have to serve. This is in most cases an overestimation, though it does give a measure of a system's usefulness to a node since the more copies of an item are available, the higher a download rate can be achieved by splitting downloads, and the more reliable the system is as a "backup" of that item. If we simply use the potential number of replicas served as a measure of the load of each node, we find that, fairly obviously, nodes with more items, and more popular items see the highest loads. It is fairly reasonable to assume, however, that nodes with larger item caches and more popular items make more use of the system, and are thus willing to contribute more. We therefore divide the load a node potentially sees by the load it potentially creates. We do not consider the cost of providing negative replies to queries, on the assumption that this will be small compared to the cost of serving file downloads.

3.3 Data Sets

The data sets we study consist of a set of N nodes and a set of F unique files, or items. Each node corresponds to a user and has a *file cache* which contains a set of replicas of files from F, in which the user is interested. We consider two data sets, one of measurements from an eDonkey peer-to-peer file sharing system, the second of user ratings of movies from the Movielens recommendation system.

The eDonkey data set is presented in [1] by Le Fessant *et al.* It was obtained by crawling the eDonkey network during a week in November 2003, recording the actual file cache contents of nodes. The full dat set contains data for 37,044 nodes (11,872 with 1 or more file) and 923,718 files. Le Fessant *et al.* present an analysis of file replication and sharing distributions and measure node and file correlations for this data set. They find that there is a significant amount of correlation between the file caches of certain nodes, showing that semantically-similar nodes exist.

Since in this study we are only interested in comparing semantic search networks, we create a subset of the eDonkey data that contains only the nodes and files that can contribute to semantic similarity and successful searches. We thus remove all of the files for which there is only one replica, and all of the nodes that subsequently do not contain any files. This gives us a data set in which, in the best case, all nodes can find a replica of any file they hold in their cache. This refined data set has 11,545 nodes and 104,722 files. Nodes have between 1 and 1059 files in their file caches. Files have between 2 and 344 replicas.

The eDonkey data sets contains a large number of nodes with very small file caches, and a large number of files with very few replicas. These factors together make search difficult; nodes with small file caches may not be worth querying and the many unpopular files will be hard to find. In an ideal file sharing network all nodes would contribute files and even unpopular files would have several replicas. It is fairly reasonable to guess that in the eDonkey system users are actually interested in more files than appear in this data set. The low number of files measured is probably partly due to the short period over which the data was gathered, and to the fact that many users could be removing files from their eDonkey caches once they have been downloaded. In the future it is hoped that incentive mechanisms can be used to fix this weakness. We thus also study a second data set, taken from the Movielens recommendation system [2]. Since this data set comes from an internal measurements of a successful recommendation system, built on the premise that users with similar tastes will rate movies in similar ways, we can assume that a useful amount of semantic similarity exists between nodes.

We consider a scenario in which a user's files consist of the movies he has rated with 4 or 5 stars in the Movielens data set, thus assuming that each user will keep and share recordings of his favorite movies. As with the eDonkey data set we remove all movies that appear only once, and all users that subsequently store no movies. The original Movielens data set contains ratings for 3592 movies made by 6039 users, each of which rated at least 20 movies. The subset we study contains 3381 movies (items/files) and 6038 users (nodes). Nodes contain replicas of between 1 and 1433 movies. Files are replicated on between 2 and 2853 nodes. Compared to the eDonkey data, these nodes share more files, and files are more widely replicated. As in the eDonkey data, most nodes have smaller numbers of files, and most files have smaller numbers of replicas.

4 Experimental Results

4.1 Hit Rates

Figure 1 compares average hit rates for each of the search methods. The x-axes give the search neighborhood size, s, and y-axes give the total fraction of items found over all nodes. For direct best-neighbors search s is the size of the neighbor cache, which may or may not be filled, depending on how many potential neighbors a node has. For friends-of-friends search (fof) points are plotted for a query forwarding radius of between 1 and 4. Results are plotted for neighbor cache sizes of 3, 4, 5, and 6. We consider s to be the number of nodes that could potentially have been reached in this number of hops. In actuality, the number of nodes queried is slightly lower since cycles can result in some nodes being queried twice. Accounting for this difference however

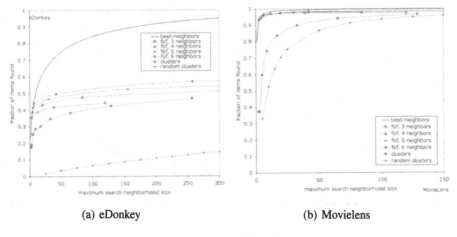

(a) eDonkey	(b) Movielens

Fig. 1. Average Hit Rates

does not change the overall performance ordering of the methods. The figure also plots results for two clustered overlays with the maximum cluster size determining the search neighborhood size (s). We compare clusters created at random to clusters created by an algorithm that attempts to maximize hit rates, described in Section 4.3. For the random clusters we plot the average result of 10 random clusterings.

Direct best-neighbors search gives the highest possible hit rate for a give search neighborhood size, since each node is able to query the nodes which it knows will produce the most hits. Friends-of-friends and cluster-based search should, in all but the extreme case, produce lower hit rates since nodes do not get to directly choose all of their search neighborhood. In the eDonkey graph we see that choosing search neighborhoods directly gives a large advantage. Increasing the friends-of-friends query radius improves hit rates, but by a very small amount compared to the number of additional nodes queried. Similarly, creating clusters also produces fairly poor search neighborhoods. The fact that a carefully considered clustering performs much better than a random clustering indicates that a semantic grouping of nodes does exist. However, the mediocre performance of the friends-of-friends and cluster based searches indicates that this grouping is not entirely clear cut. For the Movielens data set both friends-of-friends and cluster-based search perform much better. However, random clusters also produce good search neighborhoods, indicating that the improved performance is more due to the fact that there is a greater amount of item replication in the Movielens data than due to the fact that better groupings exist.

4.2 Load Balancing

From Figure 1 it would appear that direct best-neighbors search should always be used. Hit rates are, however, only one aspect of search performance. Figure 2 plots the largest load ratio seen by any node in the network on the y-axes, with again the maximum search neighborhood size on the x-axes. For this measure cluster-based search should

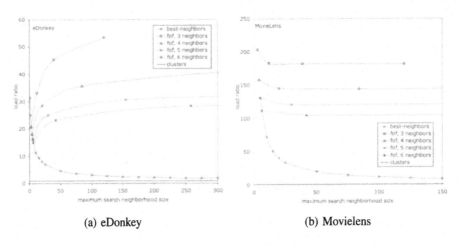

(a) eDonkey   (b) Movielens

Fig. 2. Maximum Load Ratios

produce the best results. All the nodes a node queries in its cluster will also query it in return, resulting in a load ratio of 1. In a best-neighbors overlay, on the other hand, while the out-degree of a node is fixed, the in-degree is unlimited. Thus some nodes with many or very popular items could be disproportionately popular, and receive an inordinately large number of queries, resulting in large load ratios. The plot for best-neighbors search in the eDonkey data set shows that this does happen for low neighbor-cache sizes. As neighbor-cache size increases, however, nodes find more replicas in new outgoing neighbors than they must serve to new incoming neighbors. Thus for larger neighbor cache sizes loads appear to be reasonably well balanced. With a neighbor cache size of 150 the maximum load ratio is only 2.5. Friends-of-friends search, on the other hand, results in a larger proportion of queries being forwarded to more popular nodes as the query radius increases, while those nodes do not benefit much from a larger search neighborhood. Thus for friends-of-friends search loads become more imbalanced as query radius increases. The Movielens data shows more of an imbalance; for direct best-neighbors searches at a neighbor-cache size of 150 the maximum load ratio is 8.7. This indicates that the Movielens data set contains nodes which many other nodes choose as neighbors. Such nodes are more likely to occur in the Movielens data set which has more users than items than in the eDonkey data set in which there are many more items than users.

Maximum load ratios, however, only tell part of the story; the load distribution over all of the nodes gives a clearer picture of how balanced a system is. Figure 3 plots load ratio distributions for direct best-neighbors search with neighbor cache-sizes that produce good hit rates. Figure 3(a) gives the distribution for the eDonkey data set with a neighbor cache size of 120. Figures 3(b) and 3(c) give the distribution for the Movielens data set with a neighbor cache size of 5. Overall, the eDonkey nodes are fairly evenly balanced, only 13.6% of nodes have a ratio over 1, and 8.8% are exactly balanced with a load ratio of 1. The worst-off node serves 2.5 times more files than it receives, and the majority of nodes receive a little more than the system than they give, but these

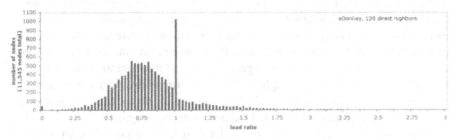

(a) eDonkey, $s = 120$, load ratios divided into intervals of 0.025

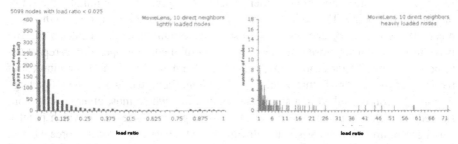

(b) Movielens lightly loaded nodes, $s = 5$, in-tervals of 0.025

(c) Movielens heavily loaded nodes, $s = 5$, in-tervals of 0.25

Fig. 3. Example Load Ratio Distributions for Best-Neighbors Overlays

imbalances would probably be considered reasonable by users. For the Movielens data sets the distribution is much worse. Some nodes give much more to the system then they receive, with the worst off having a load ratio of 72, and only 1.6% of nodes have a load ratio of 1 or above. Of more concern, however, is the fact that most nodes provide much less to the system than they receive, with 20.5% of nodes contributing nothing at all. Thus, even though all nodes provide files in this data set, a large percentage end up free riding due to the structure of the network. With a larger cache size of 120 this distribution improves, the maximum load ratio is 10.4, 5.6% of nodes have a load ratio of 1 or above, and only 3.3% of node contribute nothing. However, the distribution still remains heavily skewed so that most nodes provide much less than they receive.

4.3   Determining Clusters

The hit ratio for cluster-based search depends heavily on the clustering of the nodes created by the clustered-overlay. When groupings are straightforward most algorithms will produce a reasonable clustering of a data set. We tested two basic algorithms, k-means and a hierarchical top-down minimal-spanning-tree algorithm (MST). We found that for our measure of distance, the number of files two nodes have in common, nei-ther of these produced good clusters. MST produced one large cluster and many single point clusters, due to the high dimensionality of the data and low similarity between nodes. For k-means, which depends on finding poor initial clusterings, then gradu-ally improving them by moving points to new clusters, points were so much more similar to themselves than to any other point that the initial clusterings could not be much improved upon. The failure of these two algorithms to produce reasonable clusterings indicates that obvious clusters do not exist within the data sets. This is not very surprising considering the high dimensionally of the data and the sparsity of the user-item matrix. Given more data on user preferences, and thus a more accurate measure of similarity between nodes we might be able to determine clusterings more easily. On the other hand, it is also likely that such clusterings simply do not exist. While users are similar to some other users, they do not fall into clear cut categories.

For the experiments in this paper we used a staged, size-limited, bottom-up hierarchical clustering algorithm, which, though trial and error, provided the best clusterings we could find. This algorithm considers a set of clusters, which is initially the set of individual data points. For each cluster, c_1, its nearest neighbor, c_2, for which the combined size of c_1 and c_2 does not exceed some maximum value M is calculated. The two clusters which are closest together are then combined. This operation is repeat until no more combinations can be made. The distance metric used was the reciprocal of the number of new "hits" that would result by combining the two clusters. For large M this procedure resulted in a single cluster forming, which most other clusters considered their closest neighbor. This cluster would grow to size M, at which point it could accept no new members, thus allowing a next favorite to grow. To force clusters to grow in parallel we divide the process into phases in which M is slowly increased. A series that prevented the largest existing clusters from joining together each phase appeared to work the best. For the clustered-overlays measured above we used the series, $M = 2, 3, 5, 9, 17, 33, 65, 129, 257$. Cluster sizes can end up being smaller than the largest value of M, thus actual cluster sizes varied from the maximum size plotted in the graphs.

5   Conclusions and Discussion

We have presented a comparison study of peer-to-peer search in two fundamental forms of semantic-overlay network. We compared search performance in terms of hit rates and load balancing, given the best possible overlay configurations for two typical file sharing data sets. We found that high hit rates can be achieved in a simple overlay in which each node is directly linked to a small number of best neighbors. For the Movielens data set, in which item replication was high, only 10 neighbors per node were needed for nodes to be able to find copies of 90% of their files in neighboring nodes. For the eDonkey data set, which contained many rare files, still only 175 neighbors per node were required to achieve a 90% hit rate. Methods for building overlays that reduce the number of direct neighbors per node, by assuming that nodes fall into interest groups, were not as effective, indicating that though node groupings exist to some extent they are not well enough defined to be exploited in this way. Creating groups of nodes, however, may prove useful in situations where the fairness of resource usage is a an issue. We observed that in the Movielens data set allowing nodes to individually choose their best neighbors resulted in a network in which a large number of nodes did not receive queries, and thus did not participate equally in the file sharing network.

Creating clusters of nodes avoided this problem, and, because of the high item replication within the data set, still allowed for reasonably high query hit rates.

These observations have interesting implications for the application of peer-to-peer techniques in multi-agent systems. The choice between using a best-neighbors or a clustered overlay involves a trade-off between search performance and fairness. In peer-to-peer systems, which are often concerned with data-centric applications, performance often takes priority. In multi-agent systems, in which agents are already complex and transactions can be expensive, the importance of fairness might justify the extra cost of building clusters. Further, the data-set characteristics for an application, and in particular the degree of replication, can play a large role in this choice. Peer-to-peer applications, which are often quite open about the peers they accept, are likely to have less item replication than multi-agent applications in which a smaller variety of agents usually exist.

In this study we only considered abstract overlay structures, not the performance of actual peer-to-peer systems. In a real best-neighbors network it is possible to make load distributions in the network more fair by capping the contribution of popular nodes [5]. This, and other incentive mechanisms, can prevent popular nodes from becoming overloaded. Incentive mechanisms, however, do not necessarily solve the problem that unpopular nodes simply never get a chance to contribute. In an actual peer-to-peer system we would also face the problem that methods for determining the best possible semantic overlay do not usually exist. This will lower hit rates in both best-neighbors and clustered overlays. However, the fact that an overlay containing random clusters also performed reasonably for the Movielens data set indicates that in some applications finding the exact best structure for the network might not be particularly important.

References

1. Fessant, F.L., Handurukande, S., Kermerrec, A.M., Massoulie, L.: Clustering in peer-to-peer file sharing workloads. In: Voelker, G.M., Shenker, S. (eds.) IPTPS 2004. LNCS, vol. 3279, pp. 217–226. Springer, Heidelberg (2005)
2. Miller, B., Konstan, J., Riedl, J.: Pocketlens: Toward a personal recommender system. ACM Transactions on Information Systems 22, 437–476 (2004)
3. Cohen, E., Shenker, S.: Replication strategies in unstructured peer-to-peer networks. SIGCOMM Computer Communication Review 32, 177–190 (2002)
4. Chawathe, Y., Ratnasamy, S., Breslau, L., Lanham, N., Shenker, S.: Making gnutella-like p2p systems scalable. In: Proc. 2003 Conference on Applications, Technologies, Architectures, and Protocols for Computer Communications, pp. 407–418 (2003)
5. Cholvi, V., Felber, P., Biersack, E.: Efficient search in unstructured peer-to-peer networks. In: Proc. 16th ACM Symposium on Parallelism in Algorithms and Architectures, pp. 271–272 (2004)
6. Sripanidkulchai, K., Maggs, B., Zhang, H.: Efficient content location using interest-based locality in peer-to-peer systems. In: Proc. of the 22nd INFOCOM Conference (2003)
7. Voulgaris, S., van Steen, M.: Epidemic-style management of semantic overlays for content-based searching. In: Cunha, J.C., Medeiros, P.D. (eds.) Euro-Par 2005. LNCS, vol. 3648, pp. 1143–1152. Springer, Heidelberg (2005)
8. Yang, B., Vinograd, P., Garcia-Molina, H.: Evaluating guess and non-forwarding peer-to-peer search. In: Proc. 24th Int'l Conference on Distributed Computing Systems, pp. 209–218 (2004)

9. Cohen, E., Fiat, A., Kaplan, H.: Associative search in peer-to-peer networks: Harnessing latent semantics. In: Proc. of the 22nd INFOCOM Conference (2003)
10. Crespo, A., Garcia-Molina, H.: Semantic overlay networks for p2p systems. Technical report, Computer Science Department, Stanford University (2002)
11. Garbacki, P., Epema, D., van Steen, M.: A Two-Level Semantic Caching Scheme for Super-Peer Networks. In: Proc. IEEE 10th Int'l Workshop on Web Content Caching and Distribution (2005)
12. Nejdl, W., Wolpers, M., Siberski, W., Schmitz, C., Schlosser, M., Brunkhorst, I., Löser, A.: Super-peer-based routing and clustering strategies for rdf-based peer-to-peer networks. In: Proc. 12th Int'l World Wide Web Conference, pp. 536–543 (2003)
13. Ogston, E., van Steen, M., Brazier, F.: Group formation among decentralized autonomous agents. Applied Artificial Intelligence 18, 953–970 (2004)

Mitigating the Impact of Liars by Reflecting Peer's Credibility on P2P File Reputation Systems

So Young Lee, O-Hoon Kwon, Jong Kim, and Sung Je Hong

Dept. of Computer Science and Engineering,
Pohang University of Science and Technology
{soyoung,dolphin,jkim,sjhong}@postech.ac.kr

Abstract. Liars that submit wrong feedbacks can subvert the reputation systems by inducing false detection of untrustworthy downloads. In this paper, we propose a reputation management scheme which mitigates the impact of liars and reduces the untrustworthy downloads on the P2P file reputation system. Our scheme uses global file reputations and local peer credibilities to build the trust of downloaded files. Simulation results show that the proposed scheme effectively reduces the untrustworthy downloads with low false detection rate even when the high rate of untrustworthy files and liars exist.

1 Introduction

Since all peers have equal capabilities in a fully decentralized P2P system, no peer has the special power or responsibility to monitor and restrain the others' behaviors. This nature of P2P frees the malicious peers to behave badly and spread untrustworthy files such as fake files that cheat their contents and corrupted files that harm the others' systems. To protect the systems and innocent users from these malicious behaviors without the help of any central authorities, several reputation based P2P systems have been proposed [1,2,3,4,5].

There are some notions related to the P2P reputation systems. Since our focus is on the P2P file sharing systems, terminologies are based on the file sharing applications. *Trust* of a file represents whether the file is trustworthy or not. The trust value of a file is weighted on the aggregation of feedbacks from the past users. The positive feedbacks increase the trust value of the file and negative feedbacks decrease it. A file with high trust value is regraded as trustworthy. However, since all users do not always leave correct feedbacks, the feedbacks are weighted by the feedback senders' *Credibility*. A peer's credibility is built based on its past feedback. If a peer's past opinions are credible, the peer has high credibility value. *Trust* of a peer is determined by the trust of the files provided. If a peer provides many trustworthy files, it has a high trust value.

There are two different approaches in P2P reputation system such as using *Peer Reputation* and using *File Reputation*. The difference of two systems is the target of the evaluation. Assume that peer i downloads the file f from peer j and peer i leaves its feedback. In the peer reputation system, the target of the feedback is peer j. On the other hand, in the file reputation system, the target of the feedback is file f. The use of file reputation gives some benefits such as preventing malicious peers who change their

S. Joseph et al. (Eds.): AP2PC 2006, LNAI 4461, pp. 111–122, 2008.

identities and reducing the message overhead for managing reputation data. Most of the previous works use peer reputation [2,3,4,5] and [1] uses the combined reputation of resources and peers based on Gnutella. In [6], we have proposed a reputation management scheme using file reputation and peer reputation together based on the structured P2P system.

Since the reputation system highly depends on the feedbacks left by the past users, the credibility of the feedback sender is very important. But, the previous studies for the P2P reputation system have emphasized on detecting and punishing peers who provide untrustworthy files and are negligent to the *Liars* who send incorrect feedbacks. Such liars can subvert the reputation system by polluting the feedbacks. Therefore, the reputation system should take the liars into considerations and diminish their negative impact. To confirm the correctness of a feedback, some studies [2,5] use the trust value of the feedback sender or feedback receiver, by making assumptions that the peers with high trust value always give the correct feedback or decent file. However, these assumptions are not always true. Sometimes, good peers who provide trustworthy files can submit wrong feedbacks in order to upgrade their reputation by degrading other peer's reputation. And malicious peers can build a good reputation and later send untrustworthy files to maximize their influence. Therefore, the correctness of feedback itself should be considered as a criterion for the peers' credibility [4,3]. That is, peers can judge the other's credibility by comparing the feedbacks of themselves with those of others for the same target. All of the proposed methods to reflect peer's credibility have been proposed on peer reputation systems while none of them is based on file reputation systems.

In this paper, we propose a method to mitigate the impact of liars by reflecting peer's credibility on the file reputation system. The proposed scheme has two characteristics. Firstly, the scheme is based on the file reputation system and secondly, we take an approach to compare the feedbacks of the peers for the same file and use the similarity of the feedbacks as credibility metric. This paper is organized as follows. In Section 2, we briefly overview the previous works. In Section 3, we describe the file reputation system without considering the credibility of the feedbacks. In Section 4, we explain considerations for supporting the credibility of the feedbacks in the file reputation system. In Section 5, we describe the reputation management protocol. Then, we show the simulation results in Section 6. Finally, we summarize this paper and discuss concluding remarks and future works in Section 7.

2 Related Works

In EigenTrust [2], after a transaction is performed, a peer evaluates whether the transaction is positive or negative and stores the rating in its local storage. A local trust value s_{ij} is defined as the sum of the ratings of all transactions that peer i has downloaded from peer j. Multiple score managers of peer i aggregate the local trust values and build the global trust value of peer i when other peers request the trust value of peer i. In the aggregation process, score managers ask their neighbors on their opinions about peer i and the opinions are weighted by the trust value of the opinion senders. Since they use the trust value of the opinion sender as the credibility, they cannot prevent liars with high trust value.

In [5], they define a *suspicious transaction* to detect the peers who provide false feedbacks. A *suspicious transaction* is one in which the feedback is different from the one expected for the file provider whose trust value is known. That is, when the trust value of the file provider is positive but the feedback for the provider is negative, the transaction is regarded as suspicious. If α_i is the ratio of the number of suspicious feedbacks sent by peer i over the total number of feedbacks sent by peer i, the credibility of peer i is represented $(1-\alpha_i)$. They implicitly assume that a highly reputable peer always provides decent files and judges the correctness of the feedback by the provider's trust value. If malicious peers once build a good reputation and later send untrustworthy files, this method will cause false detection.

In [3], peers store their evaluations to its local storage and build local trust values. A peer selects a file by the provider's trust value. If it doesn't have enough information about file providers, it queries others about the unknown providers. After downloading a file, if its evaluation is positive, the trust rating of the file provider is upgraded. Otherwise, the trust rating of the provider and the rating of those who contributed to its selection are downgraded. And the credibility of a peer who has expressed an opinion on other peer is updated when the peer's trust rating is updated. If the peer's trust rating is upgraded and the opinion is positive or the peer's trust rating is downgraded and the opinion is negative, the peer's credibility rating is upgraded. Otherwise, the value is downgraded. In PeerTrust [4], peer i uses a personalized similarity measure to rate the credibility of another peer j through peer i's personalized experience. If peer i wants to compute peer j's credibility, peer i retrieves the common set of peers that have interacted with both peer i and j. The feedback by peer i and the feedback by peer j over common set of peers are represented as two vectors and the similarity between the two feedback vectors is defined as the credibility. In [3,4], peers build the credibilities of other peers by comparing their own judgements and the others' feedbacks for the same peer. Their approaches are similar to ours in comparing the feedbacks for the same target. However, they compare the feedbacks for the same peer, whereas we comapre the feedbacks for the same file.

3 Feedback Only Reputation Scheme

In [6], we have proposed a reputation management scheme using file reputation on structured P2P system, and explain our scheme based on Chord [7]. Every peer that takes part in the system has a unique identifier ID_{peer} which is the hash value of the peer's IP address. And each file has two identifiers; ID_{key} which is generated by hashing the file name and $\text{ID}_{content}$ which is generated by its contents. Every peer is responsible for some part of the file index information and manages the reputation data of the files using *File Reputation Repository*. The file reputation repository is organized as a table with attributes (*ID_{key}, $ID_{content}$, Recommenders, Non-Recommenders, File Owners, and Description*). The repository stores the information about the file including who left a positive evaluation and a negative evaluation and who has the file using two keys, ID_{key} and $\text{ID}_{content}$. The value of Recommenders column is the list of the peers that left positive evaluations and Non-Recommenders is the list of the peers that left negative evaluations for the file. After using a file, the consumer sends its evaluation as positive or negative to the file reputation manager. If the peer sends a positive evaluation, the ID_{peer} of the peer is added to the list of Recommenders. Otherwise, it is added to the list of Non-Recommenders. When a peer sends a search query and receives the list of files, the files are classified into 3 levels by their file reputation: *Trustworthy, Unknown, and Untrustworthy*. The reputation level of each file is decided by the following two conditions.

$$|Positive| + |Negative| >= T \qquad (1)$$

$$\frac{|Positive|}{|Positive| + |Negative|} >= P \qquad (2)$$

The two parameters, T and P, are system-wide parameters. The parameter T is a data confidence threshold, which represents the minimum number of evaluations required and P is a trust threshold, which represents the ratio of positive evaluations. The files that do not satisfy Condition (1) are classified as *Unknown*. Namely, the number of evaluations are not enough to decide whether the file is trustworthy or not. The files which satisfy Conditions (1) and (2) are classified as *Trustworthy*. These files have been evaluated enough times and are perceived as trustworthy, whereas, the files which satisfy Condition (1) but do not satisfy Condition (2) are classified as *Untrustworthy*. A peer selects one among the files classified as *Trustworthy* or *Unknown*. In this scheme, we do not consider the credibility of the feedback sender. In the following, we refer to this scheme [6] as the Feedback Only Reputation Scheme (FORS).

4   Considerations for Credibility

To detect liars, peers build the other's credibility based on feedback comparison for the same file and store the credibility value in their local repository. And these credibility values are used for computing trust value of files.

4.1   Credibility Repository

The credibility repository is organized as a table with attributes (ID_{key}, *Credibility Vector*). We reference the scheme which is proposed by Selcuk et al. [3] to store and compute the credibility value. Each peer stores the similarity of its opinion and others' opinion in the credibility repository. To compute the similarity, a peer compares its feedback and other's feedback for the same file. The result of feedback comparison is

Table 1. Credibility Repository

ID_{key}	Credibility Vector
N_5	00101
N_8	000111
N_{26}	1110

stored in the credibility vector, which is a binary vector with maximum l bits. The bit value 1 represents that the peer's feedback accords with its own. The bit value 0 represents that the feedback discords with its own. If a peer sends a search query, it can obtain the list of Recommenders and Non-Recommenders. By referencing their recommendation (or non-recommendation), the peer decides to download the file. If the peer downloads and uses the file, it evaluates the file. If its evaluation turns out positive, it gives Recommenders the bit value 1 and Non-Recommenders the bit value 0. If negative, it gives Non-Recommenders the bit value 1 and Recommenders the bit value 0. The result of the most recent comparison is written at the most significant bit, shifting the present bits to the right. Table 1 shows the *Credibility Repository* of peer N_3. The credibility vector of peer N_5 in that repository is 00101. It means that the opinion of peer N_5 accords with that of N_3 twice and discords three times. If N_5's opinion agrees with N_3 again, its credibility vector changes from 00101 to 100101. To prevent the credibility vector from being large, the vector size is limited by l.

4.2 Credibility Computation

Peer v's credibility computed at peer u is expressed by two values, credit rating $Cr(u, v)$ and discredit rating $\overline{Cr(u, v)}$. We define the credit rating $Cr(u, v)$ as the similarity between peer u's and peer v's feedback for the same file and the discredit rating $\overline{Cr(u, v)}$ as the dissimilarity. These two values are computed by using the credibility vector. A credibility vector with length l is read as an l-bit integer and divided by 2^l for conversion into a scalar *credit rating* in the [0,1) interval. And *discredit rating* is computed from the complement of the credibility vector. An example of computing credit rating and discredit rating is shown in Fig. 1.

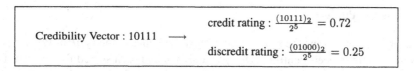

Fig. 1. Computing credit rating and discredit rating

4.3 Trust Computation of File

Trust of file i computed at peer u is expressed by its two values; trust rating $Tr_i(u)$ and distrust rating $\overline{Tr_i(u)}$. We compute the trust and distrust ratings of file i using its recommender's and non-recommender's credit rating and discredit rating. Trust rating of file i, $Tr_i(u)$, is expressed as the average of recommender's credit rating and non-recommender's discredit rating:

$$Tr_i(u) = \frac{1}{\alpha + \beta} \left\{ \sum_{k=1}^{\alpha} r_k + \sum_{k=1}^{\beta} \overline{n_k} \right\} \tag{3}$$

where the recommender's credit rating $R = \{r_1, r_2, ...r_\alpha\}$ and the non-recommender's credit rating $N = \{n_1, n_2, ...n_\beta\}$. The distrust rating of file i, $\overline{Tr_i(u)}$, is defined as the average of non-recommender's credit rating and recommender's discredit rating:

$$\overline{Tr_i(u)} = \frac{1}{\alpha + \beta} \{\sum_{k=1}^{\alpha} \overline{r_k} + \sum_{k=1}^{\beta} n_k\} \tag{4}$$

The file i's trust value which is computed at peer u and denoted by $Tf_i(u)$ is defined as Eq. (5) and the file is regraded as *Trustworthy* when the value of $Tf_i(u) > 0$, *Untrustworthy* when the value of $Tf_i(u) < 0$, and *Undetermined* when the value of $Tf_i(u) = 0$.

$$Tf_i(u) = Tr_i(u) - \overline{Tr_i(u)} \qquad \begin{cases} > 0 \; Trustworthy \\ < 0 \; Untrustworthy \\ = 0 \; Undetermined \end{cases} \tag{5}$$

If the file is regarded as *Untrustworthy*, peer u does not download the file and chooses one of the file among *Trustworthy* or *Undetermined*.

5   The Reputation Management Protocol

We explain how the proposed scheme works based on the steps of file sharing system. These steps consist of the following phases: *Join and Publish*, *Query and Response*, *Select File*, *Update Credibility*, and *Submit Feedback*.

5.1   Join and Publish

In this phase, a peer joins the system and publishes its files to the system. When a peer joins the system, a peer identifier ID_{peer} is assigned and each shared file receives two identifiers such as ID_{key} and $ID_{content}$. A peer publishes its file by sending publish messages to the file reputation manager: *Publish (ID_{key}, $ID_{content}$, ID_{peer}, Description)*. The file reputation manager that received the publish message updates its file reputation repository. If the repository does not contain the information of published file, the manager adds a new row to its repository and adds the ID_{peer} value to the list of owner column in that row. If the information already exists in the repository, the manager just adds the ID_{peer} value to the owner's list.

As shown in Fig. 2, peers N_{10} and N_{20} both publish a file whose name is the same as "Music1" but whose contents are different. Since the two files have the same name, they are assigned with the same ID_{key} and published to the same file reputation manager N_3. The manager N_3 updates its repository using the received message. The file of N_{10} is a newly appeared one because no entry matches its two identifiers, K_3 and F_7. Thus, N_3 adds a new row with file owner N_{10}, whereas the file of N_{20} with K_3 and F_6 already exists in the repository and the other peer N_4 also has the same file. In this case, N_3 just adds N_{20} to the owner's list.

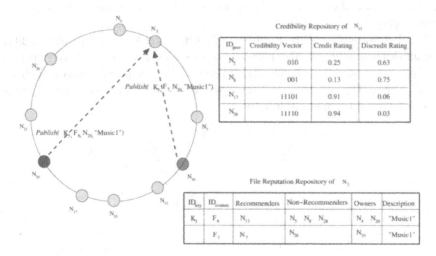

Fig. 2. Join and Publish

5.2   Query and Response

In this phase, a peer sends a search query to find a desired file and receives a response which contains the information of files from the manager. The peer sends a query message to the proper file reputation manager; *Query (ID_{key})*. The file reputation manager retrieves the list of owner, the list of recommenders and the list of non-recommenders of the file which has the same ID_{key} as sent on the query from its repository. If several versions of files which have a same ID_{key} but different $ID_{content}$ exist, the result can be several sets. The manager sends the response message to the requester: *Response(set of {ID_{key}, $ID_{content}$, list of owners, list of recommender's, list of non-recommenders, description})*.

In Fig. 2, if N_3 has received a query to search K_3 from N_{12}, it can find that there are two different versions of files whose $ID_{content}$ are F_6 and F_7 with the same key identifier K_3. From this result, manager N_3 sends the following *Response* to the querier N_{12}: *Response ({$K_3,F_6,N_{13},\{N_5,N_8,N_{28}\},\{N_4,N_{20}\}$,"Music1"}, {$K_3,F_7,N_7,N_{26},N_{10}$, "Music1"})*

5.3   Select a File

In this phase, a peer computes each file's trust value and select a file. A peer which has received the *Response* computes each file's trust value referring to its local credibility repository. The peer obtains the list of recommenders and non-recommenders from *Response*, and finds the credibilities of recommenders and non-recommenders from its *Credibility Repository*. Only the opinions of the peers whose credibility exist in *Credibility Repository* are used to compute the trust value of each file and the others are ignored. Using the credibility vector, the peer can compute the recommenders' and non-recommenders' credit rating and discredit rating. And using this credibility value, it can compute each file's trust value. The peer selects one of the files which are classified as *Trustworthy* and *Undetermined*. The files classified as *Untrustworthy* are excluded from its choice.

Fig. 2 shows the *Credibility Repository* of file requester N_{12} and computed credit rating and discredit rating of other peers. Among recommenders and non-recommenders, the opinions of peer N_{13}, N_5, N_8, and N_{26} are used to compute the trust of a file. Let the file whose $ID_{content}$ is F_6 be f_1 and the file whose $ID_{content}$ is F_7 be f_2. The file f_1's trust value is computed as follows;

$$
\begin{aligned}
Tf_1(N_{12}) &= Tr_1(N_{12}) - \overline{Tr_1(N_{12})} \\
&= \frac{0.91 + 0.63 + 0.75}{3} - \frac{0.06 + 0.25 + 0.13}{3} \\
&= 0.61 \quad\quad\quad (6) \\
Tf_2(N_{12}) &= Tr_2(N_{12}) - \overline{Tr_2(N_{12})} \\
&= 0.03 - 0.94 \\
&= -0.91 \quad\quad\quad (7)
\end{aligned}
$$

By Eqs (6) and (7), the file f_1 is regarded as trustworthy and f_2 is regarded as untrustworthy. Therefore, peer N_{12} will decide to download the file f_1.

5.4 Update Credibility and Submit Evaluation

In this phase, the peer evaluates the file and applies the evaluation to the credibility repository and file reputation repository. After using the file, the peer evaluates its trustworthiness as positive or negative. If the file turns out trustworthy, it increases the recommender's credibility and decreases the non-recommender's credibility. If not, it decreases the recommender's credibility and increases the non-recommender's credibility. And it sends the evaluation to the file reputation manager. If the peer sends positive evaluation, the file reputation manager adds ID_{peer} of it to the list of recommenders. And if it sends a negative one, the manager adds it to the list of non-recommenders.

6   Performance Evaluation

We have performed six experiments to show the effect of the proposed scheme on reducing untrustworthy downloads with low false detection rate. In the first four experiments, we have compared the proposed scheme which is referred to as the Feedback Credibility Reputation Scheme (FCRS) with the Feedback Only Reputation Scheme(FORS) [6]. These experiments show the effect of using the concept of credibility on the file reputation systems. In the fifth and sixth experiments, we have compared FCRS with the Loubna's scheme [5] which defines *suspicious transaction* for detecting liars. These experiments compare the file reputation systems and the peer reputation systems with the concept of credibility.

As performance metrics, we use the Untrustworthy Downloads Rate (UDR) and False Detection Rate(FDR). UDR and FDR are defined as follows:

$$
UDR = \frac{N(ud)}{N(t)} \quad , \quad FDR = \frac{N(fp) + N(fn)}{N(t)} \quad , \quad\quad (8)
$$

where $N(t)$ denotes the total number of requests and $N(ud)$ denotes the number of untrustworthy downloads. And $N(fp)$ denotes the number of blocked trustworthy files (false positive) and $N(fn)$ denotes the number of allowed untrustworthy files (false negative) by a wrong trust computation. Therefore, UDR represents the effect of the scheme for reducing untrustworthy downloads and FDR represents the accuracy of the scheme for distinguishing untrustworthy files from trustworthy files.

The experiments are performed under a static P2P network with 1,000 peers and the identifiers of peers and files are 32-bit random number. Every peer has 20 different kinds of files, thus the total number of files is 20,000 and the number of distinct files are 4,000. Also, the system-wide parameters T, P, l are fixed as 5, 0.7 and 10. In experiments, we vary the percentile of untrustworthy files from 10% to 80% and that of liars also from 10% to 80%.

6.1 Simulation Results

In the first experiment, we measured the UDR of two schemes by fixing the rate of untrustworthy file with 10% and varying the rate of liars from 10% to 80%. Fig. 3.(a) shows the result of FCRS and Fig. 3.(b) shows the result of FORS. The results show that the UDR decreases as the total number of requests increases in both schemes. However, as the rate of liars increases, FORS does not effectively decrease the UDR, whereas, FORS is not affected by the rate of liars.

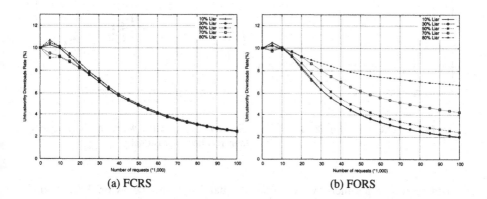

(a) FCRS   (b) FORS

Fig. 3. UDR under various rate of liars

In the second experiment, we have changed the rate of untrustworthy files from 10% to 80%. In this experiment, the rate of liars are the same as the rate of untrustworthy files. Fig. 4 shows the result of the second experiment. In case of FCRS, as shown in Fig. 4.(a), UDR decreases rapidly under the high rate of untrustworthy files. But, as shown in Fig. 4.(b), FORS does not work well under the high rate of untrustworthy files.

In the third experiment, we have compared FDR of two schemes when the rate of liars is 10% and 50%. Fig. 5 shows that FCRS distinguishes trustworthy files and

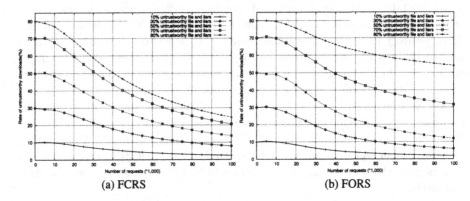

Fig. 4. UDR under various rate of untrustworthy files

untrustworthy files accurately with both low rate (10%) and high rate (50%) of liars. However, FORS regards many trustworthy files as untrustworthy by wrong feedbacks from the liars.

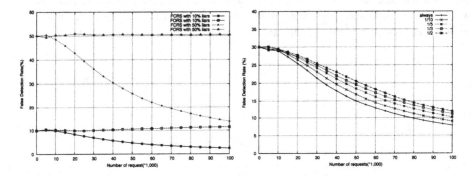

Fig. 5. FDR of the two schemes

Fig. 6. FDR of FCRS when the liars change their feedback occasionally

In the fourth experiment, we consider the liars' dynamic behavior. That is, liars change their feedbacks occasionally to hide their misbehaviors. We have performed an experiment under 30% of untrustworthy files and 30% of liars. The liars send wrong feedback with some probability such as 10%, 20%, 33%, 50%, once every 10 times when the probability is 10%. Fig. 6 shows that the liars' dynamic behavior has little influence on FDR of the proposed scheme.

In the fifth and sixth experiments, we have compared the UDR of FCRS to the UDR of the Loubna's scheme [5]. Since FCRS is based on the file reputation system and Loubna's scheme [5] is based on the peer reputation system, we set the simulation parameters more variously than the previous experiments. Table 2 shows the distribution of the peers and their behavior patterns of the fifth experiment. We can expect 45% ($50\% \times 10\% + 10\% \times 20\% + 10\% \times 80\% + 30\% \times 100\%$) of untrustworthy files in

Table 2. Distribution of peers and Behavior type

Type	Rate of Peers	Pro. of sending untrustworthy files	Pro. of submit wrong feedback
Good Peer	50%	10%	0%
Malicious 1	10%	20%	80%
Malicious 2	10%	80%	80%
Malicious 3	30%	100%	100%

Table 3. Distribution of peers and Behavior Type

Type	Rate of Peers	Pro. of sending untrustworthy files	Pro. of submit wrong feedback
Good Peer	30%	10%	0%
Malicious 1	20%	20%	80%
Malicious 2	20%	80%	80%
Malicious 3	30%	100%	100%

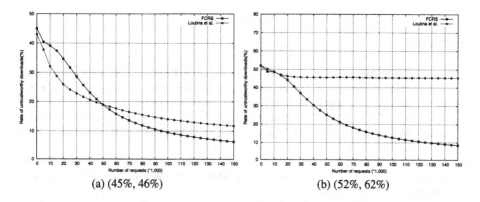

(a) (45%, 46%)   (b) (52%, 62%)

Fig. 7. UDR of FCRS and Loubna's scheme [5] (Rate of untrustworthy files, Rate of liars)

average and 46% ($10\% \times 80\% + 10\% \times 80\% + 30\% \times 100\%$) of wrong feedbacks in average from the parameters of Table 2. Table 3 shows the distribution of peers and their behavior patterns of the sixth experiment. We can expect 52% ($30\% \times 10\% + 20\% \times 20\% + 20\% \times 80\% + 30\% \times 100\%$) of untrustworthy files in average and 62% ($20\% \times 80\% + 20\% \times 80\% + 30\% \times 100\%$) of wrong feedbacks in average from the parameters of Table 3. Fig. 7(a) shows the result of the fifth experiment and Fig. 7(b) shows the result of the sixth experiment. Since Loubna et al.'s scheme stores the reputation and credibility data in supernodes, the credibility of a peer is built more rapidly than FCRS. In comparison, since FCRS uses the local credibility repository, it needs some time to build the other's credibility. Nevertheless, FCRS steadily reduces the rate of the untrustworthy downloads even though the rate of liars is high.

7   Conclusion and Future Works

We have presented a reputation management scheme which mitigates the impact of liars and reduces the untrustworthy downloads on file reputation system. The proposed scheme can reduce the untrustworthy downloads even in case of existing high rate of liars and high rate of untrustworthy files. Also the simulation results show that the false detection rate is reduced gradually as the number of file requests increases. It means that the proposed scheme can accurately detect the untrustworthy files and trustworthy files. And finally, we show that the proposed scheme still works well when the liars' opinions are occasionally changed. However, to encourage peers to leave feedbacks, some incentive mechanisms are needed and a method to share the local credibility data will be helpful to rapidly build credibility.

Acknowledgments

This research was supported by the MIC(Ministry of Information and Communication), Korea, under the ITRC(Information Technology Research Center) support program supervised by the IITA(Institute of Information Technology Assessment). (IITA-2005-(C1090-0501-0018))

References

1. Damiani, E., di Vimercati, D.C., Paraboschi, S., Samarati, P., Violante, F.: Reputation-based approach for choosing reliable resources in peer-to-peer networks. In: Proceedings of the 9th ACM Conference on Computer and Communications Security (2002)
2. Kamvar, S.D., Schlosser, M.T., Garcia-Molina, H.: The eigentrust algorithm for reputation management in p2p networks. In: Proceedings of the 12th International World Wide Web Conference (2003)
3. Selcuk, A.A., Uzun, E., Pariente, M.R.: A reputation-based trust management system for p2p networks. In: Proceedings of the International Workshop on Global and Peer-to-Peer Computing, IEEE/ACM CCGRID (2004)
4. Xiong, L., Liu, L.: Peertrust: Supporting reputation-based trust for peer-to-peer electronic communities. IEEE Transactions on Knowledge and Data Engineering 16, 843–857 (2004)
5. Mekouar, L., Iraqi, Y., Boutaba, R.: Detecting malicious peers in a reputation-based peer-to-peer system. In: The IEEE Consumer Communications and Networking Conference (CCNC) (2005)
6. Lee, S.Y., Kown, O.H., Kim, J., Hong, S.J.: A trust management scheme in structured p2p system. In: Despotovic, Z., Joseph, S., Sartori, C. (eds.) AP2PC 2005. LNCS (LNAI), vol. 4118, Springer, Heidelberg (2006)
7. Stoica, I., Morris, R., Karger, D., Kaashoek, F., Balakrishnan, H.: Chord: A scalable Peer-To-Peer lookup service for internet applications. In: Proceedings of the 2001 ACM SIGCOMM Conference (2001)

A Comparative Study of Reasoning Techniques for Service Selection*

Murat Şensoy and Pınar Yolum

Department of Computer Engineering, Boğaziçi University, Bebek, 34342, Istanbul, Turkey
{murat.sensoy,pinar.yolum}@boun.edu.tr

Abstract. Open multiagent systems do not provide guarantees about the quality of the service of its providers. This makes it difficult for service consumers to find correct service providers. Many existing approaches share the intuition that service consumers can share their knowledge about service providers to help locate useful service providers. However, representing existing past knowledge and reasoning about this knowledge are two important challenges. A traditional approach for dealing with these challenges is to represent past dealings with ratings and to aggregate the ratings. However, rating-based approaches lack the expressiveness to articulate objective information about service dealings. To enable richer representations, we have developed an objective experience-based approach for service provider selection, in which consumers record their *experiences* with service providers rather than the overall, subjective ratings for a provider. A consumer's experience with a service provider is represented using an ontology that can capture subtle details including the context in which the service was requested. When a service consumer decides to share her experiences with a second service consumer, the receiving consumer evaluates the experience using its own context and evaluation criteria. In this work, we tackle the problem of reasoning about the collected experiences. We study different reasoning techniques for consumer agents to use in selecting service providers. We formulate these techniques into agent strategies and examine their strengths and weaknesses through simulations.

1 Introduction

Finding service providers for specific needs is difficult when service providers offer services at varying levels. A consumer agent can try various service providers on its own and choose a provider solely based on its previous experiences. But, that means many trial-and-errors on the consumer side. A more acceptable solution is to enable consumers to exchange knowledge about service providers, so that each agent can reason about the knowledge it gathers from other agents.

The simplest form of such exchange is that of ratings, commonly employed in today's e-commerce sites. The basic idea is that the consumers rate the providers that they interact with and reveal their ratings publicly [1] or privately to certain agents. The

---

* This research has been supported by Boğaziçi University Research Fund under grant BAP06A103 and The Scientific and Technological Research Council of Turkey by a CAREER Award under grant 105E073. We also thank the anonymous referees for helpful comments.

S. Joseph et al. (Eds.): AP2PC 2006, LNAI 4461, pp. 123–134, 2008.

agents then examine these ratings and decide if any of the service providers are satisfactory for their own purposes [2]. Rating-based approaches reflect the subjective opinion of the raters. Most of the time, the context of the ratings are not made explicit. Hence, it is hard to judge what the rating would correspond to in a different setting. Furthermore, even if the context of the ratings is made explicit, these ratings may still mislead the consumers, because the satisfaction criteria of the consumer using these ratings may be different from the satisfaction criteria of those who give the ratings in the first place.

The reasoning process is inherently dependent on how the knowledge is represented. For example, since the ratings represent previous knowledge compactly, it is difficult to interpret what the numbers mean in different settings and to reason on these ratings. Thus, reasoning elaborately on others' knowledge will require the knowledge to be expressed in greater detail.

We have recently proposed an approach for distributed service selection that allows consumers to capture their experiences with the service providers using ontologies [3]. The ontology represents the details of the requested service description and the received service. The consumers can then exchange their detailed experiences of service providers rather than plain ratings. A consumer that receives another agent's particular experience evaluates the received experiences individually considering her own context to decide on which service provider to select. Whereas rating-based approaches reflect the subjective opinion of the raters, the experience-based approach allows the objective facts of the experience to be communicated to the other party.

The proposed approach enables experiences to be expressed in detail. The immediate question is how the agents will use these experiences to select a service provider. We had previously employed a parametric classification technique using Gaussian model. Here, we also develop a strategy in which agents use case-based reasoning to select a service provider. Our results show that when service providers do not change the quality of their service, both reasoning techniques perform equally well in finding service providers. However, case-based reasoning finds the service providers in a shorter time than the parametric classification. On the other hand, if the service providers vary their service offering even a small percentage, then case-based reasoning performs worse than the parametric model.

The rest of this paper is organized as follows: Section 2 gives a brief overview of our representation of experiences and Section 3 explains how agents interact to exchange their experiences. Section 4 and Section 5 explain parametric classification using Gaussian model and case-based reasoning respectively and how they can be used for selecting providers using a set of experiences. Section 6 explains our experimental setup, simulations, and results of comparisons. Section 7 summarizes our contribution and compares it to relevant literature.

2   Representation of Experiences

Rating-based approaches reflect the subjective opinion of the raters. Even though the context of the ratings is explicitly expressed, these ratings may still mislead the consumers, because the satisfaction criteria of the consumer using these ratings may be different from the satisfaction criteria of those who give the ratings. Even if their service interests are the same, consumers rate the same service differently depending on their satisfaction criteria. The main question at this point is how to get rid of subjectiveness of ratings in the service selection.

Instead of ratings, consumers can record their interactions with service providers in a great detail within an experience structure [3]. An experience contains the consumer's service demand and the provided service in response to the service demand. Actually, an experience expresses the story between the consumer and the provider regarding a specific service demand. So, any consumer receiving an experience can evaluate the service provider according to its own criteria using the objective data in the experience. This approach removes the subjectiveness of the rating-based approaches.

Experiences require representational power of ontologies. For each domain, a different ontology for the representation of experiences is necessary. We represent a base level ontology for domain independent concepts and a domain ontology for domain dependent ones. The base level ontology covers domain-independent infrastructure of the experience ontology. It is centered around the *Experience* class, whose instances represent experiences of service consumers. This is motivated by the concept of experiences in real life. An experience is a combination of what we have requested from a service provider and what we have received at the end. So, in the ontology, an experience consists of a service demand and supplied service for the demand. For this purpose, *Demand* and *Service* classes are included in the base ontology. Both demand and supplied service concepts are descriptions of a service for a specific domain and hence share a number of properties. Domain level ontology captures domain specific properties and concepts. For example, a domain level ontology for online shopping may include concepts such as *hasShoppingItem*, *toLocation*, *hasDeliveryType*, *hasDelivery-Duration*, *hasShipmentCost*, and *hasPrice*. Since our focus in this paper is on reasoning, we do not give the details of our representation. Details of base level and domain level ontologies used for simulations can be found elsewhere [3].

Service consumer will need to interact with other service consumers with similar demands. Since the definition of a similar demand varies from one agent to another, we allow each consumer to define its understanding of a similar demand using the ontology and the Semantic Web Rule Language (SWRL) [4].

When a consumer agent has a particular service demand and a list of others' experiences, then it can apply the SWRL rule to select those experiences in which the service demands were similar to that of her own. If the consumer makes its SWRL rule for similar demands public, other consumers can also use this expression of similarity to reason about whether their past service demands were similar to the demand of the consumer or not.

3   Retrieving Experiences

The service consumers are organized in a peer-to-peer multiagent system. Each service consumer knows only a subset of all consumers in the society and lists these consumers in its *acquaintance list*. An acquaintance list is a dynamic list of service consumers having service demands classified as similar demand by the owner of the list. When a new service consumer joins the society, its acquaintance list is populated with a small number of randomly chosen service consumers. Each consumer collects others' experiences in an *experience repository*. Each time a service consumer makes a service selection, it uses the experiences in this repository for decision making. Service consumers refresh and update their repositories periodically by removing old experiences and adding newly found ones. Initially, service consumers do not have any experiences.

When a service consumer decides to receive a service, it checks its experience repository. If number of experiences in the repository is small, the service consumer collects new experiences. However, in order to collect new experiences, the consumer should have sufficient number of acquaintances. If it does not have enough acquaintances, then it increases the number of its acquaintances by first discovering other service consumers having similar demands and by populating its acquaintance list with those service consumers. This procedure is summarized in Algorithm 1.

In order to discover new acquaintances, a service consumer X uses two messages: *Peer Discovery Message (PDM)* and *Request for Acquaintances Message (RAM)*. Both PDM and RAM messages contain a SWRL rule that expresses the similar demand criteria of the message originator. When a consumer Y receives a PDM message, it checks if its service demands are similar to that of the originator X. If so, it notifies X and X adds Y as a new acquaintance entry in its acquaintance list. This entry contains identity of Y and its demands classified as similar demand by similarity criteria of X. The consumer Y also forwards the request to a set of service consumers in its acquaintance list if these consumers have similar demands with respect to similarity criteria in the PDM message. If there is no such consumer, Y randomly selects consumers from its acquaintance list. How long the request is going to be forwarded is controlled using a time-to-live field. All other consumers that receive the request act the same way Y does. When, Y receives a RAM message from the originator X, it checks its acquaintance list for the consumers having similar demands with respect to similarity criteria in the RAM message. Then, Y sends identities of these consumers to X. So, X can add these consumers to its acquaintance list. After having sufficient number of acquaintances, the consumer uses *Request for Experience Message (REM)* to collect new experiences. A REM message also contains a rule for expressing similar demand criteria of the sender. When service consumer Y gets a REM message from service consumer X, it evaluates its service demands in its own experiences using the similarity criteria in the REM and sends its experiences to X if these experiences have similar demands with respect to similarity criteria in the REM. So, X can populate its repository with these experiences. The details of the peer-to-peer discovery protocol is described elsewhere [5].

4   Service Selection Using Parametric Classification

Unlike subjective ratings, different AI techniques can be applied on objective experience data, because experiences contain much more comprehensive, detailed, and noise-free information. Information in the experiences can be used for the modeling of provider behaviors for different service demands. For this purpose, a parametric classification method, multivariate Gaussian model (GM), is used in our previous work [3]. In this method, a service consumer models each service provider by building a multi-dimensional Gaussian model using the collected experience data. There are two classes

Algorithm 1

1: Check Experience Repository
2: **while** (Not Have Enough Experience) **do**
3:     Check Acquaintance List
4:     **if** (Not Have Enough Acquaintance) **then**
5:         Get New Acquaintances: Using PDM or RAM
6:     **end if**
7:     Get Experiences: Using REM
8: **end while**
9: Select Provider Using Experiences

---

for each model: satisfied and dissatisfied. These classes represent the experiences in which the supplied services are classified as satisfactory and unsatisfactory with respect to the satisfaction criteria of the consumer. Then, for each of the models, a discriminant function is defined to compute the probability of satisfaction [6]. The service consumer performs this computation for every service provider and chooses the provider with the highest satisfaction probability. Modeling of providers may require a high volume of experiences concerning different providers. Collecting that many experiences may be costly in terms of time and messaging complexity.

5   Case-Based Service Selection

Non-parametric methods such as case-based reasoning (CBR) can also be used for service selection. CBR is an approach for problem solving and learning in which old problems and their solutions are encapsulated into a case structure and stored in a case-base. When a new problem is encountered, the most similar past cases are retrieved from the case-base and solutions in these cases are modified to conform to the new situation [7]. The idea is that if two problems are similar, the solutions to these problems will probably be similar, too. The concept of similarity plays a crucial role in CBR.

The most important challenge in the CBR is the selection of metrics for the similarity, because performance of CBR systems critically depends on these metrics. Another challenge is that most CBR approaches are centralized. This implies that ill-constructed metrics for the similarity could drastically affect the performance of the whole system. The proposed approaches in Section 2 and Section 3 can be combined to construct a context-aware, flexible and distributed CBR approach for the service selection. In this approach, each consumer uses consumer society as a distributed case-base. Additionally, unlike the classic CBR systems, each consumer can represent its own similarity metrics using an OWL ontology and SWRL rules. Using this well defined similarity metric, the consumer queries the consumer society for similar experiences using the procedure explained in Section 3. After retrieving the similar experiences, the consumer computes a score for each retrieved experience. The computation depends on the following factors:

- Recency: The new experiences are preferred over old experiences since they are likely to hold again in the near future. For this reason, each experience is assigned a recency value. The newer the experience, the larger the recency value.

- Similarity: This is a factor that measures the similarity of the current demand with the examined experience. The similarity value ranges between 0 and 1, where 0 denotes total difference and 1 denotes identical demands.
- Satisfaction: This is an important factor that measures how satisfied the current consumer agent would be, had it lived the examined experience itself. The consumer evaluates the supplied service depending on its current service demand and its own satisfaction criteria and obtains its expected degree of satisfaction.

We combine these factors using the formula below:

$$S_i = recency_i \times sim_i \times sat_i \tag{1}$$

where, S_i is the computed score for the experience i, $recency_i$ is the recency factor, sim_i is the similarity factor and sat_i is the satisfaction factor. After computing the scores for each experience, the consumer picks the experience with the highest score and selects the provider supplying the service within this experience. This approach is unique from different perspectives. To the best of our knowledge there is no CBR system using OWL ontologies for the representation of cases and there is no distributed CBR approach in which similarity metrics are defined individually by each user using SWRL rules.

6 Simulations

In order to demonstrate the performance of the proposed methods, we implemented a simulator and conducted simulations on it. In the simulator, three types of service provider selection strategies are implemented and tested. Those strategies are shortly explained below.

- **Service Provider Selection Using CBR and Experiences** (SPS_{CBR}): This strategy uses the proposed CBR approach for the service provider selection in Section 5.
- **Service Provider Selection Using Gaussian Model** (SPS_{GM}): This strategy is proposed in [3] and shortly explained in Section 4.
- **Service Provider Selection Using Selective Ratings** ($SPS_{ratings}$): For a new service demand, a service consumer agent can select a service provider using ratings from other consumer agents. Ratings reflect the aggregation of consumers' entire history of interactions with providers. In this strategy, in order to make satisfaction-targeted decisions, a consumer requests ratings only from those consumers who have similar demands with respect to similarity criteria of the consumer.

Essentially, all three strategies actually use information from the same service consumers for a given decision process. These strategies are compared with each other in terms of achieved satisfaction. In the simulations, if an agent decides to receive a service, it uses these strategies to make three (possibly different) selections. As is the case with real world, service consumers periodically change their service demands. If a consumer does not have any previous experience related to her new demand, service decisions become very hard. That is the most challenging situation in the problem we are addressing. To focus on this challenge, the simulations enforce agents to make decisions based on others' experiences rather than their previous experiences.

6.1 Simulation Environment and Settings

In order to compare performance of the service provider selection strategies, a simulator is implemented in Java and KAON2 is used as OWL-DL reasoner [8]. Simulations are run on a PC with 1.8 GHz CPU and 256 MB RAM under Windows OS. Simulations are repeated 10 times in order to increase the reliability. In the simulations, performance of different strategies are measured using two metrics; computation time and average satisfaction ratio, which is the ratio of service selections resulted in satisfaction on the average.

Simulation environment is created using the same methodology in our previous work [3]. Each property of *Service* class in the experience ontology has a predefined range and represents a dimension in a multidimensional service space. Each service provider has a randomly generated multi-dimensional region called service region in this service space. Service region covers all of the services produced by the service provider. When a service demand is made, the provider produces a service within its service region so that the produced service will overlap with the service demand as much as possible. Demand of a service consumer is generated as follows. Demand space is constructed by removing dimensions of service space that do not belong to *Demand* class. Then, for each consumer, a region named demand region is chosen randomly. Center of this region represents the demanded service. If provided service for this demand stays within the margins of the demand region, the service consumer having this demand gets satisfied, otherwise she gets dissatisfied. So, consumers having exactly the same service demand may have different satisfaction criteria.

When the simulations start, agents do not have any prior experiences. As the simulations advance, agents gain and collect experiences. There are several, important factors in the simulations:

Variations in service demand. Each service consumer changes its demand characteristics after receiving a service with a predefined probability denoted as P_{CD} and collects experiences for its new demand. Each service consumer has a probability of requesting a service for any epoch. This probability is uniformly chosen between 0 and 1. In other words, only around 50% of consumers consume a service at a given epoch.

Variations in service satisfaction. Even though a service consumer X regards the service demand of consumer Y as a similar demand, this does not mean that Y and X share the same satisfaction criteria. Hence, a service dissatisfying Y may satisfy X and vice versa. This fact is also imitated in the simulations. A parameter called misleading similarity factor (β) defines what ratio of the service consumers having similar service demands with respect to similarity criteria of X will have satisfaction criteria conflicting with the satisfaction criteria of X. So, ratings of these consumers will probably mislead the consumer X during service selection.

Variations in service quality. Some providers may have nondeterministic nature and may supply marginally different services at different instances of time for the same service demand and conditions. In our simulations, with a very small probability, providers deviate from their expected behavior. This probability is called probability of indeterminism (PI). Think of a provider who usually produces unsatisfactory services for a specific service demand. If this provider produces a perfect service for this service demand in a transaction with a consumer, this kind of indeterminism may mislead the consumers in their future decisions. So, PI is an important parameter in our simulations.

By varying the aforementioned factors (i.e., service demand; service satisfaction; and service quality), we are interested in understanding the strengths and weaknesses of the proposed strategies. The simulation environment is setup with 20 service providers and 400 service consumers. Simulations are run for 100 epochs. Experiences expire after 20 epochs to keep experience repositories fresh and small. The ratio of satisfaction and the required computational time for selecting services are used as metrics to evaluate each strategy.

6.2 Simulation Results

This section summarizes the results of the simulations. There are three primary parameters in the simulations: P_{CD}, β and PI. Initially, PI is set to 0. Note that this shows that the service providers always provide the same quality of service. After setting PI to 0, we measure the average satisfaction ratio of the strategies when β equals 0 and 0.5 as well as when P_{CD} varies from 0 to 1. Remember that the P_{CD} value denotes how much service consumers change their demands. In Table 1, we immediately note that for all values of P_{CD}, both SPS_{GM} and SPS_{CBR} achieve a high average satisfaction ratio, while $SPS_{ratings}$ achieves a decreasing average satisfaction ratio. We had observed this behavior also in our previous work [3]. When consumers change their demands frequently, the ratings they communicate to others about their service dealings may not coincide with the service demands of others. This causes a drop in the average satisfaction ratio. Similarly, when the β value is increased, there will be many consumers with similar demands but different satisfaction criteria. Hence, receiving ratings based on demand will not guarantee satisfaction. Since, $SPS_{ratings}$ is not robust to variations on β and P_{CD}, it cannot be used in real life settings. Unlike the rating-based approaches such as $SPS_{ratings}$, SPS_{GM} and SPS_{CBR} are robust to β and P_{CD}. Moreover, for $PI=0$, performance of these two strategies are impressive and equivalent. Hence, we continue our experimentation with studies of SPS_{GM} and SPS_{CBR}.

Table 1. Average ratio of satisfaction with respect to different β and P_{CD} values, given $PI=0$

P_{CD}	SPS_{GM}		SPS_{CBR}		$SPS_{ratings}$	
	$\beta = 0$	$\beta = 0.5$	$\beta = 0$	$\beta = 0.5$	$\beta = 0$	$\beta = 0.5$
0.0	0.97	0.97	0.96	0.97	0.95	0.53
0.1	0.97	0.96	0.94	0.96	0.72	0.35
0.2	0.97	0.97	0.95	0.96	0.56	0.28
0.4	0.98	0.98	0.96	0.97	0.42	0.18
0.6	0.98	0.97	0.95	0.95	0.37	0.15
0.8	0.97	0.98	0.97	0.98	0.32	0.13
1.0	0.98	0.98	0.96	0.97	0.28	0.12

Although the performance of SPS_{GM} and SPS_{CBR} are almost the same, the time they use to select the providers are different. Figure 1 shows the time consumed by each approach for different number of experiences. For small number of experiences, the time required by these approaches looks similar. However, as the number of experiences increases, the time consumed by SPS_{GM} exceeds the time consumed by SPS_{CBR} dramatically. For the modeling of consumers using GM, size of dataset, namely number of experiences, is important. Size of the data set should be large enough to remove the bias [6]. However, increasing the number of experiences will increase the time required for the computations considerably.

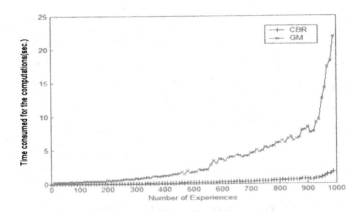

Fig. 1. Time consumed by GM and CBR for different number of experiences

Note that so far we assumed that PI equals to 0, which means that there is no indeterminism in the behavior of providers. So, a provider will either satisfy or dissatisfy a specific service demand all the time. In the settings where behaviors of providers are predictable and free of indeterminism, SPS_{CBR} can easily replace SPS_{GM}. Moreover, in terms of computational efficiency, SPS_{CBR} outperforms SPS_{GM} in these settings. By knowing almost the same or highly similar service demands and the corresponding services supplied by the providers for these demands in the past, a consumer can easily make correct service decisions using SPS_{CBR}. In the origin of the CBR approach, there is an assumption that if a provider satisfies a service demand which is very similar to or the same as the current demand of a consumer, the provider will probably satisfy the consumer's demand, too. When PI is set to zero, this assumption always holds. Providers produce similar services for the same or very similar service demands. These services deviate insignificantly from each other so that the deviation does not considerably affect the consumers' degree of satisfaction. However, in realistic environments, some providers may infrequently provide marginally different services for the same or similar service demands. The experiences containing these service instances may be misleading for the consumers. In order to simulate this situation, PI is set to very small probability values. In our simulations, each provider deviates from its usual service characteristic in favor of consumers with these probabilities.

Figure 2 and Figure 3 show simulation results for $PI = 0.001$ and $PI = 0.01$, respectively. The performance of SPS_{CBR} in terms of archived satisfaction is sensitive to PI parameter and considerably decreases with an increase in the value of PI. However, the performance of SPS_{GM} is robust to variations in PI. In other words, performance of SPS_{GM} does not change with changing PI and it is constant around 100% satisfaction. The performance of SPS_{CBR} further decreases with time, since each time new misleading experiences are added to the environment, the number of misleading experiences increases with time.

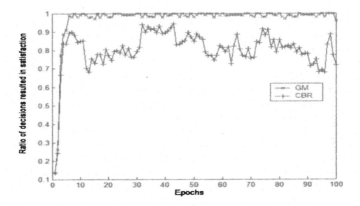

Fig. 2. Simulation results for $PI = 0.001$

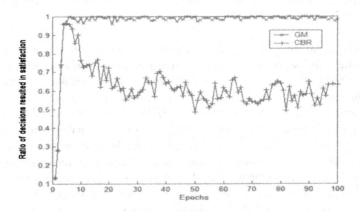

Fig. 3. Simulation results for $PI = 0.01$

7   Discussion

Previous research on service selection is mainly based on ratings, which depend on subjective opinions of the raters. We propose to use ontology-based objective experience data instead of subjective ratings. In our model, service consumers collect experiences from other service consumers with similar service demands and then different methods can be applied on the experiences to make services selections. We have previously proposed to use GM strategy on top of the experience data.

In this paper, we propose a variation by replacing the Gaussian model with case-based reasoning. Through simulations, we show that both CBR and GM increase the overall satisfaction significantly compared with the rating-based strategy. If indeterminism is observed, GM outperforms CBR in terms of average satisfaction ratio. However, CBR runs faster than GM and thus can find service providers in a shorter time.

Yolum and Singh study properties of referral networks for service selection, where referrals are used among the service consumers to locate the service providers [9]. Current applications of referral networks also rely on exchanging ratings. It would be interesting to combine referral networks with the ontology representation here so that agents can exploit the power of ontologies for knowledge representation as well as referrals for accurate routing.

Maximilien and Singh develop a QoS ontology to represent the quality levels of service agents and the preferences of the consumers [10]. Their representation of QoS attributes is richer (such as availability, capacity, and so on). However, their system does not allow reasoning by agents individually as we have developed here. Their ontology can be used as a supplementary ontology to represent and enrich *Quality* concept in the experience ontology.

CBR is used in centralized recommendation systems to automatically estimate consumer preferences. Aguzzoli *et. al.* propose a collaborative cased-based recommendation system for the music market [11]. The proposed system is hosted by an online shopping site. During their online shopping, consumers choose sound tracks and add them to their shopping chart, which is called a partial compilation. The system inspects the partial compilation of a consumer and recommends new sound tracks using a case-base. This case-base is composed of the recorded compilations of consumers, who have previously visited the website and used this system. Matching of sound tracks between the partial compilation and the compilations in the case-base is used for the computation of similarity between compilations. Then, sound tracks included in the similar compilations are recommended to the consumer. A similar approach for recommending restaurants is proposed by Burke [12]. This system is hosted by a website, which records the browsed restaurants as cases and recommends new restaurants to the users depending on their browsing histories.

Limthanmaphon and Zhang propose a web service composition approach that uses CBR for service discovery [13]. Definitions of previous composite service cases are stored in a case-base. Definition of a composite service includes the set of sub-services it includes and relationships between these sub-services. When a user comes up with a new request for a composite service, similarity measure is used to find the closest cases in the case-base. Their similarity is measured by matching the definitions of composite services. Then, the previous service with the highest similarity value is suggested to the user.

As a future work, we plan to study other reasoning methods for service selection and compare their performances with the strategies that we have examined here.

References

1. eBay (1995), http://www.ebay.com
2. Sabater, J., Sierra, C.: Reputation and social network analysis in multi-agent systems. In: Proceedings of the 1st International Joint Conference on Autonomous Agents and MultiAgent Systems (AAMAS), pp. 475–482 (2002)
3. Sensoy, M., Yolum, P.: A context-aware approach for service selection using ontologies. In: Proceedings of Fifth International Joint Conference on Autonomous Agents and Multiagent Systems (AAMAS) (2006)
4. SWRL: A Semantic Web Rule Language Combining OWL and RuleML (2004)
5. Sensoy, M., Yolum, P.: Experience-based service provider selection in agent-mediated e-commerce. Engineering Applications of Artificial Intelligence (in press, 2006)
6. Duda, R.O., Hart, P.E., Stork, D.G.: Pattern Classification. John Wiley and Sons, West Sussex (2001)
7. Aamodt, A., Plaza, E.: Case-based reasoning: Foundational issues, methodological variations, and system approaches. Artificial Intelligence Communications 7, 39–59 (1994)
8. KAON2: Kaon2 web site (2005),http://kaon2.semanticweb.org
9. Yolum, P., Singh, M.P.: Engineering self-organizing referral networks for trustworthy service selection. IEEE Transactions on Systems, Man, and Cybernetics A35, 396–407 (2005)
10. Maximilien, M., Singh, M.P.: A framework and ontology for dynamic web services selection. IEEE Internet Computing 8, 84–93 (2004)
11. Aguzzoli, S., Avesani, P., Massa, P.: Collaborative case-based recommendation systems. In: Craw, S., Preece, A.D. (eds.) ECCBR 2002. LNCS (LNAI), vol. 2416, Springer, Heidelberg (2002)
12. Burke, R.: A case-based reasoning approach to collaborative filtering. In: Advances in Case-Based Reasoning, pp. 370–379. Springer, Heidelberg (2000)
13. Limthanmaphon, B., Zhang, Y.: Web service composition with case-based reasoning. In: Australasian Database Conference, pp. 201–208 (2003)

PROSA: P2P Resource Organisation by Social Acquaintances

Vincenza Carchiolo, Michele Malgeri, Giuseppe Mangioni, and Vincenzo Nicosia

Dipartimento di Ingegneria Informatica e delle Telecomunicazioni
Facoltà di Ingegneria – Università di Catania
Viale A. Doria 6 – 95100 Catania, Italy
{car,malgeri,gmangioni,vnicosia}@diit.unict.it

Abstract. P2P overlay networks have been deeply studied in the last few years. The main problems of such networks are resources distribution and retrieving. In this paper *PROSA* is presented. It is based on a novel adaptive algorithm to build an efficient and semantically searchable P2P system. This algorithm is inspired by human relationships, since social communities possess some interesting properties (such as being "small–worlds") that allow fast and efficient routing of queries for resources.

1 Introduction

Peer-to-Peer (P2P) systems are computer networks where all hosts have the same functionalities and role. In P2P networks there is no difference between "client" hosts and "servers": a peer acts as a "client" host if it requests a resource from the network, and it acts as a "server" if it is requested a resource it is sharing. From this point of view, P2P networks differ a lot from Internet and, in general, from client–server networks.

In the last years the interest for overlay P2P networks has increased, mainly because bandwidth, computing power and cheapness of personal computers allow to implement such kind of "logic" networks. Examples of overlay networks include Gnutella, Freenet [1], CAN [2], Tapestry [3]. Each of them focuses on a particular aspect of P2P computing: Gnutella is totally unstructured, Freenet is practically anonymous, CAN is search–efficient and so on.

Some P2P structures proposed till now face the problem of efficient resources retrieval. In particular one of the more desirable feature in a P2P network is the possibility to perform query based on semantic resource description. Semantic queries are interesting because they are similar to the natural way a user describe concepts.

In unstructured networks, such as Gnutella, semantic query for resource can be performed, but for each request most part of the network is flooded, and there are no response guarantees either if the requested resource is present ([4]). In networks organised as Distributed Hash Tables (DHT) [1][2][3] semantic queries are not allowed, since resources are described by a certain hash of their content or description, so no "semantic proximity" can be neither defined nor used to discover them.

Some recent works [5][6] proposed to organise a P2P network in semantic groups of "similar" peers, to facilitate resource search and retrieval based on semantic queries.

S. Joseph et al. (Eds.): AP2PC 2006, LNAI 4461, pp. 135–142, 2008.

Our attempt is to define a P2P structure in which semantic proximity of resources is mapped onto topological proximity of peers. We propose a P2P network named **PROSA** inspired by social relationships and their dynamics, because social networks characteristics can be exploited to optimise query forwarding and answering. The paper is organised as follows: in Section 2 we point out some interesting aspects of social networks; in Section 3 we show how social relationships arise and how can be used to speed up information retrieval; in Section 4 we discuss our proposal and Section 5 presents a plan for future work.

2 Social Relationships and Small–World

The way social contacts and relationships are arranged, how they evolve and how they end, is matter for psychologists and social scientists research. Nevertheless some studies about social groups and their connections reveal that a "social network", i.e. the network of relationships among people from simple acquaintance to friendship, has many interesting properties that can be exploited in a real–world P2P structure. The Milgram experiment of 1966 [7] showed that a message from a "source" to a "destination" person can be delivered by forwarding it step–by–step to just one of the related people, in the direction of the destination. This experiment opened the research in the field of "small-world" networks [8]. A small–world network presents both small network diameter (i.e. the maximum distance, in number of hops, between two generic nodes of the network) and high clustering degree (i.e. good connections among similar or related nodes). The small–world property seems to be a characteristic of many human communities, such as mathematicians, actors, scientists. Our target is to develop a P2P system using rules and concepts inspired by human behaviours and relationships dynamics.

3 The Social Model

At the beginning of his life, a child has a small number of "social connections": his relatives. These contacts are the only interface between the baby and the outside world and are sufficient to a baby to grow. When a child goes to school, he is introduced to his teachers and class-friends. These relations are new "social links". We can call them "acquaintance–links". Having an acquaintance–link with somebody requires simply to know him. Naturally, not all social links have the same importance: if a child needs to solve a mathematic problem he will probably ask help to his math teacher or to the top student of the class (both of them being acquaintance–links), not to a randomly chosen person. Since the top student of the class probably can be useful in solving math problems, he becomes a "semantic–link" in the field of math for our child. Note that a semantic–link is not symmetric because the child knows that the math teacher is an expertise in the field of math (he solved some problems the child was not able to solve), but the teacher considers the child no more than a person that is probably interested in math (a simple acquaintance–link!): if he is not able to solve a math problem, he will not ask the child, but probably a colleague.

It is clear that a semantic–link is more than a simple acquaintance–link: having a semantic–link with somebody requires at least an acquaintance–link plus some additional information about his interests, culture, abilities, knowledge etc. In real life no great effort is needed in order to establish a semantic–link with somebody: you have just to share a knowledge field or a passion or simply an interest with a person and meet him in some circumstances, have a talk with him and no more. Once you know somebody shares a certain knowledge or passion with you, a semantic–link in that field with that person is established and you're ready to use that link the next time you need information, help, assistance or collaboration in that field. In real life we massively use semantic–links to speed up information retrieval. *PROSA* uses the social model as a reference to build an efficient small–world semantic–searchable P2P network, exploiting the power of social links.

4 Building a Social P2P Network

In a P2P system the performance of searching and retrieving resources is heavily dependent on the organisation of the network.

Our target is to create a P2P network based on acquaintance– and semantic–links, where peers join the network in a way similar to a "birth", then achieve more links to other peers according to the social model, i.e. by linking (semantically) with peers which have similar interests, culture, hobbies, works and so on, and maintaining a certain number of "random" acquaintances. If *PROSA* catches the dynamics of the social model, the resulting network should be a small–world. To implement such a model we need i) a system to model knowledge, culture, interests, and ii) a network management algorithm as much as possible similar to the social model.

4.1 Modelling Knowledge

In *PROSA* , knowledge (each resource shared by peers) is represented using the Vector Space Model (VSM) . In this approach each document is represented by a state–vector of (stemmed) terms called Document Vector (DV); each term in the vector is assigned a weight based on the relevance of the term itself inside the document. This weight is calculated using a modified version of TF–IDF [9] schema, as follows:

$$w_t = 1 + \log(f_t) \tag{1}$$

where f_t is the term frequency in the document. It has been proved [10] that this way of calculating relevance is a good approximation of TF–IDF ranking schema. The VSM representation of a document is necessary to calculate the relevance of a document with respect to a certain query. We model a query by means of a so–called Query Vector (QV), that is the VSM representation of the query itself. Since both documents and queries are represented by state–vectors, we define the relevance of a document (D) with respect to a given query (Q) as follows:

$$r(D, Q) = \sum_{t \in D \cap Q} w_{t,D} \cdot w_{t,Q} \tag{2}$$

Using VSM we obtain also a compact description of a peer knowledge. This description is called "Peer-Vector" (PV), and is computed as follows:

- For each document hosted by the peer, the frequencies of terms it contains are computed ($F_{t,D}$).
- Terms frequencies for different documents are summed together, obtaining overall frequency for each term:

$$F_t = \sum_t F_{t,D}$$

- Then a weight is computed for each term, using:

$$w_t = 1 + \log(F_t)$$

- Finally all weights are put into a state–vector and the vector is normalised.

The obtained PV is a sort of "snapshot" of the peer knowledge, since it contains information about the relevant terms of the documents it shares. The relevance of a peer (P) with respect to a given query (Q) is defined as follows:

$$r(P,Q) = \sum_{t \in P \cap Q} w_{t,P} \cdot w_{t,Q} \qquad (3)$$

This relevance is used by the **PROSA** query routing algorithm. It is worth noting that a high relevance between a QV and a PV means that probably the given peer has documents that can match the query.

VSM is an effective way to represent a peer knowledge. If we take a look at a typical DV, we can see that it gives an idea of the corresponding document. For example in figure 1 the DV corresponding to the manual page of the Unix command "mount" is shown.

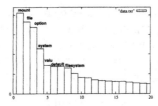

Fig. 1. A sample DV

You can see that the most relevant (stemmed) terms are: mount, file, option, system, valu, default, filesystem. Just six or seven terms give a precise idea of what kind of document we are dealing with. On the other hand if a user is searching for help about the "mount" command, he will probably build a query containing these terms, for example "mount default filesystem"; if a user is searching info about compiling sources with gcc, his query could look like "gcc compile source". The relevance of the first query with the "mount" manual page is about 0.014. The relevance of the second query is zero, since the document doesn't contain those terms (and it is not related with compiling source code!). So we can argue that the VSM is a good choice to rank resources with respect to a given query.

4.2 Managing Connections

In **PROSA** we want to use some principles inspired by observations about natural evolution of social groups. In particular we want to simulate the way people "link" to other people. As stated above, relationships among people are usually based on similarities in interests, culture, hobbies, knowledge and so on. And usually these kind of links evolve from simple "acquaintance–links" to what we called "semantic–links". To implement this behaviour three types of links are introduced: i) Acquaintance–Link (AL) ii) Temporary Semantic–Link (TSL) iii) Full Semantic–Link (FSL). TSLs represent relationships based on a partial knowledge of a peer. They are usually stronger than ALs and weaker than FSLs.

Since relationships are not symmetric (remember the case of the child and the teacher), it is necessary to specify what are the source peer (SP) and destination peer (DP) of a link. Figure 2(a) shows the representations for the three different types of links.

Remembering links. To efficiently use the right link in any given situation, each peer maintains a list of known peers, that we call Peer List (PL). Each entry of the PL contains two fields: an address and a vector. For example, if the network overlays a TCP/IP network, the address of the linked peer is the couple IP address/TCP port. If the link is a simple AL, the peers doesn't know the corresponding PV: in this case an empty PV is placed into the vector field. If the link is a TSL, then the peer doesn't know the PV of the linked peer, but a Temporary Peer Vector (TPV) is built based on the query received in the past from that peer. Finally, if the link is a FSL, the PV is put in the vector field.

A new peer was born. A new peer which wants to join **PROSA** , just searches other peers (for example using broadcasting, or by selecting them from a list of peer that are supposed to be up, as in Freenet or Gnutella) and adds some of them in his PL as ALs. The joining phase is represented in figure 2(b), where "N" is the new peer; N chose some other peers (P) at random as initial ALs. These peers are connected, via ALs, TSLs or FSLs to other peers into **PROSA** , and allow N to start forwarding queries until it meets other peers.

Links dynamics. In **PROSA** links dynamics are strictly related to queries. When a user of **PROSA** requires a resource, he performs a query and specify a certain number

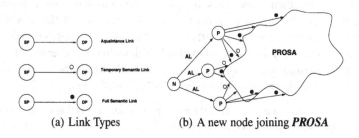

(a) Link Types   (b) A new node joining **PROSA**

Fig. 2.

of results he wants to obtain. The relevance of the query with the resources hosted by the user's peer is first evaluated, using equation 2. If none of the hosted resources has a sufficient relevance with respect to the query, the query has to be forwarded to other peers. The mechanism is quite simple:

- A query message containing the QV, a unique QueryID, the source address and the required number of results is built.
- If the peer has neither FSLs nor TSL, i.e. it has just AL, the query message is forwarded to one link at random.
- Otherwise, the peer computes the relevance between the query and each entry of his Peers–List.
- It selects the link with a higher relevance, if it exists, and forward the query message to it.

When a peer receives a query forwarded by another peer, it first updates its PL. If the requesting peer is an unknown peer, a new TSL to that peer is added in the PL, and the QV becomes the corresponding Temporary Peer Vector (TPV). If the requesting peer is a TSL for the peer that receives the query, the corresponding TPV in the list is updated, adding the received QV and normalising the result. If the requesting peer is a FSL, its PV is in the PL yet, and no updates are necessary. [1] After PL update, the relevance of the query and the peer resources is computed. There are three possible cases:

- No document has a sufficient relevance. In this case the query is forwarded to an-other peer, according to link relevance.
- The peer has a certain number of relevant documents, but they are not enough to full-fill the request. In this case a response message is sent to the requester peer, specifying the number of matching documents and the corresponding relevance. The message query is forwarded to all the links in the PL whose relevance with the query is higher than a given threshold (semantic flooding). The number of matched resources is subtracted from the number of total requested documents before for-warding.
- The peer has sufficient relevant documents to full-fill the request. In this case a result message is sent to the requesting peer and the query is no more forwarded.

This situation is showed in figure 3(a), where peer "N" forwards a query to one of his ALs randomly chosen, since it has niether TSLs nor FSLs. In our example the chosen peer is "P1". As soon as P1 receives the QV, it automatically establish a TSL with N (see figure 3(a)) and then it forwards the query if needed. When the requesting peer receives a response message it presents the results to the user. If the user decides to download a certain resource from another peer, the requesting peer contacts the peer owning that resource and asks it for download. If download is accepted, the resource is sent to the requesting peer, together with the Peer Vector of the serving peer. This case is illustrated in figure 3(b), where peer "N" received a response from peer "Pr"

---

[1] In **PROSA** a TPV is similar to a "hint"; the assumption made here is that a peer querying for a certain resource would eventually find it, and could successfully answer similar queries in the future. So it makes sense to save a weak link to a querying peer, since that link could be useful to answer future queries.

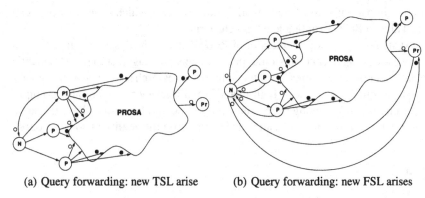

(a) Query forwarding: new TSL arise   (b) Query forwarding: new FSL arises

Fig. 3.

and decided to download the corresponding resource. Note that Pr established a TSL with N, because it received a QV from it, and N established a FSL with Pr, because it successfully received a resource from it.

4.3 Comments on the Algorithm

The algorithm presented in Sections 4.1 and 4.2 is an attempt to model human relationships and their behaviour in a P2P system.

The network management system used in **PROSA** , allows links to move from simple acquaintance to weak relationship, and the algorithm proposed works in a way similar to relationships dynamics in real world. A Temporary Peer Vector can be considered as a partial description of a person you don't know very well. It's just an approximation, but is is better than nothing. It is also worth noting that the proposed algorithm allows the growth of fuzzy "semantic groups". A semantic group is a group of peers with similar knowledges. It is the algorithmic transposition of "social groups". In real life people may belong to different social groups, according to their interests. Peers that are "interested" in a particular topic, usually perform query in that topic. When they receive responses, they acquire new semantic links to peers sharing resources belonging to that topic. This is quite similar to "moving" in the direction of the semantic group made of all the peers sharing that kind of knowledge. On the other hand, if a peer changes his interests (i.e. if different topics are required) it smoothly "discards" links to unwanted topics, because the size of the PL is limited: if new semantic links are put into the PL, the old ones will be gradually pushed out. The PL represent the current "social" state of a peer, a "snapshot" of the semantic groups he belongs to.

5 Conclusions and Future Work

In this paper a novel adaption algorithm for P2P system organisation has been presented. The algorithm is heavily based on observation of the social world. In particular it emulates the way social relationships among people naturally arise and evolve. Our hope is that the resulting system could present some of the desirable properties of social communities, in particular the "small–world" characteristic, which is peculiar of social groups and allow efficient routing and high clustering.

The next step is to develop a simulator of *PROSA* to test the described algorithm. In particular we are going to check if similar peers are clustered together to form "semantic groups" and "social communities". Another interesting research is measuring the quality of responses to query, in terms of both quantity and relevance. We are also going to introduce weighted links among peers, since not all social relationships have the same relevance in a person life, and this can heavily impact on the quality of social groups.

References

1. Clarke, I., Sandberg, O., Wiley, B., Hong, T.W.: Freenet: A distributed anonymous information storage and retrieval system. In: Federrath, H. (ed.) Designing Privacy Enhancing Technologies. LNCS, vol. 2009, Springer, Heidelberg (2001)
2. Ratnasamy, S., Francis, P., Handley, M., Karp, R., Shenker, S.: A scalable content addressable network. Technical Report TR-00-010, Berkeley, CA (2000)
3. Zhao, B.Y., Kubiatowicz, J.D., Joseph, A.D.: Tapestry: An infrastructure for fault-tolerant wide-area location and routing. Technical Report UCB/CSD-01-1141, UC Berkeley (2001)
4. Loo, B., Huebsch, R., Stoica, I., Hellerstein, J.: The case for a hybrid p2p search infrastructure. In: Voelker, G.M., Shenker, S. (eds.) IPTPS 2004. LNCS, vol. 3279, Springer, Heidelberg (2005)
5. Bawa, M., Manku, G.S., Raghavan, P.: Sets: search enhanced by topic segmentation. In: SIGIR 2003: Proceedings of the 26th annual international ACM SIGIR conference on Research and development in informaion retrieval, pp. 306–313. ACM Press, New York (2003)
6. Zhu, Y., Yang, X., Hu, Y.: Making search efficient on gnutella-like p2p systems. In: Parallel and Distributed Processing Symposium, 2005. Proceedings. 19th IEEE International, pp. 56a–56a. IEEE Computer Society, Los Alamitos (2005)
7. Milgram, S.: The small world problem. Psychol Today 2, 60–67 (1967)
8. Watts, D.J., Strogatz, S.H.: Collective dynamics of 'small-world' networks. Nature 393, 440–442 (1998)
9. Salton, G., Buckley, C.: Term weighting approaches in automatic text retrieval. Technical report, Ithaca, NY, USA (1987)
10. Schutze, H., Silverstein, C.: A comparison of projections for efficient document clustering. In: Prooceedings of ACM SIGIR, Philadelphia, PA, pp. 74–81 (1997)

Reliable P2P File Sharing Service

Jung-Hwa Shin[1], Weon Shin[2], and Kyung-Hyune Rhee[3,*]

[1] Department of Computer Science, Pukyong National University,
599-1 Daeyeon 3-Dong Nam-Gu,
Busan, 608-737, Republic of Korea
shinjh@pknu.ac.kr
[2] Department of Information Security, TongMyung University,
535 Yongdang Dong Nam-Gu,
Busan, 608-711, Republic of Korea
shinweon@tu.ac.kr
[3] Division of Electronic, Computer and Telecommunication Engineering, Pukyong
National University
khrhee@pknu.ac.kr

Abstract. A P2P service is a popular for sharing various information through direct connection among two or more peer entities. This service which does not require a dedicated server can be used for finding and exchanging information freely. P2P file sharing systems have become popular as a new paradigm for information exchange. All users who use file sharing service can use shared files of each other freely by equal access privilege. Therefore, P2P file sharing service can suffer from free rider that only downloading without sharing on file. Also, some users can provide malicious files such as virus, worm. Recently, reputation information has been used to solve these problems. Hence, we propose the reliable P2P file sharing service model that can restrict a "free rider" and guarantee the reliability of shared files and users using reputation information.

1 Introduction

A P2P network is a computer network that does not have fixed clients and servers but a number of peer nodes that function as both clients and servers to the other nodes in the networks. By the nature of its architecture, a P2P file sharing systems provide an open and unrestricted environment for content sharing. However, this openness also makes it an ideal environment for attackers to spread their malicious contents. Also, P2P networks introduce a range of security threats, as they can be used to spread malicious software, such as viruses and Trojan horses, and easily bypass firewalls. And, there is also evidence that P2P networks suffer from free riding. Reputation systems are well suited to fight these problems. Reputation-based systems are widely used to establish trust among the members of on-line communities where the parties have no prior

---

* Corresponding author.

S. Joseph et al. (Eds.): AP2PC 2006, LNAI 4461, pp. 143–150, 2008.

knowledge of each other [1]. A user can evaluate the party it dealt with after a transaction, and the accumulation of such evaluations makes up a "reputation" for the involved parties. By these records of earlier transactions, a new user is able to distinguish the trustworthy parties from untrustworthy ones. In this paper, we can decrease the impact of free rider using trust value based on reputation information. Also, we can restrict use of shared files against users that provide harmful files such as virus or worm, low quality file, or file whose contents have no connection with the title. The rest of this paper is organized as following: In section 2, we describe the concept of P2P, the considerations in P2P file sharing service, and reputation-based file sharing systems. In section 3, we describe a reliable P2P file sharing service model using trust value. In section 4, we analyze the proposed model and conclude in section 5.

2   Related Works

2.1   Peer-to-Peer

P2P computing is a novel Internet-based computing paradigm which is being studied widely in recent years. In P2P systems, peers are acting as service consumer and provider simultaneously. Two main architectures of P2P networks are available today, the pure P2P model and the hybrid model [2][3]. Pure P2P models are decentralized without any central server. This kind of system is built on participating peers only, connected to each other. No central administrator unit will be involved to distribute information within the community. The network environment will be formed automatically when peers log into the system and establish connections to other peers. Hybrid P2P models are centralized in the sense that they depend on some central server. This model have the one-point failure problem. The server is not holding any data itself, it is mainly used to organize the network. According to system function, current P2P systems can be classified to three categories : file sharing, distributed processing and instant messaging. In this paper, we focus on the file sharing service.

2.2   The Consideration in P2P File Sharing Service

In P2P file sharing, the balance between resource providers and consumers must be considered. Like their counterparts in the real world, P2P communities depend on the presence of a sufficient base of communal participation and cooperation in order to function successfully. But, in the P2P context, this might mean downloading files but not sharing any for upload, or initiating queries without forwarding or answering queries from others. At best, such behavior just means increased load for everyone else; at worst, it can significantly harm the functioning of the system. A recent study on Gnutella file sharing system shows that as many as 70% of its users don't share any files at all [4]. This means that these users use the system for free. This behavior of an individual user who uses the system resources without contributing anything to the system is the first form of the Free Riding problem. Such users are referred to as free riders. Free riders use the resources available in the P2P network, but do not make any resources available. Free riding reduces the availability of information as well as the level of network performance [5][6]. Reputation can be used to solve the "free riding" in P2P file public ownership service as file or information that can display believability about user. It collects and aggregates the feedback of participants' past behaviors, which is known as reputation, and publishes the reputations so that everyone can view it freely. The reputation informs the participant about other's ability and disposition, and helps the participant to decide who to trust. Furthermore, reputation system also encourages participant to be more trustworthy and discourages those who are not trust worthy.

2.3   Reputation-Based File Sharing System

Reputation, a summary of a peer's past behavior, is a powerful tool for predicting the peer's future action. The reputation scheme helps to build trust among peers based on their past experiences and feedback from other peers. The reputation values will be used as selection criteria among peers. The goal of reputation is to maximize user satisfaction, and decrease the sharing of corrupted files.

Kazaa [7] defines a participation level for each peer based on the Mbytes it transfers and the integrity of the files it serves. Each user rates the integrity of the files it downloads as excellent, average, poor, or delete file. Based on the ratio of Mbytes uploaded and downloaded and the integrity rating of the files, the peers are assigned to three categories: low, medium, and high. The participation level score varies between 0 and 1000. A new user starts at a medium participation level of 100. The participation level score is used in prioritizing among peers during periods of high demand. The security aspects in peers modifying their locally stored participation level values are not addressed.

EigenRep [8] is a reputation management system for P2P networks. Each peer locally stores its own view of the reputation of the peers it does transactions with. The global reputation of each peer is computed by using the local reputation values assigned to it by other peers, but weighted by the global reputation of the assigning peers. This method of reputation inference rules out the possibility of malicious peers maligning the reputation of other peers.

3   Reliable P2P File Sharing Service Model

Our model based on hybrid P2P model. We intend to solve the "free riding" problem and guarantee the reliability of shared files and users using trust value based on reputation information. Also, we can restrict use of shared files against peers that provide harmful files. In our model, the server manages the trust value and shared file list on peers. When any peers query about specific files to the server, the server notifies a peer list and trust value on peers. File requester refers to their trust and select a target peer and request the file download to selected peer. File provider can permit or deny downloading by comparing the trust value of itself with the trust value of provider.

3.1 Notations

- MS : Management Server
- P_X : the identity of peer
- f_i : shared file list
- r_{old} : the latest reputation value
- r_{new} : the new reputation value
- fn_{old} : a number of shared files before transaction
- fn_{new} : a number of shared files after transaction
- GR_{old} : the sum of good reputation before transaction
- GR_{new} : the sum of good reputation after transaction
- BR_{old} : the sum of bad reputation before transaction
- BR_{new} : the sum of bad reputation after transaction
- TP_X : trust value of peers
- dn : the speed of download
- α_X : the ratio of shared files

3.2 Operations

The proposed scheme consists of four steps. At the first step, peers log in the server and register list of sharing files into the server. The second step is a query and response. Peers query to obtain a file and received a response from the server. The third step is download on the file and final step is evaluation on the file and update of the reputation and trust value.

[Step 1] Login and Registration

1. $P_i...P_n \rightarrow MS$: Login, $MS \rightarrow P_i...P_n$: Success
   Peers log in the server and the server identifies a correct user, and then sends the message that login is successful.

2. $P_i...P_n \rightarrow MS$: Register $(f_i...f_n)$
   Peers receive a response message from the server and register the file list that they want to share with other peers. The server maintains following information on peers.

$$\langle P_i...P_n, f_i...f_n, TP_i...TP_n \rangle$$

[Step 2] Query and Response

1. $P_i \rightarrow MS$: Query(f)
   The P_i sends a query to obtain a file to the server.

2. $MS \rightarrow P_i$: Info$((P_i, TP_i), ..., (P_n, TP_n))$
   The server sends the peer list and their trust value.

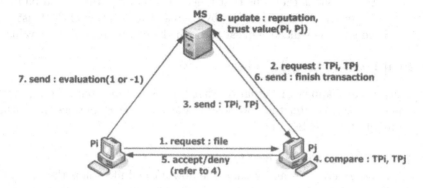

Fig. 1. Download and Evaluation

[Step 3] Download

Fig. 1 depicts the operation of download and evaluation on file.

1. The P_i chooses a peer by referring to trust value of peers and requests information for connection to the peer.

2. $MS \rightarrow P_i$: Send(IP_{P_j}, pn_{P_j})
   The server sends the message including IP address and port number of the P_j.

3. $P_i \rightarrow P_j$: Request(f)
   The P_i sends the message about file download to the P_j using the information received from the server.

4. $P_j \rightarrow MS$: Request(TP_i, TP_j)
   Before the P_j permit downloading to the P_i, he requests the trust value of the P_i and P_j to the server.

5. P_j : Compare(TP_i, TP_j)
   The server sends the trust value to the P_j and P_j compare itself trust value with the trust value of P_i.

6. $P_j \rightarrow P_i$: download accept/deny
   If the trust value of the P_i is greater than the trust value of the P_j, the P_j permit the downloading, else denies it.

$$TP_i \geq TP_j : \text{permit downloading request}$$
$$TP_i < TP_j : \text{deny downloading request}$$

By the trust value is the value that reflect on good reputation and bad reputation, peer can select the target peer by means of verification of the trust value and he decides the download request through the comparison of trust value.

[Step 4] Evaluation and Update

1. Since it can happen the situation that the P_i does not send the reputation value on the P_j, after the download is finished, the P_j notifies the finish of transaction to the Server.

2. $P_i \rightarrow MS$: $Send(r_{P_j} : 1 \text{ or } -1)$
   After the P_i executes and verifies the downloaded file, sends the reputation on the P_j. If the file is executed correctly and is identical with the requesting file, the P_i sends 1, otherwise -1. The server receives the transaction finish message from the P_j. And then, if the server does not receive the reputation value of the P_j for a specified period of time, he increased the bad reputation value of the P_i by the ratio of shared files.

3. MS : $Update(GR_{P_i}, BR_{P_i}, TP_i, \alpha_{P_i}, GR_{P_j}, BR_{P_j}, TP_j, \alpha_{P_i})$
   The server updates the reputation value and trust value of the P_j using evaluation value received from the P_i. We can divide update method into four state according to reputation value received from latest reputation and current reputation of the P_j. Table 1 depicts the update of reputation value on file provider.

Table 1. Reputation update of the file provider

r_{old}	r_{new}	GR	BR
1	1	$GR_{old} + |r_{new}| * \alpha$	BR_{old}
1	-1	GR_{old}	$BR_{old} + |r_{new}|$
-1	1	$GR_{old} + |r_{new}|$	BR_{old}
-1	-1	GR_{old}	$BR_{old} + |r_{new}| * \alpha$

If the P_j received the good evaluation from latest transaction and current transaction, we increased by α the good reputation of the P_j. On the other hand, if the P_j received the bad evaluation from latest transaction and current transaction, we increased by α the bad reputation of the P_j. If peers received different evaluation value from latest transaction and current transaction, we reflect on evaluation value received from current transaction.

By the α is the ratio of shared files, we use to give peers incentive. The computation of α is as follows.

$$\alpha = \frac{fn_{old}}{fn_{new}}$$

The computation of the P_j's trust value based on good and bad reputation is as follows.

$$TP_j = \frac{GR_{new} - |BR_{new}|}{GR_{new} + |BR_{new}|} * dn_{P_j}$$

The reputation value of file requester(P_i) is computed as follows.

$$GR_{new} = GR_{old} * \alpha$$
$$BR_{new} = BR_{old} + \alpha$$

If the P_i sent the evaluation on the P_j, we decrease by α the good reputation of the P_i. If the P_i does not send the evaluation, we increase the bad reputation of the P_i. Therefore, the trust value of the P_i decreases.

4   Analysis

In this paper, we can solve the "free riding" problem using trust value based on reputation information. Also, we can restrict use of shared files against users that provide malicious file including virus or worm, low quality file, or file whose contents have no connection with title. Therefore, we can guarantee the reliability of shared files and peers. We have performed experiment to show the effect of the proposed scheme on change of trust value on peers. Simulation parameters are as follows. a number of peers : 7, a number of shared files : 100, upload rate (100%, 80%, 60%, 40%, 0%), initial reputation and trust value : 1. Fig. 2 depict the change of trust value on peers through simulation.

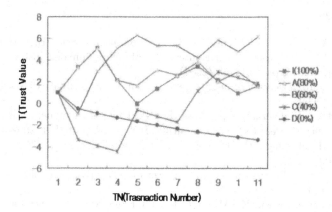

Fig. 2. The change of trust value on peers

If peers upload the file and receive the good reputation continuously, their trust value increase. On the other hand, if peers upload the file and receive the bad reputation from many peers, their reputation value decrease gradually.

Therefore, we can know that when peers provide the file and received the good reputation,their reputation increase.

Our model manages the reputation and trust value of peer using the server. Therefore, peer can not manipulate the reputation and trust value themselves and can trust the reputation and trust value that is provided by the server. Also, if a peer does not send the evaluation on the file provider after the transaction, the server decreases the reputation value of the file requester.

5 Conclusion

In this paper, we diminished the impact of free riders and malicious users by comparing the trust value of peers. In our model, if peers do not share files, they can not obtain download authority for the shared files of other peers with low trust value. Also, if peers share harmful files, they received a bad reputation from file requester and restricted download authority. Therefore, we can improve the reliability on shared files among peers and restrict the participation of free rider and malicious user by referring to the trust value of peers.

Acknowledgement

This research was supported by the Program for the Training of Graduate Students in Regional Innovation which was conducted by the Ministry of Commerce Industry and Energy of the Korean Government.

This work was supported by grant No. R01-2006-000-10260-0 from the Basic Research Program of the Korea Science and Engineering Foundation.

References

1. Selcuk, A.A., Uzun, E., Pariente, M.R.: A Reputation-Based Trust Management System for P2P Networks. In: IEEE International Symposium on Cluster Computing and the Grid, 2004, pp. 251–258 (2004)
2. Aslund, J.: Authentication in peer-to-peer system, Undergraduate thesis, Linkoping University (2002)
3. Milojicic, D.S., Kalogeraki, V., Lukose, R., Nagaraja, K., Pruyne, J., Richard, B., Rollins, S., Xu, Z.: Peer-to-Peer Computing, HP TechReport HPL-2002-57 (2002)
4. Adar, E., Humberman, B.: Free Riding on Gnutella,TechRept:SSL-00-63,Xerox PARC (2000)
5. Oram, A.: Peer-to-Peer:Harnessing the Power of Disruptive Technologies. O'Reilly, Sebastopol (2002)
6. Golle, P., Leyton-Brown, K., Mironov, I., Lillibridge, M.: Incentives for sharing in peer-to-peer networks. In: Fiege, L., Mühl, G., Wilhelm, U.G. (eds.) WELCOM 2001. LNCS, vol. 2232, pp. 75–87. Springer, Heidelberg (2001)
7. Kazaa, http://www.kazaa.com
8. Kamvar, S.D., Schlosser, M., Garcia-Molian, H.: EigenRep:Reputation Management in P2P Networks. In: Proceedings of the 12th International World Wide Web Conference, pp. 123–134. ACM Press, New York (2003)

Studying Viable Free Markets in Peer-to-Peer File Exchange Applications without Altruistic Agents

David Cabanillas and Steven Willmott

Technical University of Catalonia,
Software department,
Campus Nord, Omega building
Jordi Girona Salgado, 1-3
Barcelona (08034), Spain
{dconrado,steve}@lsi.upc.edu

Abstract. File sharing networks are among the most popular applications of Peer-to-Peer (P2P) technology to date [1] and have been widely studied in terms of performance, behavior, topology and other properties. A persistent theme throughout this research has been the evidence that many P2P file sharing systems rely on the presence of *altruistic users*, who provide files, network capacity or some other goods without obvious personal gain and are potentially damaged by the presence of too many *free-riders* (users who consume resources but do not provide to others in return). In this paper we will explore the use of simple market mechanisms for P2P file sharing which function without the need of altruistic users and consider the conditions under which such markets may be viable.

1 Introduction

Many P2P file sharing systems are known to rely heavily on the presence of *altruistic* users which act as sources for content which benefits others but not necessarily themselves [2][1]. But experiences with P2P file sharing systems confirms that large resources owners are not always altruistic [4]. Economic market based systems have been proposed widely (and in some trial systems also adopted [5]), as a regulatory mechanism to provide incentives for users to provide content/resources to a system rather than relying on the altruism to others. Systems such as Karma [6] and MojoNation[2] are well known for introducing "virtual currency" based markets in order to facilitate exchange. Systems based on reputation [7], ranking [8], or other means have also been suggested.

---

[1] In some P2P systems a non–negligible percentage of peers were proven to be altruistic. In Gnutella for example, 1% of peers served about 37 % of the total file shared [3].

[2] MojoNation has ceased operations, although information is still online: web.archive.org/web/*/mojonation.net/*.

S. Joseph et al. (Eds.): AP2PC 2006, LNAI 4461, pp. 151–158, 2008.

The majority of the analysis of such systems [9], however have focus on free riders – actors who take more than their fair share of the benefits or do not shoulder their fair share of the costs of their use of a resource – and how to eradicate them. The danger for a system is that the presence of too many free-riders will reduce or force to zero the number of altruists in the population – thus stopping a system from functioning. In this context, an additional question arises: *can a market-based system for P2P file exchange function at all without the presence of altruistic agents?* and if so *what are the conditions necessary for it to function?* It seems intuitive that the answer to the first question should be *yes* since digital content can arguably been seen as a good like any other. However, as is argued in this paper, there are a number of pitfalls in implementing a functioning market system. In the work described, we study the conditions under which a file exchange market mechanism based on a "virtual currency" such as those tried in Karma and MojoNation can facilitate viable file-exchange. The paper is organized as follows: Section 2 describes the environment, Section 3 characterizes different types of markets, Section 4 are analysis experimental results for different market configurations and finally Section 5 provides conclusions and outlook. A longer version of this paper is available as [10].

2 Token Based Markets for P2P File Sharing Environments

File–sharing applications provide the means for interchanges of content between users. Specifically, users typically have in their possession a certain amount of content but they would like to obtain other files they currently do not possess. Other users, in turn may wish to access the content a user may have. In an ideal world, a user would like to obtain all the content of interest to him/herself without incurring any infrastructure costs (note that in certain systems costs for content itself may apply - these are not considered here). Other members of the community however have a similar aim and given that there are inevitably some infrastructure costs incurred from providing content files to others, such as bandwidth, continual connectivity etc. the question arises as *how should these costs be shared between participants?*

Given the assumption that no agent in the world is willing to altruistically incur costs simply in support of the community, as in human economic systems, a balance therefore needs to be struck between a member of the community providing content and their ability to download access content. A powerful mechanism to achieve this is the use of a concrete means of transferable value which can be earned by providing content and spent by downloading it.

3 Types of Market Scenario

A market provides a mechanism to regulate exchange between members of a community in which each member of the community wishes to maximize its utility [11]. A natural step is to create market places which use a type of artificial currency in order to simulate transferable value between users in a system – and hence facilitate exchange. As is shown in this section however, there are pitfalls to doing this. In particular the types of markets envisaged include: Time limited markets, content limited markets, and time and content unlimited markets. The model for file interchange, described in [10], has three main elements: are content distribution, monetary system, and agent behavior. The most relevant aspects to look on as is that the model are:

- The model is composed by two markets. The inner market model used to study the application and the outer market model which models a real world currency.
- Agents select their strategies (offer/download content) depending on the quantity of tokens that they have/do not have via a set of thresholds.

3.1   Time Limited Markets

In this case, the number of interactions in a given market place is limited (time limited). Concretely, this means that in a time the system will cease functioning (for example if all files are exchanged, a certain deadline passes or after some signal is given). In a time unlimited market, members cooperate with the objective of getting a benefit in a long term future.[3] However, when the time is limited, the hope of a future benefit is not apparent because members know that in a concrete time the game will finish.

.To understand the effect of this fact given that players know that a game has exactly n rounds. Then, no matter which round has been reached (say $n-1$) the agent is aware that the currency used in the inner market will no longer be useful after the end of the game. Hence no agent will offer content in the last round (round n). Subsequently this also means that the currency is no use not only after the end of the game but also not in the last round. Similarly no agent will offer content in round n-1 and so forth. By repeating this argument many times, rational agents would deduce that they should not offer content at all. In a simulation where an agent can chose between two strategies, the only difference between the two strategies (s_1,s_2) and (s_1',s_2) is that in the period t the first strategy chooses C (cooperate – offer content) and the second strategy chooses D (defect – not offer content). Until the end T of all iterations the benefits of choosing the strategy (s_1',s_2) will be greater than (s_1,s_2). This concept is clearly analogous in the well known game theory known as the Prisoner's Dilemma (PD) [12] result for games of known duration.[4] The conflict between the individual and collective interests is expressed in this game, which has implications in real life in areas like the policy, society, economy. Concretely the relation is with a subset of PD, named PD with finite repetitions.

---

[3] The shadow of the future [12].

[4] PD rules are explained in detail in [13].

3.2 Content Limited Markets

This hypothesis considers that the content is limited even if time were unlimited. In such world the number of total different content items is finite and unchanging. In an ideal world all members in the market should obtain all content items that they want. If agents are aware of this fact, this goal will not be achieved. When an agent obtains all the content that it desires (satisfied agent) it is conscious of the fact that it has all it may want so a rational agent would cease offering content. The reason is similar to that in the previous case: the agent will, in the future, not derive benefit from the inner–market tokens (IMT) obtained. This fact entails that other non-satisfied agents may not obtain all the content they desire if some of it is held by satisfied agents. The tokens have value for an agent if they can be exchanged for something desirable. Once it is known that there is no more new content to obtain, the value of tokens tends to zero. In turn, this causes the agent to become resistant to offering content before all possible useful exchange have been made. Only altruists would continue once they had obtained everything they needed.

3.3 Time and Content Unlimited Markets

In the previous section it was argued analytically that markets limited in time or/and content function sub–optimally, if at all. In this section, we move on to the case of behavior of the market without these limitations. With respect to the cost of offering a piece of content versus the satisfaction that someone can obtain from obtaining outer–market tokens (OMT), we have the following alternatives:

A. If the cost of offering is less than the benefit obtained: In this case, agents have interest in offering their contents because they can obtain benefit of it in return – a benefit that in the future the agent can re–invest.
B. If the cost of offering is equal to the benefit obtained: In this case, no net benefit is generated through offering content on average.
C. If the cost of offering is greater than the benefit obtained: In this case file exchange generates a net loss for the community over time and most likely for the individual – increasing with the number of transactions carried out.

For the three options above it is probable that A and B could function in some form (although option B only in a very limited manner), while option C appears to be unsustainable in the long run since agents in the system will all incrementally loose satisfaction.

4 Experimental Evaluation

In this section we describe a number of simulations which help to clarify the nature of the dynamics of a token–based P2P market under the scenarios listed in the previous section – Time and content unlimited markets.

Table 1. Initial experiment parameters

Symbol	Meaning	Value
A	n of agents	200
F	n of files	200
C	n of categories	5
CxA	n of categories x agents	2
$Cimt_{f_x}$	Cost per file (IMT)	500
$Bimt_{f_x}$	Benefit per file (IMT)	500
$Comt_{f_x}$	Cost per file (OMT)	Minimum $Bomt_{f_x}$
$Bomt_{f_x}$	Benefit per file (OMT)	Greater than $Comt_{f_x}$

Agents in the system[5] do not act altruistically[6] and this is concretely inter-
preted as a fixed rule: agents only offer content to generate IMT up to a set limit
(threshold) which is *the level the agent expects to be able to usefully spend on
new content.* Further, since an agent cannot buy content if it has less IMT. By
means of these thresholds, the period where agents offer content is constrained
by need. When an agent has more tokens than supply threshold, none of its content will be offered, although the agent wishes to purchase some content from
the market. If an agent has less tokens than the demand threshold and wishes
to purchase content in the market, it will automatically begin to offer content.

4.1 Experimental Results

In this section we analyze the results of experiments simulating options 2 and 4
above. Different cases considered for option 2 are:

Simulation 1: At this case agents have a quantity of 2900 IMT, near to threshold related with the supply.
Simulation 2: At this case 2000 IMT per agent.
Simulation 3: At this case 600 IMT per agent, near to the demand threshold
related with the demand.

In option 4, three cases are considered:

Simulation 4: Half of the members 600 IMT and the other half 2000 IMT.
Simulation 5: Half of the members 200 IMT and the other half 2000 IMT.
Simulation 6: Half of the members 200 IMT and the other half 6000 IMT.

Figures 1 a) and 1 b) show the cumulative density function of the different scenarios proposed above, in terms of quantity of files exchanged in the system and
times that agents did not have enough tokens to buy contents when they would

---

[5] Table 1 describes the system settings.
[6] However when the system starts to work in the initial state some agents are randomly
selected and forced to offer their contents. Without this jump start, no agents would
offer content initially.

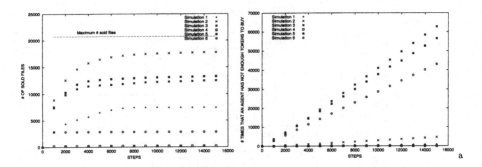

Fig. 1. a) Experiment showing the number of sold files x simulation b) Experiment showing the number of times that agents in the system did not have enough tokens

have liked to (indicating inefficiency of the market as an exchange mechanism) respectively. The first figure shows the relationship between quantity of tokens and number of files on sale. The second figure relates the threshold and quantity of times an agent in the system does not have enough IMT to buy content. Both figures show the importance of the amount of tokens that the agents in the system runs.

4.2   Evaluation Results and Discussion

The simulations show the following results:

- The first observation is that at the beginning all simulations show a significant increase of activity due to different facts: initially, agents have enough money to buy at least one file; also we may think about many agents having an interest in the content offered by the rest of members.
- Simulations 1, 2 and 3 reveal that the quantity of tokens in the system modifies the behavior of the market, in terms of global number of files exchanged (at satisfaction level). Reviewing values shown in figures 1 a) and 1 b), in a first glance it is shown that in simulations 2, 6 and specially 3, in many cases agents want to buy content but they do not have enough tokens to buy anything, showing that it is not a optimum market. Reviewing in detail different steps in the simulation 3, it can be seen that the distribution of tokens is not appropriate to the right working of the system: Some agents pass boundary of supply, so they can't offer anything; and other agents do not have enough tokens to buy content. This creates a deadlock in which potential sellers of this desired content in turn cannot obtain funds to buy the content they desire – a clear liquidity problem.
- Simulation 4 shows that selfish agents can actually prevent the system from working correctly. This occurs because; if an agent have more tokens than threshold supply they will not offer their content. And, in this case, the remaining agents have a number of tokens near to the threshold supply. Hence once a few files have been purchased, they also pass this quantity and

cease offering files. This confirms the stability of market fails in the case of token oversupply.

- In simulation 5, agents that have fewer tokens than the purchasing threshold can trade to move above the threshold. Limited trade becomes stable in token undersupply situations.
- In simulation 6, agents that have more tokens than the threshold supply can trade with agents that have fewer tokens. A transferring of tokens is generated from agents that have tokens to agents who do not have tokens.

Throughout this paper we have discussed which market conditions which are/are not viable for P2P file sharing systems. While the restrictions discussed in this paper do not apply to all P2P systems they may certainly arise in systems. Examples could include: 1) limited content a system of interchange of contents could exist specialized. In particular file categories, 2) limited time markets in special short–term corporate promotions (where tokens loose validity after a certain date) or 3) in time/content unlimited scenarios where the balance between cost and benefit is very narrow. The analysis and experiments show that:

- Markets finite in time or content are likely to fail (either because agents can reason about the eventual collapse of the token currency, or because content is withdraw from sharing to early once some agents gather all the files they are interested in).
- That even in markets with infinite time and content, where token based economies can function, barriers still exist to fluid interchange even if the cost/benefit of trading files is above zero.
- Money supply issues in infinite time and content markets play a large role in success/failure (as implicitly does new content supply). This mirrors real world inflation/deflation/money supply issues in a simple way which is unsurprising. However, in such limited environments, effects are more dramatic and further the existence of upper and lower bounds suggest that optimal values may exist which would need to change over time with the amount of users and content.

The first result suggests that artificial currencies would not be a good solution for time/content limited scenarios and in these cases, despite the added cost/complexity, real currency approaches may need to be used. The second two statements suggests that even in cases where virtual currency approaches could be applied, careful management of the currency in question needs to be carried out – most likely regulating the money supply over time to ensure efficient functioning.

5   Conclusion and Outlook

The results presented here provide a rough classification of types of token-based markets. In order to understand these phenomena in detail however, more work is needed in particular to: establish the range of conditions under which such a phenomena arise, analyze the detailed dynamics of those cases under which the system works. The overall aim of further work would be to explore money supply and market policy issues in order to manage the economy of the inner market to keep it in the identified functional zone. Each of the model changes considered above would likely change the visible market dynamics but the underlying results of a relatively narrow set of market conditions being viable seems likely to be stable.

References

1. Androutsellis-Theotokis, S., Spinellis, D.: A survey of peer-to-peer content distribution technologies. ACM Comput. Surv. 36, 335–371 (2004)
2. Ntarmos, N., Triantafillou, P.: Aesop: Altruism-endowed self-organizing peers. In: Ng, W.S., Ooi, B.-C., Ouksel, A.M., Sartori, C. (eds.) DBISP2P 2004. LNCS, vol. 3367, pp. 151–165. Springer, Heidelberg (2005)
3. Adar, E., Huberman, B.A.: Free riding on gnutella. First Monday 5 (2000)
4. Ranganathan, K., Ripeanu, M., Sarin, K.R., Foster, A.,,, I.: Incentive mechanisms for large collaborative resource sharing. In: Proc. of the 4th IEEE/ACM International Symposium on Cluster Computing and the Grid (CCGrid 2004), Chicago, USA (2004) (accepted)
5. Antoniadis, P., Courcoubetis, C.: Market models for p2p content distribution. In: Moro, G., Koubarakis, M. (eds.) AP2PC 2002. LNCS (LNAI), vol. 2530, pp. 138–143. Springer, Heidelberg (2003)
6. Garcia, F.D., Hoepman, J.H.: Off-line karma: A decentralized currency for peer-to-peer and grid applications. In: Ioannidis, J., Keromytis, A.D., Yung, M. (eds.) ACNS 2005. LNCS, vol. 3531, pp. 364–377. Springer, Heidelberg (2005)
7. Wang, Y., Vassileva, J.: Trust and reputation model in peer-to-peer networks. In: Peer-to-Peer Computing, p. 150. IEEE Computer Society, Los Alamitos (2003)
8. Kamvar, S.D., Schlosser, M.T., Garcia-Molina, H.: The eigentrust algorithm for reputation management in p2p networks. In: WWW 2003: Proceedings of the 12th international conference on World Wide Web, pp. 640–651. ACM Press, New York (2003)
9. Kamvar, S.D., Schlosser, M.T., Garcia-Molina, H.: Incentives for combatting freeriding on p2p networks. In: Kosch, H., Böszörményi, L., Hellwagner, H. (eds.) Euro-Par 2003. LNCS, vol. 2790, pp. 1273–1279. Springer, Heidelberg (2003)
10. Cabanillas, D., Willmott, S.: Studying viable free markets in peer–to–peer file exchange applications without altruistic agents. Technical Report LSI-06-12-R, Department of Computer Science, University of Catalonia (2006)
11. Ranganathan, K., Ripeanu, M., Sarin, A., Foster, I.: To share or not to share an analysis of incentives to contribute in file sharing environments. In: Workshop on Economics of Peer-to-Peer Systems, Berkeley, CA, USA (2003)
12. Axelrod, R.M.: The Evolution of Cooperation. Basic Books (1984)
13. Poundstone, W.: Prisoner's Dilemma. Doubleday, New York (1993) (Based On Work By-John Von Neumann)

Distributed Multi-layered Network Management for NEC Using Multi-Agent Systems

Richard Vaughan, James Wise, Paul Huey, Michael Alcock,
Jonathan Vaughan, Steven Shingler, and Graham Atkins

General Dynamics United Kingdom Ltd.
Bryn Brithdir, Oakdale Business Park, Blackwood, Wales, NP12 4AA
richard.vaughan@generaldynamics.uk.com

Abstract. Within the military environment it is important that effective communication lines are maintained so that critical messages are able to reach their destinations and remain secure. Currently the bulk of the communications infrastructure is preplanned prior to mission start, and requires manual intervention when reality fails to match the plan. The communication systems need to be highly flexible, and adaptable in the face of (unforeseen) hostile and adverse conditions.

We believe that this is where a combination of a distributed agent-based system and a reconfigurable peer-to-peer overlay network can be used help to provide a communication system that is robust and highly adaptable in the face of ever changing and adverse conditions with a minimal amount of planning and enable us to reduce the burden placed on dedicated staff in the field.

1 Introduction

During a military mission, the communications network must be structured to support the commander's intent for the mission in all circumstances, which may change several times as the situation unfolds. The combination of constraints (including very low bandwidth channels, high mobility, zero (or minimal) infrastructure and a very adverse environment) and success criteria [1] make this a particularly challenging application domain.

The management of such a network within a dynamic and hostile environment presents a number of problems to which there is no static or single point solution. No control system can accurately and instantly discover the global state of a network, deduce the ideal global state, and enact a change to the ideal state.

We propose to augment the existing planning and management approach by implementing a distributed multi-agent system (MAS) capable of making delegated decisions about the communications infrastructure on behalf of users[2] which will run on the devices in the network.

Section 2 of this paper describes the current approach to management of such a network, section 3 describes our approach to the problem, section 4 describes

---

[1] i.e. Completion of the mission, irrespective of network performance.
[2] or peer services.

S. Joseph et al. (Eds.): AP2PC 2006, LNAI 4461, pp. 159–166, 2008.

the experimentation environment we have constructed with which to explore the problem space, section 5 defines the military case study within whose boundaries we conduct our experiments, section 6 presents our results and in section 7 we present our conclusions.

2   Management of Existing UK Military Radio Networks

As we discuss in [1], the management of the existing UK military radio networks is a manually intensive, off-line process requiring expert input from signalling staff. The main issues with this management approach are that:

- **Configuration is created off-line prior to mission start.** Flaws in the configuration can lead to invalid communication plans when applied to the devices on the network. These flaws are corrected off-line and the updated plans manually reapplied to the devices.
- **The management applications are separated from the targets of control.** There is a risk that a flaw or network problem that prevents automatic update can can lead to isolated 'islands' which are outside automatic control.
- **Unforeseen changes.** As the situation unfolds on the battlefield an entity might find itself in a position that was not planned to be in. This might mean that it is unable to communicate with other nearby entities as they do not have the correct frequency allocation or cryptographic keys to enable communication. The solution for this requires an element of off-line re-planning and manual re-application of the plans to the devices in the network. However, it may not be possible to get the updated configuration out to the entities in time due to the fluid nature of the battlefield.

3   Our Approach

We propose to augment this planning and management approach by creating a distributed multi-agent system capable of making delegated decisions in a dynamic environment running on the devices in the network rather than simple augmentation of existing logic with agents. The system is capable of determining the appropriate configurations for itself as the system is running, and has the ability to enact the configurations accordingly based on high level plans fed into the system at run-time.

By adding intelligent agents into the system we are able reduce the detail required for the planning stage since the agents will be responsible for the management and implementation of the plan. For example, this means that instead of having to specify which individuals can communicate, the plan can be defined at a higher level so as to identify only the groups or roles that must communicate. Users will be assigned to one or more groups and roles at mission start and identified to the system through their data terminals. The agents are able to fuse this information together at run-time to produce the highly detailed plan and configurations necessary to manage the communications network. This approach offers a great deal of flexibility since it means a user can be removed from one group or role and assigned another while the system is running. The agent system will detect this and be able to reconfigure the communications system accordingly as the (dynamic) policies of the system dictate.

Agents[12], or agent-based systems, are not a panacea but we believe they can provide a more appropriate mapping between the control system and the system being controlled, and allow us to automate many of the resulting control mechanisms. They can also accept delegation of those decision-making and collaborative functions that are more suited to machines than people, easing the burden on operators and providing a management system that can operate in an autonomic[7] manner given appropriate high-level direction[1].

The agent-based system is shielded from the complexities of the underlying system(s) through a layered service architecture capable of presenting information fused from disperate sources and is able to enact the resulting decisions (described further in [1]). The following layers have been identified (see Figure 1):

- An external-facing layer, that will enable external applications to interact with the system as a whole.
- The agent layer itself.
- A P2P layer, which allows the agents to form an overlay network atop the underlying networking and facilitates inter-agent messaging
- A network access layer that allows the agents to influence and retrieve information from the networking sub-system or network management system(s).
- An OS abstraction layer that allows the agent system to interact with the underlying operating system.

We acknowledge that even this MAS will not be able to see the entire network at any moment in time, but, by having the agents know about changes and influences within their local zone³, we 'believe the agents will be able to make informed decisions more rapidly and efficiently than an equivalent centralised system that can only see traffic passing through, or logged to, its local node.

The agents are governed in their decisions and actions by policies. These policies are updated dynamically as the system runs, as well as being defined up-front during the planning stage(s). Policies will be set by the commanders to inform the agents how their section of the network should be managed to best meet their intent. These policies may be further refined by the agents to direct network or system components under their control or influence as needed.

3.1 System Policies

Policy is defined in the dictionary as: *"A plan or course of action, as of a government, political party, or business, intended to influence and determine decisions, actions, and other matters"*[18]. We have refined this definition to *"an expression of rules intended to govern the behaviour of the system"*.

---

³ For example, peers within 2 network hops.

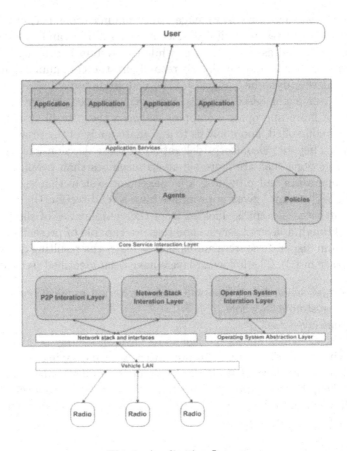

Fig. 1. Application Layers

Having researched recent papers on policy (e.g. [9], [13]), and having looked at some of the available toolkits, we have found no single policy model that embraces all of our requirements and no currently available implementation deals with the adaptive and dynamic nature of our environment appropriately and effectively. This means that we need to extend existing work to create a policy engine and associated verification mechanisms that can operate in our mobile, decentralised environment. Therefore it would appear that the approaches taken by either (or both) Imperial College on the Ponder[10] toolkit, and the work currently underway at DeMontford University on SANTA[11] could be a good base, since, both of these allow for an expression of both management and security policies.

4   Experiment Case Study

Our research has been conducted within the context of the military case study shown in Figure 3: An agile military mission group is moving through an environment where other networks (military or otherwise) are present. The terrain

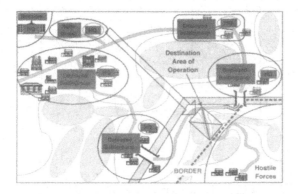

Fig. 2. Basic Mission Scenario

through which the group is travelling contains various features that can block (or disrupt) radio transmissions. The radio network must be managed such that:

1. It is always possible to communicate back to HQ (directly or indirectly).
2. The available radio network is used in the most effective manner.
3. Minor problems with the radio network are detected, analysed, and, fixed.
4. If a fix for the problem is beyond the system's capability, a human is informed to guide corrective action.
5. Most importantly, the current commander's intent for the mission must be supported effectively at all times.

5   Results

Our initial research has led us to implement an initial release of the framework for conducting these experiments and prototypes of the agents and P2P services required by our architecture[1].

We have agents that are capable of detecting simple kinds of interference on the radio network, and of making a decision as to whether the system should change radio channel given the changing nature of the user requirements and environmental conditions. This channel change is propagated across all vehicles considered to be on the local vehicle network.

The agents in the agile group (through the P2P layer) are able to maintain communications with peer agents within the headquarters network. The P2P layer is responsible for the actual maintenance of the network routes and data pipes, but the agents monitor and direct the P2P layer accordingly.

Figure 5 shows how this basic control flow occurs in the system.

1. An application requests access to some resource on another network or vehicle.
2. The local agent talks to the remote agent (via a local P2P service) and requests the service.

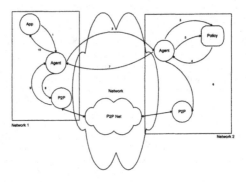

Fig. 3. Basic control flow in the network

3. The remote agent checks the request against his current policies to see if it is allowed.
4. The policies indicate that it is allowed.
5. The remote agent creates a new policy for his P2P service to allow the P2P layer to set the service up.
6. The remote agent informs his local P2P layer about the new policy.
7. The remote agent communicates the access to the local agent.
8. The local agent instructs the local P2P service to setup the user service.
9. The local P2P layer notifies the agent when the user service is ready.
10. The local agent notifies the application that the user service is ready and he can start using it.

The design of our test environment constrains our inter-agent chatter to only that which is necessary, and forces them to use a specific managed pipe (across the P2P overlay network) when it wants to communicate to an agent outside of it's local node rather than allowing the agent-framework to dictate what messages are sent, when, and how. This is important in military networks as the mobile sections are unlikely to have bandwidth to waste, and we do not want an agent to update all of it's peers to the detriment of the networks intended use.

6   Conclusions

We believe that we have defined an authentic case study in which agents can provide a benefit as part of a system level solution. This is important for the agent community, as, without authentic, customer focused, case studies based on domain specific problems, we cannot prove whether solutions incorporating agents or agent-based systems will offer an advantage over those that do not[19].

Along the way we have discovered just how complex distributed multi-agent systems are to implement. Since we have chosen to implement a complete end-to-end system (rather than a section or component of a system) we have had to deal with the complexities of the many interactions between the components that comprise the system and which all need to be defined, implemented, tested, and debugged.

Whilst, at this time we cannot say with any certainty that we have identified a *'killer app'* for agents, we believe that military radio network control systems provide challenges that agent systems are well placed to solve. The flexibility for which deployment of a MAS provides persuasive solutions that are likely to contribute effectively to system level objectives without requiring a mass increase in the workload or expertise of the ordinary users of the communications systems.

The flexibility and complexity of the communications system will increase as new radio technologies promote an expectation of ubiquitous, always-on connectivity and provide a greater variety of connection types and capabilities at each communication node. This particularly applies with reconfigurable software radios ([22], [23]) and the consequent opportunity for selective use of adaptive protocols and policies. At this stage, direct control of radio parameters becomes infeasible, in the same way that pilots of fast jets no longer stabilise the airframe manually when flying.

Our results have shown that agents are well suited to accepting delegation of routine and remedial management tasks currently carried out by signalling staff and are able cooperate to ensure system level changes are monitored and controlled effectively and consistently in a decentralised environment.

Our results also show that the overhead incurred from the distributed solution does not overwhelm or cause the network to be ineffective in normal use. For now this is a binary test of message arrival. We are designing more experiments that will produce more accurate metrics regarding the overheads concerned in benign and emergency use cases. We will present these findings in a later paper.

We are confident that the proposed agent-based approach will enable us to build systems which are more adaptable in the face of change, and that this kind of system provides a sustainable upgrade route, since the agents, and the service layers can be replaced (or augmented) without breaking the overall system [4].

Acknowledgements

This work is supported by the UK MOD Data and Information Fusion Defense Technology Centre.

References

1. Distributed Decision-making and Control for Agile Military Radio Networks In: DAMAS 2005 (2005)
2. Project: Bowman, http://www.mod.uk/dpa/projects/bowman.htm
3. Single Channel Ground and Airborne Radio System (SINCGARS),
   http://www.fas.org/man/dod-101/sys/land/sincgars.htm
4. Clansman, http://www.army.mod.uk/equipment/cs/cs_cln.htm

---

[4] As long as appropriate design guidelines are implemented and adhered to!

5. The FreeBSD Project, http://www.freebsd.org
6. IMUNES, An Integrated Multiprotocol Network Emulator/Simulator, http://www.tel.fer.he/imunes/
7. Autonomic Computing, http://www.research.ibm.com/autonomic/
8. Network Coding, http://www.networkcoding.info
9. An Artificial Intelligence Perspective on Autonomic Computing Policies, http://www.research.ibm.com/people/w/wwalsh1/Papers/policy04-acp.pdf
10. Ponder: A Policy Language for Distributed Systems Management, http://www-dse.doc.ic.ac.uk/Research/policies/ponder.shtml
11. Janicke, H., Siewe, F., Jones, K., Cau, A., Zedan, H.: Analysis and Run-time Verification of Dynamic Security Policies. In: Thompson, S.G., Ghanea-Hercock, R. (eds.) DAMAS 2005. LNCS (LNAI), vol. 3890, pp. 92–103. Springer, Heidelberg (2006)
12. Software Agents: An Overview, http://www.sce.carleton.ca/netmanage/docs/AgentsOverview/ao.html
13. Integrating goal specification in policy-based management. In: 2nd International Workshop on Policies for Distributed Systems and Networks (2001)
14. Network Enabled Capability (NEC) - Joint Services Publication (JSP 777), http://www.mod.uk/issues/nec
15. Schumacher, M.: Objective Coordination in Multi-Agent System Engineering. LNCS (LNAI), vol. 2039. Springer, Heidelberg (2001)
16. Vaughan, R.: Agent Based Routing (not yet published)
17. Multilateral Interoperability Programme (MIP), http://www.mip-site.org
18. Definition of policy, http://dictionary.reference.com/search?q=policy
19. Wagner, Gasser, Luck: Impact for Agents. In: AAMAS (2005)
20. Probability Theory: The Logic Of Science E. T. Jaynes (ISBN 0521592712)
21. Reinforcement Learning Repository, http://www-anw.cs.umass.edu/rlr/
22. Joint Tactical Radio System, http://jtrs.army.mil
23. Next Generation Communications (XG), http://www.darpa.mil/ato/programs/XG/

Facilitating Collaboration in a Distributed Software Development Environment Using P2P Architecture

Maryam Purvis, Martin Purvis, and Bastin Tony Roy Savarimuthu

Department of Information Science, University of Otago
P O Box 56, Dunedin, New Zealand
{tehrany,mpurvis,tonyr}@infoscience.otago.ac.nz

Abstract. This paper describes efforts to facilitate collaborative work in a distributed environment by providing infrastructure that facilitates the understanding of inter-connected processes involved and how they interact. In this work we describe how our agent-based framework supports these. This distributed work environment makes use of both P2P and client-server architectures. Using an example of developing an open source software system, we explain how a collaborative work environment can be achieved. In particular, we address how the support for coordination, collaboration and communication are provided using our framework.

1 Introduction

Distributed software teams are becoming more common in today's software projects, because the teams are based on skill pools that are available in the global community rather than being constrained with local resources. Distributed software development [1,2] involves collaboration of people from distributed geographical locations. This presents challenges in day-today activities in areas, such as co-ordination, collaboration and communication [2,3]. Co-ordination and collaboration can be facilitated by the provision of flexible communication mechanisms. In the context of collaborative work, an important factor that impacts the success of the final outcome is how effectively any issues associated with the shared objective are communicated and resolved. Such communication can be direct, such as face-to-face interactions, telephone conversations, interactions by means of chat tools, email, etc; or they can be indirect through common artifacts associated with the final outcome. In the context of developing an open source software system, the artifacts associated with the final product comprise documents, process models, source code etc. A mechanism is needed that ensures these constantly evolving artifacts are easily accessible to the collaborating partners. So there is a need for a system that provides infrastructural support for the smooth functioning of a collaborative work environment.

S. Joseph et al. (Eds.): AP2PC 2006, LNAI 4461, pp. 167–174, 2008.

We will assume that in a context of an open source software development, a distributed team working on a particular project is composed of a few sub-systems. For example in the development of an operating system, the sub-systems can be developing the kernel, I/O and file system, mail system, networking, a set of tools etc. A number of interested people work towards the development of each sub-system. In this environment the following elements can be useful:

 – A model that represents the functional and behavioral aspects of the project
 – A model that represents the sub-system level activities
 – A model of the communication protocol (Interaction Protocol) between various collaborators

In this paper we describe how these capabilities are incorporated into the collaborative work environment. Using various scenarios we also explain how these features are utilized. To achieve a collaborative work environment and provide communication mechanism between interacting collaborators we use the agent based system OPAL [4]. Using this system we can model each collaborator as a software agent. The Coloured Petri Net [5] formalism is used to model the activities of the collaborators as well as the communication protocols. These models are presented in more detail in Section 3.2.

2   Background

To develop the infrastructure needed for collaborative work environments we have used Coloured Petri nets to represent process models and software agents as the building block for providing P2P support. We use Coloured Petri nets (CPN) as a formalism to model workflows in our system. The mathematical foundation behind the Coloured Petri nets makes it a useful tool for modeling distributed systems. A detailed description of CPNs can be found in [5].

We have used software agents to build our system. Some of the commonly accepted characteristics of an "agent" (listed by Bradshaw [6]) are reactivity, collaborative behaviour, communication ability, adaptivity and mobility. An important benefit is that multiagent systems facilitate distributed and open architecture. Such a system can be adaptable and is robust under conditions of local failures and changing environmental conditions.

The next section describes an open source software development scenario and explains how the P2P architecture is used.

3   Collaborative Work in Open Source Software Development

3.1   An Overview of Collaborative Work

In this section we describe the collaborative work associated with an open source software development environment. Figure 1 shows how several collaborators residing in one location (e.g Dunedin), can communicate with other collaborators in another location (e.g Wellington). Collaborators A, B, C, and D may be involved in the development of one sub-system (such as a kernel sub-system), while collaborators B and E are working on another sub-system (such as a networking sub-system). For each of these sub-systems there exists a server to which the sub-system members may commit their internally developed local artifacts. The sub-system servers periodically update their stable releases to the project server.

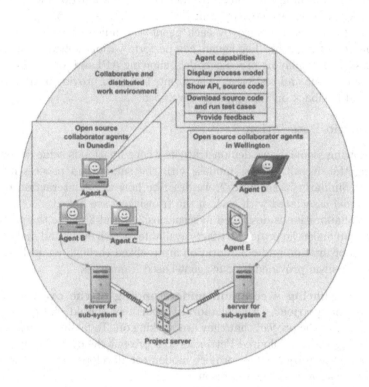

Fig. 1. An agent based collaborative software development environment

There are both inter-group and intra-group communications in the collaborative work environment. However, the inter-group communications may be more frequent, due to a possibly higher level of dependencies between the various components involved. Due to frequent changes in modules during development and the need to integrate the related modules, it is possible that members of a group will access a particular module even when it is not quite suitable for final release. For example, one member may want to obtain the API of a module, or the supporting document such as the specification, associated test cases and so on. In these circumstances the members can obtain a pre-release module for preliminary testing from the module developer directly using P2P communication. The members can thus publish pre-release modules that can be accessed by another module for integration and testing purpose. If there are any conflicts in terms of the expected interface and the current interface, it can be sent as a comment or feedback to the developer of that particular module.

On comparing with the work done by other researchers [1,2,3], our approach provides a formal and uniform way of communication mechanism between the peers by using Interaction Protocols. In addition, the collaborative agent has a built-in knowledge of the system interfaces and dependencies. This knowledge can be used in informing the collaborators to take certain actions when required in the context of software development (explained in scenario 5).

The functionalities provided by each agent are indicated inside the callout box at the top of Figure 1. The agents can perform various software engineering activities such as displaying process models, showing API and source code, downloading source code and test cases. The agents can then provide notifications on updates and feedback on the artifacts developed.

3.2   Scenario Description

In the following scenarios we demonstrate how coordination is achieved by interconnecting the overall process models with the sub-system process model in scenario 1. Similarly in scenario 2, we describe how agent interaction protocol and the model associated with each of the transitions are linked.

Group collaboration is described in scenarios 3, 4 and 5 where the participating agents can make the project artifacts available to each other and make certain requests. Coordination and collaboration are realized through agent-based peer to peer mechanism provided by our agent-based framework.

Scenario 1: Sharing a common understanding of the overall process model of the project. All collaborative partners should share a common understanding of the project that they are working on. To facilitate this common understanding we use Coloured Petri nets to represent the overall structure and behaviour of the project. The project moderator develops the process model (through discussion with related resources).

The project manager sends an XML-based process model via agent based communication modes to all the participants. The participant agents can then display the process model. The collaborators can modify the process models and send the result to the moderator agent. The moderator agent collates various process models and sends the models again to all the participants for choosing the suitable process model (perhaps by consensus).

For example the model shown in Figure 2 describes the overall project structure and the dependencies between various components. This model shows that the project is partitioned into three sub-systems, s1, s2 and s3. It can be observed that s1 and s2 can be performed concurrently. The diagram also shows that s3 depends on s1 and s2. Each sub-system in turn is represented using a CPN model which results in a hierarchy of process models that describe the overall model of the system.

Scenario 2: The process associated with the communication between agents. The generic process model describing how agents communicate with

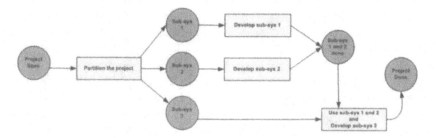

Fig. 2. Model associated with message handling (communication) in each agent

each other is given in Figure 3. Note that the interaction between collaborating members of the software development team are represented in the model by interactions between software agents, representing those team members. Each model can be executed by a collaborator agent [7] which makes use of JFern [8], a Petri net engine. The collaborator agent performs the following operations:

– Receive and parse the requests coming from other collaborator agents
– Send results to other collaborator agents

There exists a message dispatcher in the agent based framework that dispatches messages that reach the "out" node shown in Figure 3. All messages coming to a particular agent will be accumulated in the "in" node of that agent and out-going message will be placed in the "out" node of that agent [9].

When an agent recognizes a message in its "in" node, it evaluates which transition should be invoked based on information received. Each of these top-level transitions may be considered as an abstraction for a more detailed sub-model Petri net that represents a refinement of the top-level abstraction. For example the processRequest transition expands to a sub-model where the decision regarding which type of request is handled (such as show API or download source code activity) can be invoked. Once the activity is performed, the control is returned to the parent process model's transition.

Scenario 3: Group configuration. In our agent based framework, for each project, a moderator agent is created. Our framework uses OPAL's JXTA implementation [10] to facilitate peer to peer communication which allows for agent discovery, joining and leaving. Collaborator agents can join a given project by searching the projects listed in the directory service of the system. In doing so, the collaborator agents interact with the moderator (such as finding details about the overall process model). Similarly, a sub-system can be formed when one of the collaborator agents itself, chooses to become a moderator. The newly joining agents can then decide to join this specific group to implement a particular sub-system. It is also possible that one collaborator agent can be a part of two sub-systems.

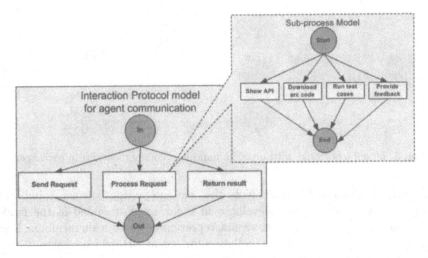

Fig. 3. Model associated with message handling (communication) in each agent

When changes are made to the artifacts produced by each sub-system, its members are notified. Also, the changes will be published to other sub-system members that have subscribed to receive these changes.

Scenario 4: Making artifacts available to the collaborators. Development team members working on each sub-system can publish their requirement specifications, API's, source code, test cases, test results etc. using a Web Service. The collaborator agents are notified of any changes made to these services. When need arises an agent can connect to a Web Service and retrieve required information. For example agent A, who is interested in updates from agent B and C, receives the notification of updates from B and C. When needed, agent A can make use of that information.

Scenario 5: Details associated with accomplishing different types of requests. Recall that Figure 1 shows that each collaborator agent can perform various services such as display process model, show API, download source code, run test cases etc. Here we describe how a collaborator agent can run test cases in a distributed environment. Assume that there are three agents belonging to three different sub-groups. Assume that agent A has to test the modules developed by B and C (as A's module interfaces both B and C). Agent A has the basic knowledge of their dependencies and can only test when both B and C have notified that their code is ready to be tested. When both the notifications are received, Agent A requests and receives the API documentation from both B and C. Agent A tests the modules developed by B and C which are exposed as Web Services and sends the results (bug report) to B and C. B and C can resolve the issues raised by A. Here we are assuming that B and C have not made any changes to their interfaces. If B has changed the interface for the module that is being developed, then A should modify the test cases and B should incorporate the changes in the Web Service that is exposed for A to test.

3.3 Infrastructural Components

In our framework the communication between agents takes place by using the infrastructure provided by the OPAL framework. Each collaborative worker in our system is represented by an agent. Each of these agents is made up of micro-agents [7]. Each micro-agent can perform certain roles. These roles could be displaying the user interface (UI micro-agent), providing communication (communications micro-agent) and process information (process micro-agent). The agents send each other messages, the contents of which are usually text-based. In our system we also use agents to execute process models.

This approach is open and scalable, since new participants may easily join the collaboration environment by registering themselves with the project moderator. The newly joined participants can interact with other team members as long as they use the agent-based infrastructure.

4   Conclusions and Future Work

In this paper we have described how an agent-based system can be used to facilitate a collaborative P2P work environment. Using different scenarios, we have demonstrated how agents can be used to coordinate, collaborate, and communicate with each other in the context of a distributed software development environment, such as an open source project. This paper reports work in progress. We acknowledge that not all possible scenarios in distributed work environment have been accommodated. In the future we plan to port the system, so that it can make use of PDAs while keeping in mind the limited capabilities of smaller devices [10].

References

1. Gutwin, C., Penner, R., Schneider, K.: Group awareness in distributed software development. In: CSCW 2004: Proceedings of the 2004 ACM conference on Computer supported cooperative work, pp. 72–81. ACM Press, New York (2004)
2. Froehlich, J., Dourish, P.: Unifying artifacts and activities in a visual tool for distributed software development teams. In: ICSE, pp. 387–396 (2004)
3. Guck, R.: Managing Distributed Software Development (2006), http://www.stickyminds.com/
4. Purvis, M.K., Cranefield, S., Nowostawski, M., Carter, D.: Opal: A Multi-Level Infrastructure for Agent-Oriented Software Development. In: The information science discussion paper series no 2002/01, Department of Information Science, University of Otago, Dunedin, New Zealand (2002)
5. Jensen, K.: Coloured Petri Nets - Basic Concepts, Analysis Methods and Practical Use, Volume 1: Basic Concepts. In: EATCS Monographs on Theoretical Computer Science, Springer, Heidelberg (1992)
6. Bradshaw, J.: An Introduction to Software Agents. In: Bradshaw, J. (ed.) Software Agents, pp. 3–46. MIT Press, Cambridge (1997)

7. Nowostawski, Mariusz Purvis, M.K., Cranefield, S.: KEA - Multi-level Agent Infrastructure. In: Dunin-Keplicz, B., Nawarecki, E. (eds.) CEEMAS 2001. LNCS (LNAI), vol. 2296, pp. 355–362. Springer, Heidelberg (2002)
8. Nowostawski, M.: JFern - Java-based Petri Net framework (2003), http://sourceforge.net/projects/jfern/
9. Purvis, M., Purvis, M., Haidar, A., Savarimuthu, B.T.R.: A distributed workflow system with autonomous components. In: Barley, M.W., Kasabov, N. (eds.) PRIMA 2004. LNCS (LNAI), vol. 3371, pp. 193–205. Springer, Heidelberg (2005)
10. Purvis, M., Garside, N., Cranefield, S., Nowostawski, M., Oliveira, M.: Multi-agent System Technology for P2P Applications on Small Portable Devices. In: Moro, G., Bergamaschi, S., Aberer, K. (eds.) AP2PC 2004. LNCS (LNAI), vol. 3601, Springer, Heidelberg (2005)

A Peer to Peer Grid Computing System Based on Mobile Agents

Joon-Min Gil[1] and Sung-Jin Choi[2]

[1] Department of Computer Science Education, Catholic University of Daegu
330 Geumnak, Hayang-eup, Gyeongsan-si, Gyeongbuk 712-701, Korea
jmgil@cu.ac.kr
[2] Department of Computer Science and Engineering, Korea University
5-1 Anam-dong, Sungbuk-ku, Seoul 136-701, Korea
lotieye@disys.korea.ac.kr

Abstract. In a peer to peer grid computing system, volunteers (i.e., re-source provides) with heterogeneous properties can freely join and leave in the middle of their computation. Thus, the system should be adaptive to a dynamic changing environment. In particular, scheduling, result cer-tification, and replication mechanisms must be dynamic and adaptive in such a system. In this paper, we propose a new peer to peer grid com-puting system based on mobile agents. The proposed system constructs volunteer groups according to volunteers' dynamic properties such as service time, availability, and credibility. For each volunteer groups, dif-ferent scheduling, result certification, replication mechanisms are used. These mechanisms are implemented as mobile agents and are conducted in a decentralized way.

1 Introduction

A peer to peer grid computing system is a platform that achieves a high through-put computing by harvesting a number of idle desktop computers owned by indi-viduals (i.e., volunteers) at the edge of the Internet using peer to peer computing technologies [1,2]. It usually supports embarrassingly parallel applications that consist of a lot of instances of the same computation with each own data.

A peer to peer grid computing is complicated by heterogeneous capabilities, failures, volatility (i.e., intermittent presence), and lack of trust [3,4]. The volun-teers that are based on desktop computers at the edge of Internet, have various capabilities (i.e., CPU, memory, network bandwidth, and latency), and are ex-posed to link and crash failures. Moreover, they are free to join and leave in the middle of execution without any constraints. Accordingly, they have various volunteering times, and *public execution* (i.e., the execution of a task as a volun-teer) can be stopped arbitrarily on account of unexpected leave. Since volunteers are not totally dedicated to a peer to peer grid computing system, the public execution can be temporarily suspended by *private execution* (i.e., the execution of a private job as a personal user). These unstable situations lead to the delay and blocking of the execution of tasks. This paper regards these situations as

S. Joseph et al. (Eds.): AP2PC 2006, LNAI 4461, pp. 175–186, 2008.
© Springer-Verlag Berlin Heidelberg 2008

volunteer autonomy failures. Volunteers have different occurrence rates for volunteer autonomy failures according to their execution behaviors. Moreover, a peer to peer grid computing system suffers from the corrupted results executed by malicious volunteers. This is due to the voluntary participation of volunteers without any constraints. Consequently, the system must detect and tolerate the erroneous results to guarantee reliable execution from such an untrustworthy environment. These distinct features make it difficult for a volunteer server to schedule tasks and manage volunteers.

In order to improve the reliability of computation and gain better performance, the peer to peer grid computing system should adapt to dynamic environment. However, existing systems do not provide adaptive and dynamic scheduling, result certification, and replication mechanisms per group basis. In addition, their mechanisms are performed only by the volunteer server in a centralized way. As a result, existing systems have high overhead and deteriorate overall performance. To solve the problems, we propose a new peer to peer grid computing system based on mobile agents. The proposed system applies different scheduling, result certification, replication algorithms to the volunteer groups that are classified on the basis of their properties such as volunteering service time, availability, and credibility; the different algorithms are implemented as mobile agents and are conducted in a decentralized way.

This paper organized as follows. Section 2 presents why mobile agents are used and describes our execution model. Section 3 presents a peer to peer grid computing system based on mobile agents in detail. In Section 4, implementation and evaluation for our mechanism will be presented. Finally, our conclusion is given in Section 5.

2   System Model

2.1   Why Mobile Agent?

Mobile agent technology [5] is exploited to make the scheduling mechanism adaptive to dynamically changing peer to peer grid computing environments. There are some advantages of making use of mobile agents in the environments.

1) *Various scheduling mechanisms can be performed at a time according to the properties of volunteers.* For example, these scheduling mechanisms can be implemented as mobile agents (i.e., scheduling mobile agents). After volunteers are classified into volunteer groups, the most suitable scheduling mobile agent for a specific volunteer group is assigned to the volunteer group according to its property. Existing peer to peer grid computing systems, however, cannot apply various scheduling mechanisms because only one scheduling mechanism is performed by a volunteer server in a centralized way.

2) *A mobile agent can decrease the overhead of volunteer server by performing scheduling, result certification, and replication algorithms in a decentralized way.* The scheduling mobile agents are distributed to volunteer groups. Then, they autonomously conduct scheduling, fault tolerance, and replication algorithms in

each volunteer group without any direct control of a volunteer server. Accordingly, the volunteer server does not further undergo the overhead.

3) *A mobile agent can adapt to dynamically changing peer to peer grid computing environments.* In a peer to peer grid computing environment, volunteers can join and leave at any time. In addition, they are characterized by heterogeneous properties such as capabilities (i.e., CPU, storage, or network bandwidth), location, availability, credibility, and so on. These environmental properties are changing over time. A mobile agent can perform asynchronously and autonomously, while coping with these changes.

2.2 Execution Model

Fig. 1 illustrates the execution model based on mobile agents in peer to peer grid computing environments. In the registration phase, volunteers register basic properties such as CPU, memory, OS type as well as additional properties including *volunteering time, volunteering service time, volunteer availability, volunteer autonomy failures, volunteer credibility,* and so on. Since these additional properties are related to dynamical execution, they are more important than basic properties. In the job submission phase, the submitted job is divided into a number of tasks. The tasks are implemented as mobile agents (i.e., task mobile agents: T-MA). In the task allocation phase, the volunteer server does not perform entire scheduling anymore. Instead, it helps scheduling mobile agents (S-MA) to perform a scheduling procedure. Initially, the volunteer server classifies and constructs the volunteer groups according to properties such as location, volunteer autonomy failures, volunteering service time, and volunteer availability. Next, scheduling mobile agents are distributed to volunteer groups according to their properties. Finally, each scheduling mobile agent distributes task mobile agents to the members of its volunteer group. In the task execution phase, the task mobile agent is executed in cooperation with its scheduling mobile agent while migrating to another volunteer or replicating itself in the presence of failures. In the task result return phase, the task mobile agent returns each result

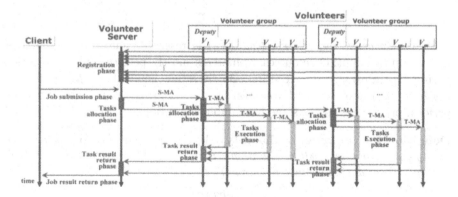

Fig. 1. Execution model based on mobile agents

to its scheduling mobile agent. When all task mobile agents return their results, the scheduling mobile agent aggregates the results and then returns the collected results to the volunteer server. In order to tolerate erroneous results, majority voting and spot-checking mechanisms are conducted. In the job result return phase, the volunteer server returns a final result to the client when it receives all the results from the scheduling mobile agents.

The main differences between our model and existing ones are as follows: 1) The new kinds of mobile agents are considered as the scheduling and task mobile agents. 2) They use the volunteer groups that are constructed according to dynamic properties of volunteers such as autonomy failures, service time, availability, and credibility. 3) Various scheduling, result certification, and replication algorithms are performed simultaneously in a decentralized way. In fact, there has been the use of mobile agents in the literature [6]. However, the migration of mobile agents in master-worker model is mainly considered.

3   Peer to Peer Grid Computing System Using Mobile Agents

This section describes a peer to peer grid computing system using mobile agents in detail. First, it provides the construction mechanism of volunteer groups. Then, adaptive scheduling, result certification, replication mechanisms are presented.

3.1   Volunteer Group Construction Mechanism

To apply different scheduling and result certification algorithm suitable for volunteers in a scheduling phase, volunteers are required to first be formed into homogeneous groups. Our construction mechanism classifies volunteers into four volunteer groups on the basis of *volunteer availability* α_v, *volunteering service time* Θ, and *volunteer credibility* C_v.

Definition 1 (Volunteering time). *Volunteering time (Υ) is the period when a volunteer is supposed to donates its resources.*

$$\Upsilon = \Upsilon_R + \Upsilon_S$$

Here, the *reserved volunteering time* (Υ_R) is reserved time when a volunteer provides its computing resources. Volunteers mostly perform public execution during Υ_R, rarely private execution. On the other hand, the *selfish volunteering time* (Υ_S) is unexpected volunteering time. During Υ_S, volunteers usually perform private execution, sometimes public execution.

Definition 2 (Volunteer availability). *Volunteer availability (α_v) is the probability that a volunteer will be operational correctly and be able to deliver the volunteer services during volunteering time Υ*

$$\alpha_v = \frac{MTTVAF}{MTTVAF + MTTR}$$

Here, the *MTTVAF* (Mean Time To Volunteer Autonomy Failures) means the average time before the volunteer autonomy failures happen, and the *MTTR* (Mean Time To Rejoin) means the mean duration of volunteer autonomy failures. The α_v reflects the degree of volunteer autonomy failures, whereas the traditional availability in distributed systems is mainly related with the crash failure.

Definition 3 (Volunteering service time). *Volunteering service time (Θ) is the expected service time when a volunteer participates in public execution during* Υ

$$\Theta = \Upsilon \times \alpha_v$$

In scheduling procedure, Θ is more appropriate than Υ because Θ represents the time when a volunteer actually executes each task in the presence of volunteer autonomy failures.

Definition 4 (Volunteer credibility). *Volunteer credibility C_v is the probability that represents correctness of the results which a volunteer will produce.*

$$C_v = \frac{CR}{ER + CR + IR}$$

Here, ER, CR, and IR mean the number of erroneous results, the number of correct results, and the number of incomplete results, respectively. The sum of ER, CR, and IR means the total number of tasks that a volunteer executes. The IR occurs when a volunteer does not complete spot-checking or majority voting on account of crash failure and volunteer autonomy failures.

When both Θ and C_v are considered in grouping volunteers, volunteer groups are categorized into four kinds of classes (A', B', C', and D') as shown in Fig. 2. In this figure, Δ and ϑ represent the expected computation time of a task and the desired credibility threshold which a task achieves, respectively.

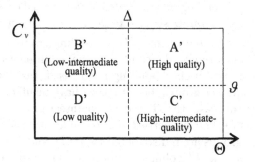

Fig. 2. The classification of volunteer groups

3.2   Group Based Scheduling Mechanism

Differently from existing scheduling mechanisms [7,8,9], our scheduling mechanism is based on volunteer group and mobile agents.

Allocating Scheduling Mobile Agents to Scheduling Groups. After constructing volunteer groups, a volunteer server allocates the scheduling mobile agents (S-MA) to volunteer groups. However, it is not practical to allocate S-MAs directly to the volunteer groups in a scheduling procedure because some volunteer groups are not perfect for finishing tasks reliably. Therefore, we need making new scheduling groups by combining the volunteer groups each other: $A'D'$ & $C'B'$, $A'B'$ & $C'D'$, and $A'C'$ & $B'D'$. In this paper, we consider the first combination in scheduling because B' volunteer group compensates for C' volunteer group with regard to volunteer availability.

The S-MA is executed in the deputy volunteer which is selected among members in A' volunteer group. Accordingly, deputy volunteers have high volunteer availability and volunteering service time. Also, they have enough hard-disk capacity and network bandwidth.

Distributing Task Mobile Agents to Group Members. A task mobile agent (T-MA) consists of a parallel code and data. After S-MAs are allocated to the scheduling groups, each S-MA distributes T-MAs to the members of the scheduling group. The S-MAs perform different scheduling, result certification, and replication algorithms according to the type of volunteer groups.

The S-MA of the $A'D'$ scheduling group performs the scheduling as follows.

1) *Order the A' volunteer group by α_v and then by Θ. 2) Distribute T-MAs to the arranged members of the A' volunteer group. 3) If a T-MA fails, replicate the failed task to a new volunteer selected in the A' volunteer group by means of the replication algorithm, or migrate the task to a volunteer selected in the A' or B' volunteer groups if task migration is allowed.*

The S-MA of the $C'B'$ scheduling group performs the scheduling as follows.

1)*Order the C' and B' volunteer groups by α_v and then by Θ. 2) Distribute T-MAs to the arranged members of the C' volunteer group. 3) If a T-MA fails, replicate the failed task to a new volunteer selected in the ordered C' volunteer groups, or migrate the task to a volunteer selected in the B' or C' volunteer groups.*

Tasks are firstly distributed to the $A'D'$ scheduling group and then the $C'B'$ scheduling group. They are also distributed to the volunteers with high α_v and long Θ. In our scheduling, if checkpointing is not used, tasks are not allocated to the B' and D' volunteer groups, because they have insufficient time to finish the task reliably. In this case, the B' and D' volunteer groups execute tasks for testing, i.e., to measure their properties. For example, the tasks executed in the A' and C' volunteer groups are redistributed to the D' and B' volunteer groups, respectively. However, the B' volunteer group can be used to assist the main volunteer groups (i.e., A' or C') if task migration is permitted. The volunteer group B' in the scheduling group $C'B'$ can be used to compensate for the C' volunteer group with regard to volunteer availability. Suppose that a volunteer in the C' volunteer group suffers from volunteer autonomy failures. If the volunteering time of a volunteer in the B' volunteer group implies the duration of volunteer autonomy failures at the failed volunteer, the suspended task can migrate to a new volunteer in the B' volunteer group.

3.3   Group Based Replication Mechanism

The group based replication mechanism automatically adjusts the number of redundancy, and selects an appropriate replica according to the properties of each volunteer group.

How to calculate the number of redundancy. If replication is used, each S-MA calculates the number of redundancy for its volunteer group. It exploits volunteer autonomy failures, volunteer availability, and volunteering service time simultaneously when calculating the number of redundancy.

In a peer to peer grid computing environment, volunteer autonomy failures occur much more frequently than crash and link failures. Moreover, the rates and types of volunteer autonomy failures are various. Accordingly, the number of redundancy must be calculated on the basis of volunteer groups that have similar rate and types of volunteer autonomy failures in order to reduce the replication overhead.

On the assumption that the lifetime of a system is exponentially distributed [7,10], the number of redundancy r for reliability is calculated by

$$(1 - e^{-\Delta/\tau'})^r \leq 1 - \gamma$$
$$\tau' = (V_0 \cdot \tau + V_1 \cdot \tau + \cdots + V_n \cdot \tau)/n \qquad (1)$$

where, τ and τ' represent the MTTVAF of a volunteer and the MTTVAF of a volunteer group, respectively; n is the total number of volunteers within a volunteer group; $V_n \cdot \tau$ means τ of a volunteer V_n; γ is the reliability threshold.

In (1), the term $e^{-\frac{\Delta}{\tau'}}$ represents the reliability of each volunteer group, which means the probability to complete the tasks within Δ. It reflects volunteer autonomy failures. The $(1 - e^{-\frac{\Delta}{\tau'}})^r$ means the probability that all replicas fail to complete the replicated tasks. If the required reliability γ is provided, the value of r is calculated using (1). Each volunteer group has different r; e.g., the volunteer group A' and C' have smaller r than the volunteer group B'.

How to distribute T-MAs to replicas. The methods of distributing tasks to replicas are categorized into two approaches: parallel distribution and sequential distribution. In the parallel distribution (Fig. 3(a)), the task T_m is distributed to all members (V_0, V_1, and V_2), and then executed simultaneously. In the sequential distribution (Fig. 3(b)), the T_m is distributed and executed sequentially.

In the case of the A' volunteer group, sequential distribution is more appropriate than parallel distribution because the former can complete more tasks. For example, in Fig. 3(b), if V_0 completes the task T_m, there is no need to execute it at V_1 and V_2. If the A' volunteer group performs parallel distribution, it exhibits the overhead of replication in the sense that volunteers execute the same tasks even though they are able to execute other tasks. In contrast to the A' volunteer group, in the case of the C' volunteer group, sequential distribution is more appropriate than parallel because the C' volunteer group frequently suffers from volunteer autonomy failures owing to a low α_v.

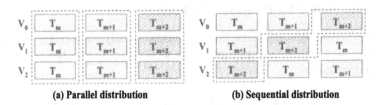

Fig. 3. Parallel and sequential distribution

3.4   Group Based Result Certification Mechanism

Result certification is dynamically applied to each volunteer group as follows: the A' volunteer group has high possibility that produce correct results. If voting is used for result certification, the sequential voting group approach is more appropriate than the parallel one because the former can perform more tasks. For example, in the case of the T_{m+2} task in Fig. 3(b), if first two results generated at V_1 and V_2 are same, there is no need to execute the T_{m+2} task at V_0 because majority (i.e., 2 out of 3) is already achieved. As a result, other tasks can be executed instead of the executions that the solid line in Fig. 3(b) includes. The B' volunteer group has high possibility that produce correct results, but it cannot complete their tasks because of lack of the computation time. Moreover, volunteer autonomy failures occur frequently in the middle of execution. In the case of task migration, a previous volunteer affects the result of the volunteer to which a task is migrated. Accordingly, the migrated volunteer must be chosen among the B' or A' volunteer groups. The sequential voting group is appropriate like the case of the A' volunteer group. The C' volunteer group has enough time to execute tasks, but its results might be incorrect. To strength the credibility, the C' volunteer group requires more spot-checking and redundancy than the A' or B' volunteer group. The parallel voting group is more appropriate than the sequential voting group. Lastly, the D' volunteer group has insufficient time to execute tasks and there is little possibility to produce correct results. Moreover, volunteer autonomy failures occur frequently in the middle of execution. Accordingly, it is beneficial that tasks are not allocated to this volunteer group.

According to the above strategies, each S-MA has its own scheduling algorithm for result certification. In general, the tasks are scheduled in the following order: A', C', and B'.

The S-MA performs scheduling for result certification as follows: 1) Order each volunteer group by α_v, Θ, and C_v. 2) Evaluate the number of redundancy or spot-checking rate. 3) Construct a sequential voting group, or choose some volunteers for spot-checking on the basis of Θ and C_v . 4) Distribute tasks in a way of sequential voting group, or allocate special tasks for spot-checking. 5) Check the collected results.

In second phase, the number of redundancy for majority voting and the number of spot-checking are differently applied to each volunteer group. The number of redundancy for majority voting is dynamically regulated by each scheduling agent. The final error rate of majority voting [7] is evaluated by

$$\varepsilon(C'_v, r) = \sum_{i=k+1}^{2k+1} \binom{2k+1}{i} (1 - C'_v)^i (C'_v)^{(2k+1-i)} \tag{2}$$

which is bounded by $\frac{[4C'_v(1-C'_v)]^{k+1}}{2(2C'_v-1)\sqrt{\pi k}}$. Here, the parameter C'_v means the probability that volunteers within each volunteer group generate correct results.

Consider the desired credibility threshold ϑ. Our mechanism calculates the number of redundancy for each volunteer group if $(1 - \vartheta) \geq \varepsilon(C'_v, r)$. Consequently, the A' and B' volunteer groups have a small r, so it can reduce the overhead of majority voting and execute more tasks. In contrast, the C' volunteer group has a large r. The large r makes the credibility high.

The rate of spot-checking q is also regulated by each scheduling agent. The final error rate of spot-checking [1] is evaluated by

$$\varepsilon(q, n, C'_v, s) = \frac{sC'_v(1 - qs)^n}{(1 - C'_v) + C'_v(1 - qs)^n} \tag{3}$$

where, n and s are the saboteur's share in the total work and the sabotage rate of a saboteur, respectively.

In a similar way of majority voting, if n and s are given, the spot-checking rate q of each volunteer group can be calculated using (3). Our mechanism calculates the rate of spot-checking for each volunteer group when $(1 - \vartheta) \geq \varepsilon(q, n, C'_v, s)$. The rate of spot-checking for the A' and B' volunteer groups are smaller than that of the C' volunteer group. Accordingly, the A' and B' volunteer groups can reduce the overhead, and thus execute more tasks. The C' volunteer group can increase its credibility.

4   Implementation and Evaluation

4.1   Implementation Status

We have developed the "Korea@Home" [9], which attempts to harness the massive computing power of the great numbers of PCs distributed over Internet. Fig. 4 shows an execution screen shot in Korea@Home. Volunteers can take part in one of four kinds of applications: new drug candidate discovery, rainfall forecast, climate prediction, and optical analysis of TFT-LCD. The CPU types of volunteers are somewhat various, but the majority demonstrates similar CPU performance. For example, the Intel Pentium 4 consists of approximately 58% of the total, the Pentium III represents approximately 13%, the Celeron represents approximately 4%, and so on.

4.2   Simulations

We compare our group-based adaptive scheduling, result certification, and replication mechanisms with eager scheduling. For three kinds of cases, we evaluate 200 volunteers during one hour (see Table 1). Case 1 is different from Case 2 with

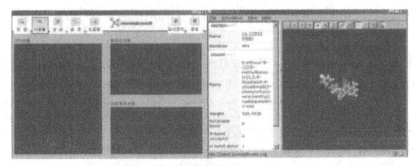

Fig. 4. Screen shot of Korea@Home

Table 1. Simulation Environment

		A'	B'	C'	D'	Total
Case 1	# of vol.	84 (42%)	26 (13%)	70 (35%)	20 (10%)	200
	α_v	0.84	0.88	0.81	0.83	0.84
	Θ	41	17	39	16	35 min.
	C_v	0.98	0.98	0.88	0.86	0.93
Case 2	# of vol.	71 (35.5%)	31 (15.5%)	76 (38%)	22 (11%)	200
	α_v	0.86	0.78	0.80	0.71	0.81
	Θ	35	17	33	16	30 min.
	C_v	0.98	0.98	0.82	0.85	0.91
Case 3	# of vol.	42 (21%)	59 (29.5%)	30 (15%)	69 (34.5%)	200
	α_v	0.80	0.70	0.78	0.69	0.73
	Θ	28	12	25	13	24 min.
	C_v	0.98	0.98	0.89	0.89	0.94

# of vol.: the number of volunteers

regard to volunteer availability and volunteer availability. On the other hand, Case 3 is different form Case 1 with respect to volunteer availability and volunteering service time. Each simulation are repeated 10 times for each case. For simulation, the mean volunteering time of volunteers is selected in the range [10, 60] min. We also assume that $MTTVAF=1/0.2\sim1/0.05$ min. and $MTTR=3\sim10$ min. A task in the application exhibits 18 minutes of execution time on a dedicated Pentium 1.4GHz. The s and n for spot-checking are assumed to be 0.1 and 10, respectively.

Fig. 5 shows total number of completed tasks for scheduling mechanism with or without result certification. In this figure, ES and GAS represents eager scheduling and our mechanism, respectively. From Fig. 5, we observe that our mechanism completes more tasks than eager scheduling for all cases. In particular, the A' volunteer group has an important role in obtaining better performance. As the number of members in the A' volunteer group increases gradually (i.e., from Case 3 to Case 1), the number of completed tasks becomes higher. In contrast, as the number of members in D' volunteer group increases, the number of completed tasks becomes lower. Also, we see that volunteer availability

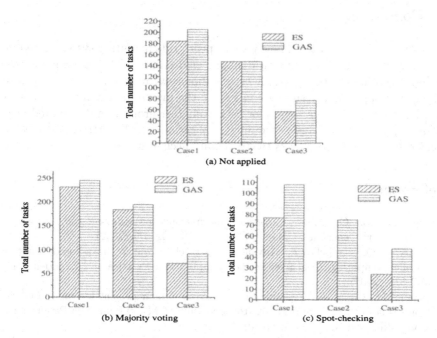

Fig. 5. The number of completed tasks

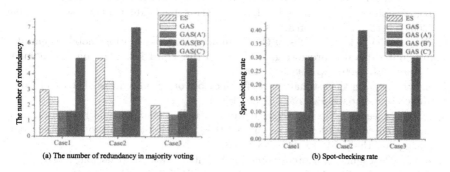

Fig. 6. The number of redundancy & spot-checking rate

is tightly related with performance; e.g., Case 1 can complete more tasks than Cases 2 and 3.

In the case of majority voting, our mechanism obtains more results of tasks than eager scheduling because it dynamically decides the number of redundancy according to properties of volunteer groups (see Fig. 6(a)). The A' and B' volunteer groups choose less redundancy than the C' volunteer group. As a result, the A' and B' volunteer groups are able to reduce the replication overhead, and so they can execute more tasks. The result of spot-checking is similar to that of majority voting (see Fig. 6(b)). This is because our mechanism can dynamically decide spot-checking rate according to properties of volunteer groups.

5   Conclusion

In this paper, we proposed a new peer to peer grid computing system based on mobile agents, which adapts to a dynamic environment. The proposed system applies different scheduling, result certification, and replication mechanisms to volunteer groups. As a result, it can reduce the overhead of a volunteer server by using adaptive mobile agents for each volunteer group in a distributed way. Moreover, the group based scheduling, replication, result certification mechanisms can complete more tasks than existing mechanism.

References

1. Sarmenta, L.F.G.: Sabotage-tolerance mechanisms for volunteer computing systems. Future Generation Computer Systems 18, 561–572 (2002)
2. Neary, M.O., Cappello, P.: Advanced eager scheduling for Java-based adaptive parallel computing. Concurrency and Computation: Practice and Experience 17, 797–819 (2005)
3. Kondo, D., Chien, A.A., Casanova, H.: Resource management for rapid application turnaround on enterprise desktop grids. In: ACM Conf. on High Performance Computing and Networking, pp. 19–30 (2004)
4. Lo, V., Zhou, D., Zappala, D., Liu, Y., Zhao, S.: Cluster computing on the fly: P2P scheduling of idle cycles in the Internet. In: Voelker, G.M., Shenker, S. (eds.) IPTPS 2004. LNCS, vol. 3279, pp. 227–236. Springer, Heidelberg (2005)
5. Lo, V., Zhou, D., Zappala, D., Liu, Y., Zhao, S.: Oddugi mobile agent system (2004), http://oddugi.korea.ac.kr
6. Ghanea-Hercock, R., Collis, J.C., Ndumu, D.T.: Co-operating mobile agents for distributed parallel processing. In: Proc. of the Third Int. Conf. on Autonomous Agents (AA 1999), pp. 398–399 (1999)
7. Zuev, Y.A.: On the estimation of efficiency of voting procedures. Theory of Probability & Its Applications 42, 78–81 (1998)
8. Li, Y., Mascagni, M.: Improving performance via computational replication on a large-scale computational grid. In: 3rd IEEE/ACM Int. Symp. on Cluster Computing and the Grid, pp. 442–448 (2003)
9. Li, Y., Mascagni, M.: Korea@home (2003), http://www.koreaathome.org/eng/
10. Trivedi, K.S.: Probability and Statistics with Reliability, Queuing and Computer Science Applications. Wiley, Chichester (2002)

Author Index

Alcock, Michael   159
Atkins, Graham   159

Bakhouya, Mohamed   63

Cabanillas, David   151
Carchiolo, Vincenza   135
Choi, Sung-Jin   175
Cholvi, Vicent   31

Despotovic, Zoran   19

Fernández, Antonio   31

Gaber, Jaafar   63
Gil, Joon-Min   175
Gylfason, Halldor Isak   74

Hong, Sung Je   43, 111
Huey, Paul   159

Joseph, Samuel R.H.   1

Kanawati, Rushed   51
Karoui, Hager   51
Kellerer, Wolfgang   19
Khan, Omar   74
Kim, Jong   43, 111
Kwon, O-Hoon   43, 111

López, Luis   31
Lee, So Young   111

Malgeri, Michele   135
Mangioni, Giuseppe   135

Nicosia, Vincenzo   135

Ogston, Elth   98

Paranjape, Raman   1
Petrucci, Laure   51
Pirro', Giuseppe   86
Purvis, Martin   167
Purvis, Maryam   167

Rhee, Kyung-Hyune   143
Rodero Merino, Luis   31
Roh, Bong-Soo   43
Ruffolo, Massimo   86

Savarimuthu, Bastin Tony Roy   167
Schoenebeck, Grant   74
Schubert, Simon   19
Şensoy, Murat   123
Shin, Jung-Hwa   143
Shin, Weon   143
Shingler, Steven   159

Talia, Domenico   86
Tse, Ben   1

Vaughan, Jonathan   159
Vaughan, Richard   159

Willmott, Steven   151
Wise, James   159

Yolum, Pınar   123

Zoels, Stefan   19

Lecture Notes in Artificial Intelligence (LNAI)

Vol. 5110: W. Hodges, R. de Queiroz (Eds.), Logic, Language, Information and Computation. VIII, 313 pages. 2008.

Vol. 5097: L. Rutkowski, R. Tadeusiewicz, L.A. Zadeh, J.M. Zurada (Eds.), Artificial Intelligence and Soft Computing – ICAISC 2008. XVI, 1269 pages. 2008.

Vol. 5078: E. André, L. Dybkjær, W. Minker, H. Neumann, R. Pieraccini, M. Weber (Eds.), Perception in Multimodal Dialogue Systems. X, 311 pages. 2008.

Vol. 5064: L. Prevost, S. Marinai, F. Schwenker (Eds.), Artificial Neural Networks in Pattern Recognition. IX, 318 pages. 2008.

Vol. 5040: M. Asada, J.C.T. Hallam, J.-A. Meyer, J. Tani (Eds.), From Animals to Animats 10. XIII, 530 pages. 2008.

Vol. 5032: S. Bergler (Ed.), Advances in Artificial Intelligence. XI, 382 pages. 2008.

Vol. 5027: N.T. Nguyen, L. Borzemski, A. Grzech, M. Ali (Eds.), New Frontiers in Applied Artificial Intelligence. XVIII, 879 pages. 2008.

Vol. 5012: T. Washio, E. Suzuki, K.M. Ting, A. Inokuchi (Eds.), Advances in Knowledge Discovery and Data Mining. XXIV, 1102 pages. 2008.

Vol. 5009: G. Wang, T. Li, J.W. Grzymala-Busse, D. Miao, A. Skowron, Y. Yao (Eds.), Rough Sets and Knowledge Technology. XVIII, 765 pages. 2008.

Vol. 4994: A. An, S. Matwin, Z.W. Raś, D. Ślęzak (Eds.), Foundations of Intelligent Systems. XVII, 653 pages. 2008.

Vol. 4953: N.T. Nguyen, G.S. Jo, R.J. Howlett, L.C. Jain (Eds.), Agent and Multi-Agent Systems: Technologies and Applications. XX, 909 pages. 2008.

Vol. 4946: I. Rahwan, S. Parsons, C. Reed (Eds.), Argumentation in Multi-Agent Systems. X, 235 pages. 2008.

Vol. 4944: Z.W. Raś, S. Tsumoto, D.A. Zighed (Eds.), Mining Complex Data. X, 265 pages. 2008.

Vol. 4938: T. Tokunaga, A. Ortega (Eds.), Large-Scale Knowledge Resources. IX, 367 pages. 2008.

Vol. 4933: R. Medina, S. Obiedkov (Eds.), Formal Concept Analysis. XII, 325 pages. 2008.

Vol. 4930: I. Wachsmuth, G. Knoblich (Eds.), Modeling Communication with Robots and Virtual Humans. X, 337 pages. 2008.

Vol. 4929: M. Helmert, Understanding Planning Tasks. XIV, 270 pages. 2008.

Vol. 4924: D. Riaño (Ed.), Knowledge Management for Health Care Procedures. X, 161 pages. 2008.

Vol. 4923: S.B. Yahia, E.M. Nguifo, R. Belohlavek (Eds.), Concept Lattices and Their Applications. XII, 283 pages. 2008.

Vol. 4914: K. Satoh, A. Inokuchi, K. Nagao, T. Kawamura (Eds.), New Frontiers in Artificial Intelligence. X, 404 pages. 2008.

Vol. 4911: L. De Raedt, P. Frasconi, K. Kersting, S. Muggleton (Eds.), Probabilistic Inductive Logic Programming. VIII, 341 pages. 2008.

Vol. 4908: M. Dastani, A. El Fallah Seghrouchni, A. Ricci, M. Winikoff (Eds.), Programming Multi-Agent Systems. XII, 267 pages. 2008.

Vol. 4898: M. Kolp, B. Henderson-Sellers, H. Mouratidis, A. Garcia, A.K. Ghose, P. Bresciani (Eds.), Agent-Oriented Information Systems IV. X, 292 pages. 2008.

Vol. 4897: M. Baldoni, T.C. Son, M.B. van Riemsdijk, M. Winikoff (Eds.), Declarative Agent Languages and Technologies V. X, 245 pages. 2008.

Vol. 4894: H. Blockeel, J. Ramon, J. Shavlik, P. Tadepalli (Eds.), Inductive Logic Programming. XI, 307 pages. 2008.

Vol. 4885: M. Chetouani, A. Hussain, B. Gas, M. Milgram, J.-L. Zarader (Eds.), Advances in Nonlinear Speech Processing. XI, 284 pages. 2007.

Vol. 4874: J. Neves, M.F. Santos, J.M. Machado (Eds.), Progress in Artificial Intelligence. XVIII, 704 pages. 2007.

Vol. 4870: J.S. Sichman, J. Padget, S. Ossowski, P. Noriega (Eds.), Coordination, Organizations, Institutions, and Norms in Agent Systems III. XII, 331 pages. 2008.

Vol. 4869: F. Botana, T. Recio (Eds.), Automated Deduction in Geometry. X, 213 pages. 2007.

Vol. 4865: K. Tuyls, A. Nowe, Z. Guessoum, D. Kudenko (Eds.), Adaptive Agents and Multi-Agent Systems III. VIII, 255 pages. 2008.

Vol. 4850: M. Lungarella, F. Iida, J.C. Bongard, R. Pfeifer (Eds.), 50 Years of Artificial Intelligence. X, 399 pages. 2007.

Vol. 4845: N. Zhong, J. Liu, Y. Yao, J. Wu, S. Lu, K. Li (Eds.), Web Intelligence Meets Brain Informatics. XI, 516 pages. 2007.

Vol. 4840: L. Paletta, E. Rome (Eds.), Attention in Cognitive Systems. XI, 497 pages. 2007.

Vol. 4830: M.A. Orgun, J. Thornton (Eds.), AI 2007: Advances in Artificial Intelligence. XIX, 841 pages. 2007.

Vol. 4828: M. Randall, H.A. Abbass, J. Wiles (Eds.), Progress in Artificial Life. XII, 402 pages. 2007.

Vol. 4827: A. Gelbukh, Á.F. Kuri Morales (Eds.), MICAI 2007: Advances in Artificial Intelligence. XXIV, 1234 pages. 2007.

Vol. 4826: P. Perner, O. Salvetti (Eds.), Advances in Mass Data Analysis of Signals and Images in Medicine, Biotechnology and Chemistry. X, 183 pages. 2007.

Vol. 4819: T. Washio, Z.-H. Zhou, J.Z. Huang, X. Hu, J. Li, C. Xie, J. He, D. Zou, K.-C. Li, M.M. Freire (Eds.), Emerging Technologies in Knowledge Discovery and Data Mining. XIV, 675 pages. 2007.

Vol. 4811: O. Nasraoui, M. Spiliopoulou, J. Srivastava, B. Mobasher, B. Masand (Eds.), Advances in Web Mining and Web Usage Analysis. XII, 247 pages. 2007.

Vol. 4798: Z. Zhang, J.H. Siekmann (Eds.), Knowledge Science, Engineering and Management. XVI, 669 pages. 2007.

Vol. 4795: F. Schilder, G. Katz, J. Pustejovsky (Eds.), Annotating, Extracting and Reasoning about Time and Events. VII, 141 pages. 2007.

Vol. 4790: N. Dershowitz, A. Voronkov (Eds.), Logic for Programming, Artificial Intelligence, and Reasoning. XIII, 562 pages. 2007.

Vol. 4788: D. Borrajo, L. Castillo, J.M. Corchado (Eds.), Current Topics in Artificial Intelligence. XI, 280 pages. 2007.

Vol. 4775: A. Esposito, M. Faundez-Zanuy, E. Keller, M. Marinaro (Eds.), Verbal and Nonverbal Communication Behaviours. XII, 325 pages. 2007.

Vol. 4772: H. Prade, V.S. Subrahmanian (Eds.), Scalable Uncertainty Management. X, 277 pages. 2007.

Vol. 4766: N. Maudet, S. Parsons, I. Rahwan (Eds.), Argumentation in Multi-Agent Systems. XII, 211 pages. 2007.

Vol. 4760: E. Rome, J. Hertzberg, G. Dorffner (Eds.), Towards Affordance-Based Robot Control. IX, 211 pages. 2008.

Vol. 4755: V. Corruble, M. Takeda, E. Suzuki (Eds.), Discovery Science. XI, 298 pages. 2007.

Vol. 4754: M. Hutter, R.A. Servedio, E. Takimoto (Eds.), Algorithmic Learning Theory. XI, 403 pages. 2007.

Vol. 4737: B. Berendt, A. Hotho, D. Mladenic, G. Semeraro (Eds.), From Web to Social Web: Discovering and Deploying User and Content Profiles. XI, 161 pages. 2007.

Vol. 4733: R. Basili, M.T. Pazienza (Eds.), AI*IA 2007: Artificial Intelligence and Human-Oriented Computing. XVII, 858 pages. 2007.

Vol. 4724: K. Mellouli (Ed.), Symbolic and Quantitative Approaches to Reasoning with Uncertainty. XV, 914 pages. 2007.

Vol. 4722: C. Pelachaud, J.-C. Martin, E. André, G. Chollet, K. Karpouzis, D. Pelé (Eds.), Intelligent Virtual Agents. XV, 425 pages. 2007.

Vol. 4720: B. Konev, F. Wolter (Eds.), Frontiers of Combining Systems. X, 283 pages. 2007.

Vol. 4702: J.N. Kok, J. Koronacki, R. Lopez de Mantaras, S. Matwin, D. Mladenič, A. Skowron (Eds.), Knowledge Discovery in Databases: PKDD 2007. XXIV, 640 pages. 2007.

Vol. 4701: J.N. Kok, J. Koronacki, R. Lopez de Mantaras, S. Matwin, D. Mladenič, A. Skowron (Eds.), Machine Learning: ECML 2007. XXII, 809 pages. 2007.

Vol. 4696: H.-D. Burkhard, G. Lindemann, R. Verbrugge, L.Z. Varga (Eds.), Multi-Agent Systems and Applications V. XIII, 350 pages. 2007.

Vol. 4694: B. Apolloni, R.J. Howlett, L. Jain (Eds.), Knowledge-Based Intelligent Information and Engineering Systems, Part III. XXIX, 1126 pages. 2007.

Vol. 4693: B. Apolloni, R.J. Howlett, L. Jain (Eds.), Knowledge-Based Intelligent Information and Engineering Systems, Part II. XXXII, 1380 pages. 2007.

Vol. 4692: B. Apolloni, R.J. Howlett, L. Jain (Eds.), Knowledge-Based Intelligent Information and Engineering Systems, Part I. LV, 882 pages. 2007.

Vol. 4687: P. Petta, J.P. Müller, M. Klusch, M. Georgeff (Eds.), Multiagent System Technologies. X, 207 pages. 2007.

Vol. 4682: D.-S. Huang, L. Heutte, M. Loog (Eds.), Advanced Intelligent Computing Theories and Applications. XXVII, 1373 pages. 2007.

Vol. 4676: M. Klusch, K.V. Hindriks, M.P. Papazoglou, L. Sterling (Eds.), Cooperative Information Agents XI. XI, 361 pages. 2007.

Vol. 4667: J. Hertzberg, M. Beetz, R. Englert (Eds.), KI 2007: Advances in Artificial Intelligence. IX, 516 pages. 2007.

Vol. 4660: S. Džeroski, L. Todorovski (Eds.), Computational Discovery of Scientific Knowledge. X, 327 pages. 2007.

Vol. 4659: V. Mařík, V. Vyatkin, A.W. Colombo (Eds.), Holonic and Multi-Agent Systems for Manufacturing. VIII, 456 pages. 2007.

Vol. 4651: F. Azevedo, P. Barahona, F. Fages, F. Rossi (Eds.), Recent Advances in Constraints. VIII, 185 pages. 2007.

Vol. 4648: F. Almeida e Costa, L.M. Rocha, E. Costa, I. Harvey, A. Coutinho (Eds.), Advances in Artificial Life. XVIII, 1215 pages. 2007.

Vol. 4635: B. Kokinov, D.C. Richardson, T.R. Roth-Berghofer, L. Vieu (Eds.), Modeling and Using Context. XIV, 574 pages. 2007.

Vol. 4632: R. Alhajj, H. Gao, X. Li, J. Li, O.R. Zaïane (Eds.), Advanced Data Mining and Applications. XV, 634 pages. 2007.

Vol. 4629: V. Matoušek, P. Mautner (Eds.), Text, Speech and Dialogue. XVII, 663 pages. 2007.

Vol. 4626: R.O. Weber, M.M. Richter (Eds.), Case-Based Reasoning Research and Development. XIII, 534 pages. 2007.

Vol. 4617: V. Torra, Y. Narukawa, Y. Yoshida (Eds.), Modeling Decisions for Artificial Intelligence. XII, 502 pages. 2007.

Vol. 4612: I. Miguel, W. Ruml (Eds.), Abstraction, Reformulation, and Approximation. XI, 418 pages. 2007.

Vol. 4604: U. Priss, S. Polovina, R. Hill (Eds.), Conceptual Structures: Knowledge Architectures for Smart Applications. XII, 514 pages. 2007.